"This volume opens a window for English-speaking readers to a rich regional folktale tradition little-known outside of Spain. It presents a delightful body of beautifully rendered literary versions of folktales, informed by oral traditions, gracefully transposed for the page, and authoritatively translated."

Joseph Sobol, Professor of Storytelling,
University of South Wales

"These folktales, rooted in the oral tradition and written in Enric Valor's rich, personal prose, are presented here for the first time in a magnificent English translation. The imaginary universe of these lovely Valencian stories thus acquires an international dimension."

Carme Oriol, Professor of Folk Literature,
Universitat Rovira i Virgili

"Enric Valor's *Valencian Folktales* conserve the memory of a strong, resilient culture. From anonymous voices and age-old traditions, Valor constructs universal stories of a timeless popular mythology. This translation will be appreciated by scholars and students of culture, literature and folklore."

Rafael Beltrán, Professor of Medieval
Literature, Universitat de València

Valencian Folktales

Enric Valor is one of the most important Valencian authors of the 20th century. This selection of his highly popular *rondalles* (folk tales) will for the first time introduce his work to an English-speaking audience. At a time when Catalan was under threat from the cultural bulldozer of the Franco regime, which condemned the use of anything but Castilian Spanish in public communication, Valor went to great lengths to disseminate knowledge of the language, through writing grammars and linguistic studies, as well as teaching it to fellow inmates when he was imprisoned by the regime for his cultural activities. These tales, collected over a number of years in small villages in the province of Alacant, were a significant part of his ongoing efforts to safeguard the Valencian language and the culture and history of the region. The *Rondalles Valencianes* have been compared to Italo Calvino's *Italian Folk Tales* and Henri Pourrat's *Treasury of French Folk Tales*. Like them, Valor aimed in rewriting the oral material to establish a common national body of folk narratives and to make the stories more appealing to Valencian readers, young and old alike. The critical Introduction provides an outline of the author's life and an overview of his work as novelist, grammarian and folklorist, as well as an assessment of the tales which identifies their place within the broader European folklore tradition.

Paul Scott Derrick is a Senior Lecturer (retired) in American literature at the Universitat de València. He has published three collections of essays in English and has co-authored a number of bilingual (English-Spanish) critical editions of works by Ralph Waldo Emerson, Emily Dickinson, Henry Adams and Sarah Orne Jewett.

Maria-Lluïsa Gea-Valor is a Senior Lecturer in English Language and Linguistics at the Universitat de València. Her research interests lie in the fields of genre analysis, written academic discourse, and literary translation. She has specialized in evaluative and promotional genres such as the blurb and the book review.

Routledge Studies in Twentieth-Century Literature

Exile as a Continuum in Joseph Conrad's Fiction
Living in Translation
Ludmilla Voitkovska

Ernest Hemingway and the Fluidity of Gender
A Socio-Cultural Analysis of Selected Works
Tania Chakravertty

The Life and Works of Korean Poet Kim Myŏng-sun
The Flower Dream of a Woman Born Too Soon
Jung Ja Choi

Boasian Verse
The Poetic and Ethnographic Work of Edward Sapir, Ruth Benedict, and Margaret Mead
Philipp Schweighauser

Valencian Folktales
Enric Valor
Translated by Paul Scott Derrick and Maria-Lluïsa Gea-Valor

The Postwar Counterculture in Novels and Film
On the Avenue of the Mystery
Gary Hentzi

Authors and Art Movements of the Twentieth Century
Painterly Poetics
Declan Lloyd

For more information about this series, please visit: https://www.routledge.com/Routledge-Studies-in-Twentieth-Century-Literature/book-series/RSTLC

Valencian Folktales
Enric Valor

Translated by Paul Scott Derrick and
Maria-Lluïsa Gea-Valor

NEW YORK AND LONDON

First published 2023
by Routledge
605 Third Avenue, New York, NY 10158

and by Routledge
4 Park Square, Milton Park, Abingdon, Oxon, OX14 4RN

Routledge is an imprint of the Taylor & Francis Group, an informa business

© 2023 selection and editorial matter, Paul Scott Derrick and Maria-Lluïsa Gea-Valor; individual chapters, the contributors

The right of Paul Scott Derrick and Maria-Lluïsa Gea-Valor to be identified as the authors of the editorial material, and of the authors for their individual chapters, has been asserted in accordance with sections 77 and 78 of the Copyright, Designs and Patents Act 1988.

All rights reserved. No part of this book may be reprinted or reproduced or utilised in any form or by any electronic, mechanical, or other means, now known or hereafter invented, including photocopying and recording, or in any information storage or retrieval system, without permission in writing from the publishers.

Trademark notice: Product or corporate names may be trademarks or registered trademarks, and are used only for identification and explanation without intent to infringe.

ISBN: 978-1-032-34870-4 (hbk)
ISBN: 978-1-032-34871-1 (pbk)
ISBN: 978-1-003-32423-2 (ebk)

DOI: 10.4324/9781003324232

Typeset in Sabon
by Deanta Global Publishing Services, Chennai, India

Contents

1 Introduction   1
MARIA-LLUÏSA GEA-VALOR

2 The Wood-Cutter of Fortaleny   27

3 The Spinster Sisters of the Penya Roja   45

4 The Castle of the Sun   56

5 King Astoret   83

6 The Envious Moor of Alcalà   111

7 The Saddle-Maker of Cocentaina   124

8 The Gambling Man of Petrer   138

9 Peret   149

10 Joan-Antoni and the Blockheads   161

11 The Tale of the Halfling Chicken   178

Index   185

1 Introduction

Maria-Lluïsa Gea-Valor

It is truly exciting to write these lines to introduce Valencian author Enric Valor to the English-speaking reader. Besides the fact that he is one of the best-known and most highly respected writers in the Catalan language, he was also my grandfather, which happily gives me a unique and privileged perspective on the public figure but also the private man: writing about Valor is writing about my family's history.

This introductory chapter is divided into three main sections. The first part aims to provide a sketch of Valor's biography, which is closely intertwined with his literary and linguistic production. The second section focuses on the *rondalla* genre by situating it in the context of Catalan folklore and establishing its connection with the broader European tradition. The third and final section discusses the peculiarities and innovations which characterize Valor's tales and make them unique.

Enric Valor: An Extraordinary Life Defined by a Profound Love of Literature and His Language

If I were asked to give a quick overview of the public figure, I would start by saying that Enric Valor is one of the most relevant Valencian authors of the 20th century. More importantly, perhaps, he is also one of the most beloved and admired figures in Valencian culture who, together with contemporary writers, intellectuals and scholars like Joan Fuster, Manuel Sanchis Guarner and Vicent Andrés Estellés,[1] devoted his whole life to defending and upholding the Valencian culture and language, which he often referred to as "our Catalan." His prolific work, which spanned the whole 20th century until his death in 2000 at the age of 88, covers numerous areas: journalism, language teaching, lexicography, grammar, fiction and folklore. He enormously contributed to the standardization of Catalan in the Valencian territory, and his linguistic and literary legacy is widely recognized: for instance, it has been established that he rescued more than one thousand words from oblivion (Casanova, 2011), while his fiction work has been considered to fill a 100-year gap in literary production in Valencian (Iborra, 1980; Salvador,

DOI: 10.4324/9781003324232-1

2011)—let's not forget that the famous writer Vicente Blasco Ibáñez, though fluent in Valencian, wrote all of his novels in Spanish.

Born in 1911 in the town of Castalla, which is situated in the heart of the countryside of Alacant,[2] Valor endured extremely adverse times from a social and political perspective. His family, quite well-off at the time though not substantively rich, were prosperous landowners mainly invested in the wine-making business. Belonging to a sort of lower aristocracy typical of the rural world of that period, Valor's family enjoyed all the comforts of their fortunate position: his father was sent to Barcelona to study for a university degree in philosophy before returning home to take care of the business, whereas his mother was a refined, cultivated lady who enjoyed art, music and literature, and was very fond of reading.

These idyllic times abruptly changed in the mid-1920s, when the family went bankrupt due to the *phylloxera* vine plague that relentlessly hit Europe and Spain. The financial crisis resulting from World War I also played a decisive role in the demise of the family business. Obviously, these adverse circumstances had a huge impact on the Valors. Traumatically, they had to leave all their properties and comfortable lifestyle behind and migrate to more prosperous lands, more specifically to the industrial town of Elda, some 20 miles away, which was at that time starting to blossom thanks to shoe manufacturing. This opened a new chapter in Enric's life: unlike his father, he was not able to attend university, though he managed to obtain a lower degree in financial law and was soon hired in posts of great responsibility in the local industry. He was only 19. He had become part of the working class and had started to witness and comprehend the so-called *class struggle*, which led him to develop a strong social conscience and to begin his political activism. These were Republican times, after all. He was no longer part of the landowning aristocracy of rural Alacant: he had become a proletarian and was happy about it. And in Elda he met Mercè Hernàndez Barrachina, his lifelong wife with whom he would have three children.

After a few years in Elda, where the family managed to stay afloat and recover financially, Enric moved to Alacant, where he started his journalistic activity and was hired as an editor for the satirical publication *El Tio Cuc*, written in Valencian. Here Valor, whose parents had infused in him a deep love and respect for Valencian, their mother tongue, convinced the director to use correct orthography, which caused quite an impact at the time.

It is necessary to stop here for a moment and describe the terrible state of decline the Valencian language was in after more than two centuries of unrelenting and ruthless repression and persecution by the powerful Castilian state, which purposely intended to eliminate all minority languages and cultures in Spain (Ferrer Gironés, 1985). The school system expressly forbade the use of Catalan, Galician and Basque, so that those who could read and write at all did so exclusively in Spanish. Paradoxically, the native language of most of the population in the Valencian territory was obviously Valencian, our variety of Catalan: very few people, especially in

Figure 1.1 The Valor family c. 1914. Enric on left holding a hoop. Source: Valor family.

rural towns and villages, understood or let alone spoke Spanish. However, nobody knew how to write in their own language, there were no spelling rules: it was linguistic chaos. In 1932, after quite a successful Valencian cultural revival, the most relevant intellectuals, writers and cultural institutions of the time signed the celebrated *Normes de Castelló* with the aim of fixing an orthographic standard for Valencian. These guidelines followed those developed by reputed Catalan linguist Pompeu Fabra,[3] considered the father of modern Catalan. Enric Valor would become an instrumental figure in applying and spreading the Fabra rules in the Southern regions of the Valencian country.

As may be surmised from all of the above, Valor's early teenage years and transition into adulthood were quite bitter and traumatic. He would reminisce about these tough times relating how, despite his young age, he could sense the predicament his parents were in (Serrano, 1995). One particularly painful memory involved walking in on his father holding a gun to his head: such was the despair of a man facing bankruptcy. His beloved father would die one year before the outbreak of the Spanish Civil War at the age of 65. That very year Valor moved to Valencia with his family. This city would become his forever home, although he returned from time to time to the Southern lands of his childhood, where he had inherited a few properties.

Franco's military *coup d'état* in July 1936 surprised Enric in Castalla, where he was spending the summer holidays with his family. The fascist insurrection put an abrupt end to the Second Spanish Republic and all its democratic and liberal reforms (i.e., women's suffrage, divorce law, freedom

Figure 1.2 Valor with wife and daughters in 1958. Source: Valor family.

of speech and association). As is well known, a cruel Civil War ensued, where Valor fought on the Republican side, the losing side. He was drafted in early 1937 and sent to the Alacant front, although he never engaged in actual fighting. However, the horrors he witnessed and the hardship he suffered in his own flesh would deeply affect him and, as he once confessed, even transform him: the war and all its consequences would become the basis for his most ambitious work of fiction, the *Cassana* Trilogy.

Let us concentrate now on Valor's writing career. From a very early age, he was an avid reader who felt a profound passion for books. His family had a well-furnished home library, and his mother would read to him and his older brother Josep all types of novels, from Alexandre Dumas's *The Three Musketeers* to Tolstoy's *War and Peace* and Victor Hugo's *Les Misérables*. When he was only ten, he picked a book he couldn't understand completely: Gustave Flaubert's *Madame Bovary*, which he enjoyed very much and which made a strong impression on such a young boy. This atmosphere awakened in him an enduring love for literature and fantasy. His dream was to become a writer, a novelist. This was his true calling. At the age of 15, Enric wrote his first short story entitled "L'experiment d'Strolowickz" (Strolowickz's Experiment), which won a prize and was published in the newspaper *El Camí*. Indeed, Valor found in the journalistic press a way to channel his writing vocation and accordingly he worked for several newspapers and magazines. In early 1936, he had finished his first novel, *El misteri del Canadian* (The Mystery of the Canadian), but the train carrying the only copy to the publishing house in Barcelona was bombarded and the book was lost forever. The outbreak of the Civil War and its aftermath thwarted his career as a novelist for quite some time. His writing passion would have to wait.

After the war came a dark, bleak period in Spanish history: the 40-year-long Franco dictatorship. In this dismal context, Valor needed to find a way to survive and make a living: after all, he was a family man with three young children who had to provide for his loved ones; so in 1942, together with his brother Josep, who had a mind for business, he set up a truck company devoted to the transportation of coal and timber, and, later on, an auto parts company, named *Valor Ltd*. With more than 300 employees, the business enjoyed unexpected success for several years until the Bank of Spain suddenly cut off all credit and hundreds of small companies, including *Valor Ltd.*, were forced to close.

In these initial post-war years in Valencia, Enric managed to combine his frenetic activity as a businessman with his literary and intellectual vocation. He continued writing for various journals and newspapers, and started to participate in intellectual and literary gatherings, where he met the most prominent and reputed figures in the Valencian cultural scene such as Carles Salvador[4] and Manuel Sanchis Guarner, with whom he became long-lasting friends. One decisive person in Valor's formative period as a linguist was Josep Giner,[5] who taught him Latin and historical grammar, although Enric

6   Introduction

may be considered a self-taught scholar who had an extraordinary talent for philology and had been blessed with an invaluable legacy: a pristine, well-preserved language with very little interference of Spanish. Giner, in his preface to the book *Millorem el llenguatge* (Let's Speak Right, 1971, p. 5), described Valor as follows:

> This is the Valencian writer who possesses the most native, popular, instinctively well used, natural and spontaneous living "language." A language that is, in addition, rigorous, painstaking, pure and cultivated, as any professional writer's should be. For all of these reasons, Enric Valor Vives is an authority in the usage of our language in its written form, both formal and colloquial. (my translation)[6]

Because of these exceptional qualities, Enric became a valuable contributor to two seminal lexicographical works in the Catalan language: Joan Coromines's[7] *Etymological Dictionary* and Francesc de Borja Moll's[8] *Diccionari Català-Valencià-Balear*. In 1949, Valor was admitted as a member of the cultural association *Lo Rat Penat*, where he also taught language courses under Salvador's mentoring. Around this period he had begun his first serious novel, *L'ambició d'Aleix* (Aleix's Ambition), which wouldn't see the light until 1960. Spurred and encouraged by Sanchis Guarner, he started writing a collection of folktales that would become the extremely popular *Rondalles Valencianes*. The first three volumes were published between 1950 and 1958, and were immediately successful. Other publications of the time include the short story "El viatge de nadal" (A Christmas Journey) and prescriptive grammar lessons in the newspapers *Jornada* and *Levante*.

However, his political and social commitment to the cause of Valencian and against the Franco regime would carry negative consequences on a personal level: in 1966, Enric and his brother were arrested and sentenced to a 28-month imprisonment. Despite these difficult circumstances, Valor was not defeated: having a strong mind and a fighting spirit, he put his prison time to good use by continuing writing his folktales, 18 in total. He often said that writing these stories felt like opening a window to the outer world, through which he could see with his mind's eye the magnificent mountains and colorful landscapes of the country he loved and knew so well. The first thing he did when he set foot out of the penitentiary in 1969 was to touch and smell the green bright alfalfa fields that surrounded the building. After prison, he continued his linguistic work with relevant titles such as *Millorem el llenguatge* (Let's Speak Right, 1971) and *Curso medio de gramática catalane referida especialmente al País Valenciano* (An Intermediate Course in Catalan Grammar with a Special Focus on the Valencian Country, 1973). He also codirected, with his dear colleague Joan Senent,[9] the literary magazine *Gorg* until the Franco regime closed it down in 1972. Interestingly, the magazine lasted for 28 months, exactly the same as Valor's prison sentence.

The whole corpus of *rondalles*, which consists of 36 tales, saw the light in a volume entitled *Obra literària completa* (Complete Literary Works) between 1975 and 1976.

During the dictatorship, Valor's literary production was heavily censored except for his folktales, where the regime saw no element of dissidence worth silencing.[10] In *L'ambició d'Aleix*, for instance, the adultery passage was eliminated by the censors, rendering the rest of the novel somewhat senseless. Surprisingly, however, Enric encountered no difficulties in publishing his linguistic work, mainly textbooks and manuals dealing with how to use Valencian in a grammatically correct way, such as *Lea valenciano en 10 días* (Read Valencian in 10 Days, 1966) and *Curso de lengua valenciana* (A Course in the Valencian Language, 1966). Not until the 1980s and the advent of democracy could Valor fully accomplish his calling as a novelist by writing the *Cassana* trilogy, composed of three novels: *Sense la terra promesa* (Promised Land Denied), *Temps de batuda* (Times of Battle) and *Enllà de l'horitzó* (Beyond the Horizon), published between 1980 and 1991. Enric was almost 70 when he started this colossal process and finished it shy of 80. His career was in full swing. After such a long period of deterioration and decay, the status of the Valencian language was slowly being recovered, and a readership eager to consume literature in their native language was gradually developing. In this context, Enric Valor's literary work was welcomed with open arms. Besides the *Cassana* trilogy, Valor published his grammar manual *La flexió verbal* (Verb Inflections, 1983), which is considered a linguistic best-seller and is used at all educational levels. He also published a collection of short stories: *Narracions intranscendents* (Ordinary Stories, 1982), *Narracions perennes* (Eternal Stories, 1988) and *Un fonamentalista del Vinalopó i altres contarelles* (An Extremist from Vinalopó and Other Tales, 1996).

In the mid-1980s and through the 1990s, Valor started to be recognized publicly and institutionally as a key figure in the process of recovery and rehabilitation of the Valencian language and culture. He received numerous literary prizes and awards, such as the *Premi de les Lletres Valencianes* in 1985, the *Premi d'Honor de les Lletres Catalanes* in 1987 and the *Creu de Sant Jordi* in 1993. He was awarded an *Honorary Degree* by five universities in Catalan-speaking territories, namely Valencia (1993), Balearic Islands (1998), Jaume I in Castelló (1999), Alacant (1999) and Valencia Polytechnic (1999), and his vast and prolific work has been the object of numerous scholarly studies, academic conferences and doctoral dissertations. Being a very modest man, he once declared that the prizes, awards and tributes he received were a little too much, for he had only done his duty.

Enric Valor passed away on January 13, 2000. He was preparing a new novel, *Un habitatge per a l'eternitat* (A Dwelling Place for Eternity). To honor his memory, thousands of streets, squares, libraries and schools around the Valencian territory have been named after him. Annual festivals, events and

Figure 1.3 Valor in his office at home. Source: Alicante Plaza.

contests are organized to celebrate his life and work. His most popular folktales have been turned into animated films (the *Catacric Catacrac* series in the *À Punt Media* corporation) and one tale in particular—*La mare dels peixos* (The Mother of the Fishes)—has been adapted into a successful opera with performances in Valencia, Mexico City and Pittsburgh, US.[11] Every year on his birthday, August 26th, at the break of dawn, fans and admirers go on a hike to the summit of the Maigmó Mountain in Alacant, a place with a special meaning to Enric. Two literary prizes carry his name: the *Premi Enric Valor de Narrativa Juvenil* established in 1980 and the *Premi Enric Valor de Novel·la en Valencià* since 1995. In 2016 the University of Alacant created the *Càtedra Enric Valor* (Enric Valor Chair), a dynamic academic forum devoted to the study and promotion of Valor's invaluable intellectual production and unparalleled civic commitment to his people and land. Moreover, a project to create a Museum (*Casa Museu*) based in Castalla, his hometown, is now underway with the support of the *Càtedra Enric Valor*, the regional government (known as *Generalitat Valenciana*) and the local city hall. It will open its doors to the public in 2023.

The *Rondalles Valencianes* in the European Folklore Tradition

Enric Valor used to say that, had he lived in less turbulent times, he would have devoted his whole life to writing novels (Serrano, 1995). By turbulent times he meant not only the terrible Civil War and the ensuing brutal dictatorship that would plunge Spain into darkness and recession for four decades but also the status of decline and deterioration of his language and culture. As discussed above, the Catalan language had been the object of systematic political persecution for more than two centuries: the *Nova Planta* decrees issued by Spanish king Philip V of the Bourbon dynasty in the early 18th century literally prohibited the use of Catalan at school, both spoken and written, and also in the courts of justice (Ferrer Gironès, 1985). More repressive policies continued in the 19th century and culminated in the attempted cultural annihilation orchestrated by the Franco regime not only against Catalan but also the rest of non-Castilian languages in Spain. With the advent of democracy in the early 1980s, the situation has been gradually reversed, although it is far from being completely normalized.

Given these adverse circumstances, Valor's vocation as a novelist was overridden by a more urgent mission: to redress the status of the Valencian language and culture by providing his fellow citizens with the necessary linguistic tools to help them achieve social and cultural normalcy, and thus become reconciled with their heritage, their traditions, their classics: in a nutshell, their identity. This was undoubtedly an extremely challenging, even a monumental task, but Enric accepted it eagerly and courageously. After all, he believed it was his moral duty. And he carried out such an enormous assignment in two ways: one was linguistic in nature and consisted of publishing several manuals, grammars and textbooks, all highly pedagogic and informative, that would offer the interested reader a rigorous yet accessible description of all aspects of Catalan grammar, with a special emphasis on the Valencian dialectal variety. The second was perhaps more appealing to Valor since it entailed writing fiction, though it was a particular type of fiction: the *rondalla*.

The term *rondalla* refers to a narrative genre, oral or written, which has gone hand in hand with the development of human societies since the dawn of time. Recent anthropological studies indicate that some tales have prehistoric roots and may date back more than 5,000 years, preceding the earliest literary records (Flood, 2016, n.d.). We can all imagine our ancestors telling stories at night beside an open fire in the dead of winter; stories filled with myths, traditions, values and popular wisdom which have been passed down from generation to generation over the centuries. Storytelling is thus inherently human and may be found in all the world's cultures. If we put our focus on Europe, the equivalents or counterparts of the Valencian *rondalla* are the *Märchen in* Germany, the Italian *fiabe*, the *conte populair* or *conte de fees* in France, and the Spanish *cuento popular/folklórico* or *cuento de hadas*, to name but a few. In English, we find two possible terms: *fairy tales*—"wonder tales involving marvelous elements and occurrences, though not necessarily about fairies" (Britannica, n.d.a)—and *folktales*— "stories originating in popular culture, typically passed on by word of mouth" (Lexico, n.d.). Out of the two, *folktale* is perhaps a more suitable translation for *rondalla*, similarly to the German term *Märchen* mentioned above. In this sense, Seago (2001, p. 171) offers an interesting explanation regarding correspondence of terms:

> The German term *Märchen* refers to a much wider type of traditional material, while *fairy tales* are closely linked to the authored *contes des fées*, popular at the end of the 17th century at the French court and widely translated into English in the 18th century.

Indeed, traditional stories have been subjected to literary adaptation from very early times, so much so that "[i]t is often difficult to distinguish between tales of literary and oral origin, because folktales have received literary treatment, and, conversely, literary tales have found their way back" (Britannica, n.d.a). Thompson (2021, n.d.) introduces two additional factors to further clarify the distinction, namely anonymity and universality: "In contrast to a literary story, with its standard text and author living in a definite time and place, the folktale is anonymous. Its originators have long been forgotten and it exists in many versions, all equally valid."

Thus, together with their anonymous origin, one essential characteristic of folktales is their universality, evidenced by the fact that multiple versions of one story may be found in widely differing countries and cultures with their own distinctive traits and particularities. In other words, each social group has adapted the essence of universal stories to their own way of feeling, thinking and viewing the world. In a sense, folktales are a window onto a people's soul and spirituality. Their cultural importance is, therefore, undeniable, not only given their intimate relation with ancient customs, traditions and beliefs but also because, just like any other element of human culture, these narratives are inextricably connected with specific historical times and geographical locations, as well as with the unique features of the society that inspired them (Oliag, 1998, p. 189). From a historic and ethnographic standpoint, it is interesting to highlight the fact that, in the late 18th century and above all during the 19th century, folktales were used as political vehicles to promote the creation of the new European nation-states, as was the case of the tales collected by the brothers Grimm in Germany (Seago, 2001, pp. 171–172). Thus, folktales contributed to the so-called *mythomoteur* (Smith, 1986), that is, to forging national mythologies which, together with other factors such as a common language and a shared religion, became the foundational basis for the new states.[12] Besides the Grimm brothers, another paradigmatic example of the use of folklore to rekindle and affirm a sense of national identity during the 19th century is that represented by Peter Asbjørnsen and Jørgen Moe in Norway, who also contributed to setting the standard for the Norwegian language (Britannica, n.d.b). And, of course, we could add examples from other regions within Europe with authors such as John Francis Campbell in Scotland, William Butler Yeats in Ireland and Karel Jaromír Erben in Czechia (Borja, 2017, p. 427).

It thus becomes obvious that folklore has been—and still is—a central ingredient for the preservation and revitalization of local cultures and minority languages, some under threat of extinction even today (Babalola, 2012; Barroso, 2013).

The role played by language and mythology in the building and asserting of national identity is unarguable. This symbiosis was not lost to Enric Valor who, already in 1935 at the age of 24, advocated for the need to recover the dignity and self-esteem of the Valencian people by restoring their language, which at that time was extremely fragile: "the language issue is a fundamental one: it constitutes the solid base for the whole doctrine of national rebirth" (Valor, 1935, p. 2). During the 17th and 18th centuries, the cultural decline in Catalan-speaking territories had been quite dramatic, reaching an almost irreversible point until the *Renaixença*, a revival cultural movement which began in Catalonia in the early 19th century with the aim of upholding the language and building a substantial body of national literature, although this partly meant neglecting the importance of the previous literary tradition (*Enciclopèdia Catalana*). The *Renaixença* also spread to the Balearic Islands and the Valencian country; however, in Valencian lands, more vulnerable to Castilian influence, it did not have the necessary impulse to redress the situation and reinstate a collective sense of identity. Regarding literature in Valencian, it was virtually inexistent at the time and the only cultivated genres tended to be satirical, obscene and scatological (Sanchis Guarner, 2001, p. 26). Salvaging the remnants of Valencian folklore, therefore, was a pressing task, given the possibility of being completely absorbed and assimilated by an ever-growing industrialized and homogenizing society. As Sanchis Guarner (1975, p. 7) explains in his preface to Valor's *Obra literària completa*:

> The task, then, is difficult and urgent, but not impossible. [...] It needs a patient and intelligent scholar to collect them [these traditional stories] with loving perseverance. Enric Valor Vives, selfless servant of the language, courageously undertook this task on his own, with no help from anyone else. For many years he has interviewed the aged and aging villagers and farmers, principally from the area surrounding the Aitana Mountain, where he has so many close connections, and from his native Castalla Valley, that is, from a part of the Valencian country where the language and folklore are still relatively pure and which has not yet been studied as it deserves to be.

As a superb storyteller with a splendid mastery of narrative resources, Valor was clearly "the right man for the job," a job that his dear friend and colleague Sanchis Guarner encouraged him to undertake in order to enlarge the Valencian folktale corpus, which was quite sparse at the time but for a few notable exceptions.[13] In contrast, Catalonia and the Balearic Islands, where the *Renaixença* had been more successful, had shown more concern about preserving their popular cultural heritage. Especially noteworthy is the extensive volume *Folklore de Catalunya* (Catalan Folklore, 1950) by eminent Catalan ethnologist Joan Amades,[14] with whom Valor maintained "a beautiful epistolary friendship which only ended with his passing" (Valor, 1975, p. 24). A few years earlier, Mallorcan Antoni Maria Alcover[15] had recovered a substantial quantity of folktales in his *Aplec de rondalles mallorquines* (A Collection of Folktales from Mallorca), consisting of 24 volumes published between 1896 and 1931, with numerous subsequent editions and adaptations.

But what were the techniques or methods used back then to collect oral tales? It must have been a slow and arduous process given the lack of recording equipment and storage devices. As Thompson (2021, n.d.) explains, assembling techniques initially consisted of "casual longhand notes and rewritings" and then evolved "at an impressive pace through various stages to mechanical recording on discs and tapes," making "possible comparative studies of all kinds, based on the oral record." Fidelity to the sources is another important consideration in collection and transcription processes: for instance, the Grimm brothers, in their *Kinder- und Hausmärchen,* aimed at "a genuine reproduction of the teller's words and ways" (Denecke, 2020, n.d.) so what they did is directly transcribe their informants' renderings. In contrast, many folktales and legends collected in the 17th century were rewritten in the predominant literary fashion of the time, as did Charles Perrault in France or Giambattista Basile in Italy.

Regarding folklore in Catalan-speaking territories, folktale collectors such as Alcover and Valor used traditional, old-fashioned tools—i.e., humble *pen and paper*—and relied on various types of sources to obtain their stories. Alcover generally interviewed (or rather chatted with) illiterate or poorly educated informants that he regarded as authentic, uncontaminated sources of popular wisdom and oral lore. He wrote down all of his annotations into notebooks, which have become themselves "documents of great ethnological value for the raw material they contain, much sought-after by folklorists" (Grimalt, 1978, p. 8). He then wrote more elaborate, literary versions of the stories, using a personal narrative style full of local and dialectical expressions in quest of the most genuine version of the tale, one which showed the true essence of the Mallorcan people.

Enric Valor, for his part, used to refer to the collection process as "fieldwork," which entailed travelling through the Southern countryside of the Valencian region and talking with the native inhabitants of remote towns and villages: farmers, hunters, woodcutters, domestic helpers, elderly men and women, etc. Being a very friendly, congenial and chatty person, it was easy for him to strike up conversations with his countrymen. According to Marín (2017, p. 28): "his kindness and affability surely facilitated his work as a writer who approached the local people with a notebook in search of old stories." Besides these rural informants, Valor also relied on the tales he had been told as a child by his parents—especially his mother—and also by a smart housemaid named Toneta (Serrano, 1995). Similarly, family friends and neighbors from his hometown, Castalla, provided Enric with arguments (quite sketchy and incomplete at times), themes, sayings and other invaluable material. In his preface to the *Obra literària completa*, Valor himself explains his principal motivation for collecting these stories (1975, p. 23):

> [T]he change from the still and silent ancestral earth to the dynamic and noisy city only strengthened in me the memory, love and nostalgia of those tales and the desire that they not fall into oblivion, that they be set down and recreated with a certain literary dignity, that they be safeguarded from disappearance.

Driven by this sense of urgency, Valor initiated his ambitious project and published his first volume in 1950, which was quite an unexpected success. This was followed by a second volume in 1951, which also received positive criticism, and a third one in 1958. As explained above, the collection of 36 tales was finished by Valor in prison, where he wrote the remaining 18 stories, largely relying on his excellent memory and adding as many details as his imagination dictated. Like Alcover had done in Mallorca, Valor transformed the stories—those he remembered from his childhood and those he had collected—into "literary tales" (Lluch, 2011, p. 45) by filling them with extraordinary lexical richness and invaluable descriptive depth. Oftentimes he had only had access to the bare bones of the plot or the characters, which he skillfully fleshed out using his lively imagination and extraordinary narrative ability. According to Oriol (2011, p. 97):

> This process of recreation consists of expanding the text by providing a detailed description of the characters and of the setting where the action takes place, while at the same time preserving the structure of the traditional tale [...] as well as the oral register typical of folk narratives.

In the speech he delivered at the *Honorary Degree* ceremony held at Universitat Jaume I in Castelló, Valor explained his three major objectives in the literary recreation of the tales (1999, p. 23): i) to give the stories a Valencian character by rooting the action in authentic, well-known geographical locations such as mountains, forests, peaks, coves, bays, towns and villages; ii) to describe the natural landscapes of the Valencian country along with their indigenous plants and trees, and to give the protagonists Valencian names, employing humorous elements to portray them; and iii) to use a plain yet correct linguistic register, rich in vocabulary, so as to write literature, not just folklore. That way, apart from entertaining, the tales would also contribute to teaching our language and restoring its social status.

There is complete agreement among critics and scholars that these objectives were fully accomplished. As Borja (2017, pp. 419–420) clearly states:

[T]he result is an original work which is not only a testimony to the vicissitudes of the very special political and cultural context that produced it, but also—and this value should be stressed—Valencia's history, geography and many of its vital idiosyncrasies. As opposed to a faithful transcription of his informants' material, we find in Valor an extreme case of personal re-creation and a literary rewriting of the oral tradition [...] in an attempt to redeem, in literary form, the Valencian landscape and the region's linguistic, natural, architectonic, historic, ethnographic and idiosyncratic patrimony. To create literature within the genre of folklore rather than folklore itself: this was his explicit aim.

In his *Obra literària completa,* Valor classified his 36 folktales into three main types: magical-theme tales, local-color tales and tales with personified animals. The magical-theme group includes 21 stories featuring characters with supernatural powers and magical objects that may help the hero or heroine in their adventures. According to Lluch & Serrano (1995, p. 47), these tales possess a fairly fixed structure, shared by all Western cultures, as well as a consistent set of features, such as an initial challenging task which the hero/heroine eventually overcomes and a magical object used by the hero/heroine to defeat evil. The second set, tales of local-color, is made up of ten stories of non-magical themes—although Valor himself notes that some magical elements may appear—which mainly include cautionary tales, scary stories featuring witches or the Devil himself and anecdotes involving stupid and dim-witted people. The third category, with only five tales, involves personified animals such as chickens and roosters, cunning foxes, spiteful crows and shy mice; hunger is typically the cause for the conflict.

A more subtle and detailed taxonomy of the *Rondalles Valencianes* is put forward by Oriol (2011, pp. 106–107), who distinguishes seven levels: i) tales of animals; ii) magical tales (with a further sublevel: magical tales involving children); iii) non-magical tales; iv) tales of stupid giants; v) anecdotes; vi) formula tales and vii) legends. This classification roughly corresponds to the major groups included in the international ATU catalogue. As is commonly known, the basic catalogue of folktales dates back to 1961 and was entitled *The Types of the Folktale*, written by Antti Aarne and Stith Thompson. According to Stein (2015, n.d.): "the principal value of the index lies in the creation of a single classification system by which culturally distinct variants are grouped together according to a common reference number." The catalogue was later developed by Hans-Jörg Uther into the Aarne-Thompson-Uther system (2004), also known as the ATU index, which is widely used in folklore studies to categorize tales into types by identifying central elements known as *motifs*, potential variants or subtypes, and main characters. Each tale type is assigned a number identifier and a title, and the entry is completed with a summary of the plot, possible combinations with other types and additional comments. The full ATU system contains more than 2,000 types divided into seven larger groups, namely animal tales (1–299), tales of magic (300–749), religious tales (750–849), realistic tales (850–999), tales of the stupid ogre/giant/devil (1000–1199), anecdotes and jokes (1200–1999) and formula tales (2000–2399) (Uther, 2004).

According to Oriol (2011, p. 99), 83.3% of Valor's *rondalles* (30 out of 36) constitute local versions of very popular tales within the European tradition and they have logically been assigned a type number. If we focus on the present collection, the ten folktales selected here have an ATU number, except for one, *The Saddle-Maker of Cocentaina*, which is often classified as a legend.[16] Their ATU classification is shown below, along with their correspondence with other versions of the tales in universal folklore,[17] should there be any (Beltran, 2007; Oriol & Pujol, 2008; Multilingual Folk Tale Database, 2014; RondCat, 2014):

1. *The Wood-Cutter of Fortaleny*

ATU classification	ATU 330: the smith outwits the devil Within the larger category ATU 300–749: Tales of magic > 300–399: supernatural adversaries.
Literary versions	*Der Schlimiel und der Teufel* (1812) by Jacob and Wilhelm Grimm; *Smeden som de ikke torde slippe inn i helvete* (1841) by Peter Asbjørnsen and Jørgen Moe; *Salta nel mio sacco!* (1956) by Italo Calvino.
Other versions	*Three Wishes* (Netherlands); *Gambling Hansel* (German); *Old Smith* (British); *Carpenter's Tale* (Indian).

2. *The Spinster Sisters of the Penya Roja*

ATU classification	ATU 877: the old woman who was skinned Within the larger category ATU 850–999: realistic tales > 870–879: the woman marries the prince.
Literary versions	*La vecchia scorticata* (1634) by Giambattista Basile; *The King Who Wanted a Beautiful Wife* (1897) by Laura Gonzenbach; *Le tre vecchie* (1956) by Italo Calvino.
Other versions	*Jealous Sisters* (Greek); *Three Crones* (Italian); *One-Tooth and Two-Teeth* (Arab).

3. *The Castle of the Sun*

ATU classification	ATU 313: the magic flight Within the larger category ATU 300–749: tales of magic > 300–399: supernatural adversaries.
Literary versions	*La Palomma* and *Rosella* (1684) by Giambattista Basile; *Fundevogel* (1812) by Jacob and Wilhelm Grimm; *Mestermø* (1842) by Jørgen Moe; *Lu Re di Spagna* (1870) by Giuseppe Pitrè; *Blancaflor* (1924) by Aurelio Macedonio Espinosa; *Il giocatore di biliardo* (1956) by Italo Calvino.
Other versions	*Green Sleeves* (British); *The Orange Tree* (French); *Billiards Player* (Italian); *Baba Yaga* (Russian); *The Witch's Daughter* (Chinese).

4. Astoret the King

ATU classification	ATU 425: the search for the lost husband Within the larger category ATU 300–749: tales of magic > 400–459: supernatural or enchanted wife (husband) or other relative > 425–449: husband.
Literary versions	*Lo Turzo D'Oro* (1634) by Giambattista Basile; *Hurleburlebutz* (1812) by Jacob and Wilhelm Grimm; *Østenfor sol og vestenfor mane* (1841) by Peter Asbjørnsen and Jørgen Moe; *Lu surciteddu cu la cuda fitusa* (1870) by Giuseppe Pitrè; *L'uomo che usciva solo di note* (1956) by Italo Calvino.
Other versions	*The Gold Ball* (French); *Tamlane* (English); *Feather of Finist, the Bright Falcom* (Russian); *Fair as the Sun* (Greek); *Snail Choja* (Japanese).

5. The Envious Moor of Alcalà

ATU classification	ATU 503: helpful elves Within the larger category ATU 300–749: tales of magic > 500–559: supernatural helpers.
Literary versions	*Die Geschenke des kleinen Volkes* (1812) by Jacob and Wilhelm Grimm; *The Wood Maiden* (1919) by Parker Fillmore; *I due gobbi* (1956) by Italo Calvino.
Other versions	*Brewery of Eggshells* (Celtic); *The Hump* (Netherlands); *Inishkeen's on Fire* (Irish); *Miser and the Fairies of the Gump* (British); *Old Men Who Had Wens* (Japanese).

6. The Saddle-Maker of Cocentaina

ATU classification	No ATU number
Literary versions	*Un aprenent de bruixot* (1912) by Francesc Martínez Martínez; *El marit de la bruixa* and *L'aprenent de bruixot* (1950) by Joan Amades; *Les bruixes de Tabarca* (1987) by González Caturla.
Other versions	-

As pointed out by Albero Poveda (2004: 150), although this tale does not have an ATU entry, it does display several motifs included in Thompson's *motif index* (1955–1958), namely:

D1901: witches induce love
F302.3.4: fairies entice men and then harm them
G269.3: witch harnesses man and leads him to dance
G242.1.2: witch rides stalk of broom
G243: witch's Sabbath

G250.1: man discovers his wife is a witch
G247: witches dance
G248: witches feast on rich food and drink
G248.1: man joins feast of witches
G249.2: witches scream
G249.3: witch enters and leaves house by chimney
G264: *La Belle Dame Sans Merci.* Witch entices men with offers of love and then deserts or destroys them

7. *The Gambling Man of Petrer*

ATU classification	ATU 1184: the last leaf
	Within the larger category ATU 1000–1199: tales of the stupid ogre (giant, devil) > 1170–1199: souls saved from the devil.
Literary versions	*Des Herrn und des Teufels Getier* (1812) by Jacob and Wilhelm Grimm.
Other versions	-

8. *Peret*

ATU classification	ATU 1539: cleverness and gullibility
	Within the larger category ATU 1200–1999: anecdotes and jokes > 1525–1724: stories about a man > 1525–1639: the clever man.
Literary versions	*The Story of a Very Bad Boy* (1910) by Andrew Lang; *La storia di Campriano* (1956) by Italo Calvino.
Other versions	*Irishman's Hat* (English); *Pedro de Urdemalas and the Gringo* (Mexican); *Si'Djeha Cheats the Robbers* (Arab); *Clever Old Man* (Indian).

9. *Joan-Antoni and the Blockheads*

ATU classification	ATU 1384: the husband hunts for three persons as stupid as his wife
	ATU 1245: sunlight carried in a bag into the windowless house
	ATU 1651: Whittington's cat
	ATU 1281: burning the barn to destroy an unknown animal
	ATU 1250A: bringing water from the well
	ATU 1286: jumping into the breeches
	ATU 1202: the grain harvesting
	Within the larger category ATU 1200–1999: anecdotes and jokes > 1200–1349: stories about a fool / 1350–1439: stories about married couples / 1525–1724: stories about a man

18 Introduction

Literary versions	*Die klugen Leute* (1812) by Jacob and Wilhelm Grimm; *Somme kjerringer er slike* (1841) by Peter Asbjørnsen and Jørgen Moe; *The History of Whittington* (1889) by Andrew Lang.
Other versions	*Th' Lad at went oot to look fer Fools* (British); *Coggeshall Jobs* (British); *The Three Sillies* (English); *Dommer as dom* (Netherlands); *Lutoniunshka* (Russian); *Woman Called Rice Pudding* (Arab).

10. *The Tale of the Halfling Chicken*

ATU classification	ATU 715: demi-coq. Within the larger category ATU 300–749: tales of magic > 700–749: other tales of the supernatural.
Literary versions	*O pinto borrachudo* (1879) by Adolfo Coelho; *Bout-d'-Canard* (1888) by Charles Marelle; *The Half-Chick* (1892) by Andrew Lang.
Other versions	*Van den halven Haan* (Netherlands); *Cock Who Went Traveling* (German); *Demi-coq* (French); *Mediopollo* (Spanish).

While the tables above show the ATU classification of the tales selected for this volume, it is worth noting that, altogether, Valor's folktale corpus includes Valencian-rooted literary versions of 41 universally recognized tale types (Borja, 2017, p. 421). In this sense, as Rodríguez Almodóvar & Lluch (1999, pp. 192–193) point out, it is truly remarkable to ascertain that folktales are substantially the same across extremely different and geographically distant cultures—especially with regard to their narrative structure—so much so that orally transmitted culture may be considered the most universal of all. At the same time, though, secondary elements such as language, customs and settings allow for those universal stories to be firmly ingrained in the collective memory—also known as *the imaginary*—of a social group who regards them as something unique and self-defining. This is the beautiful paradox of folklore: the universal meets the specific and vice versa.

Relevance, Peculiarities and Innovations of Valor's Folktale Corpus

There is no doubt that the *Rondalles Valencianes*, besides being an all-time best-seller among readers of all ages, have become canonical in the context of Catalan popular literature. Beltran (2007, p. 29) qualifies Valor's folktale collection as "the most thorough and valuable from a literary perspective" without which it is impossible to grasp the importance of the genre. Borja (2020, p. 40), for his part, states that "when we talk about the *Rondalles Valencianes*, we are referring to a unique, iconic literary monument." Along the same lines, Albero Poveda (2004, p. 265) argues that the *rondalles* "are, qualitatively speaking, among the richest in episodes and motifs of traditional Catalan folklore." And, according to Oriol (2011, p. 105–107), Valor contributes to the national folktale catalogue with a greater variety of themes—above all, tales of magic—and, more specifically, with 26 previously unpublished stories from the Southern Valencian region.

Other relevant and remarkable features of the *rondalles* that critics and scholars have pointed out are their originality, methodological rigor, rich vocabulary and descriptive depth. For instance, Montoya Abat (1999, p. 350) argues that Valor's folktales, like all of his writings, "are highly elaborated and exhibit a solid technique, a careful composition and an elegant style" without losing their folkloric appeal. This attention to detail is especially noticeable in the descriptions of the natural landscapes where the action is set, as illustrated by this extract from "The Spinster Sisters of the Penya Roja," the second folktale in this volume:

> The *Penya Roja* is a massive, elevated peak, and is not at all easy to climb. It's surrounded by sudden, steep drops into black and daunting ravines and it often lies for days, and even weeks, beneath a thick pall of clouds that rise up loaded with moisture from the Mediterranean Sea.

The reader can easily tell that Valor himself knew these mountainous areas like the back of his hand. An enthusiastic hiker and an occasional small game hunter, he had developed over the years a deep knowledge of the orography of the territory; he was also an expert in the flora and fauna of his homeland. Not only could he recite from memory the exact altitude of hills and mountains to the meter, but he could also promptly identify birds based on their flying and singing. Enric also dabbled in meteorology, especially the weather phenomena closely related with agriculture. This invaluable, first-hand knowledge permeates every page of his tales, which are a true testimony of the author's love for nature and for the land where he was born.

Valor also succeeds in preserving the fresh charming style of traditional oral narratives by means of a wide range of resources such as dialectal expressions, idioms and proverbs, onomatopoeias and interjections, attitudinal adverbs, affective suffixes, deictic elements, rhetorical questions and cliffhanging pauses (Lluch, 2011). Nods to the reader through clarifying comments, appraising remarks and similar digressions are also a staple in Valor's corpus, together with humor, irony and wordplay. To exemplify this last aspect, let us consider the names of the two protagonists in "The Envious Moor of Alcalà," tale number five in this compilation: Al-Favet and Abd al-Maduix. The former is a play on the term "fava" which literally means "bean" but has the metaphorical meaning of "fortunate" or "naive," while the second is a play on "maduixa," the Valencian word for "strawberry." Both names are indeed very sonorous and funny and have been given the Arabizing prefixes "Al-" and "Abd-al-" so as to complete the Moorish atmosphere of the story. To top it all off, the only Christian character in the tale, an apostate and a conman, is called Sanç-i-Bons, which literally means "good saints" or "good and saintly," the complete opposite.

As may be surmised from all the above, the presence of the narrator and his interaction with the reader are essential traits which contribute to evoking orality and adding expressive force to the narration. They allow the audience to feel closer to the story too. Here are some recurrent formula used by Valor to fulfil this purpose: "And what do you think happened next?," "what does he see?," "As you can well imagine," "as we know," "who knows where that came from," "we know that was the only reason she had come," "and this was strangest of all," "Exactly right!," etc.

In this respect, it is important to note that the tales were originally intended for a mixed, heterogeneous audience ranging from children to adults. Over time, there have been several adaptations of his tales to younger readers but most of the new versions have suffered very few alterations, as explained by author Rosa Serrano (1999, p. 236):

> My task was very simple. I just shortened the lengthy passages and elaborate descriptions that were not suitable for children [...]. Not only was Mr. Valor informed of this "gardening" process but he also read or rather audited the adaptations and gave his explicit consent.

As explained in the previous section, Valor intended his folktales to function as tools for teaching the Catalan language—with a special focus on the Valencian variety—and giving the Valencian people their self-esteem back. This accounts for another key feature of the *rondalles*: their educational tone, as evidenced by the delightful fragments which comment and/or describe, in more or less detail,

> the ethnological reality of our people, namely customs, house building methods, opinions about saints and other religious figures, medicinal uses of herbs, superstitions, cooking techniques, local festivities, etc. All these references make the stories become alive and help recover a bygone form of life.
>
> (Albero Poveda, 2004, p. 16)

The following extracts from "The Woodcutter of Fortaleny," the first tale in this volume, illustrate this educational intention: the first one elaborates on a historical event to help situate the story, while the second one offers information about the etymological evolution of proper and geographical names:

> A great event had occurred in Rome, and now its echoes and effects were reaching the Ribera de Xúquer with a joyful explosion of festivities. The Emperor Constantine had accepted Christianity and granted

Christians the freedom to practice their faith in public. [...] The year was 313.

To cut a long story short, in 1713 Ben Paulo was called Pauet. After more than 1,400 years of life, he was still cutting wood. He was still rich, too. His money never ran out and he lived in the same village where he had been born in Roman times. That village was no longer known as *Fortalèniun* (nor *Beniarení* as the Moors had called it during some time), nor *Fortalénio* as the Mozarabs called it, nor any other ugly-sounding name to the wood-cutter's ear. At that time it was called, as it still is today, *Fortaleny*, in the lovely and lilting Valencian tongue that was spoken throughout the Ribera.

A unique trait of the *Rondalles Valencianes*—and one that substantially distinguishes them from most European folktales—has to do with the fact that the action is not set in remote, unknown or imaginary locations; on the contrary, Valor purposely situates the story in well-known, genuine geographical locations in the Valencian territory. Furthermore, with the intention of rendering the tale more credible and strengthening its connection with the reader, we often find the phrase "it can still be seen today" or "today you can still find" in the descriptive passages, especially those found in the opening lines of the tale.

Another distinctive feature that makes Valor's folktale corpus stand out in the genre is their "humanist and progressive stance," particularly when it comes to the depiction of human relations (Albero Poveda, 2004, p. 267). Unlike most traditional folklore, issues like cruelty and violence, albeit present in some tales, are generally toned down, and the focus is placed on the accomplishment of the challenging task by the hero of the story rather than on the actual fight (Rodríguez Almodóvar & Lluch, 1999). Oftentimes, the villains' fate is described in such a way that the reader feels sorry for them; moreover, the punishment they receive is generally proportional and justified, and tends to have a moralizing function, as this passage from "The Envious Moor of Alcalà" illustrates:

> The years went by, and the heart of Abd al-Maduix, the envious Moor, grew softer through his misfortune, just as the diabolical pickle brine had softened his body. In time he was resigned to his deformity, realizing that it was a just punishment for his inordinate envy. And, by the will of Allah, he and Al-Favet became close friends and lived in peace; and thus they both grew old and were living examples of divine justice, which always allots to each and every one what they deserve.

Another aspect of interest which makes Valor's tales singular has to do with female roles, which are far from stereotypical: many of Valor's heroines are described as smart and resourceful young women that rescue the prince and save the day; they are the ones with initiative, courage and resolution. In contrast, most princes in the *Rondalles Valencianes* come across as immature and spoiled characters, greatly dependent first on paternal figures and then on the women they fall in love with or their future wives (Rodríguez Almodóvar & Lluch, 1999; Albero Poveda, 2010).

Finally, with regard to religion, Valor usually treats this issue from a historical, objective perspective, often resorting to humour to actually question the stereotypes traditionally attached to each faith—mainly Christian and Islamic. In many *rondalles* the action is set during medieval times, either under Muslim rule[18] or some centuries after King James I's conquest, which took place in 1238. In addition, we frequently find religious figures with an active role, usually Saint Peter and occasionally Jesus Christ himself, as is the case in "The Woodcutter of Fortaleny." As pointed out by Rodríguez Almodóvar & Lluch (1999, p. 198), one distinctive feature of the *Rondalles Valencianes* has to do with the fact that a handful of protagonists who try to cheat holy characters for their own advantage are not punished but amply rewarded, despite their dishonesty and deceitfulness. Finally, Valor's tales also feature antagonistic, supernatural characters such as the Devil, lesser demons and a personified Death: these actors generally find themselves defeated and mocked when trying to claim the main character's soul.

All in all, we must not lose sight of the fact that traditional oral narratives are inherently dynamic and open to variation and constant change. The treatment given to these stories by those who transcribe them and recreate them is what really makes them special and, in a way, leads them to become classics too. This is undoubtedly the case of Valor's folktales inasmuch as they constitute an essential piece in the collective memory of the Valencian people, who will always find their true identity when reading and rereading these tales.

I would like to finish this introductory chapter on a personal note. As one of Enric Valor's grandchildren, I have been extremely lucky and privileged to grow up surrounded by these fantastic stories told in my native language by an excellent, caring, naturally-talented storyteller. The translation the reader will find in this volume has succeeded in preserving the essence and the spirit of the tales: in a way, Valor speaks English here. So, as suggested by Sanchis Guarner more than 40 years ago addressing his fellow compatriots in the preface he wrote to Enric Valor's *Obra literària completa*: "Read these folktales, Valencians, and have your children read them: they are a veritable delight, both objectively and subjectively, whether enjoyed in a group or enjoyed alone" (1975, p. 8).

Notes

1 Joan Fuster (1922–1992) was a prominent writer especially known for his insightful political essays, the most influential of which is *Nosaltres els Valencians* (We the Valencians, 1962). In 1981 he suffered an attempt on his life in his own home where two bombs were planted. He was not injured but his library and other rooms were severely damaged. No one was prosecuted. Manuel Sanchis Guarner (1911–1991) was a linguist, historian and university

Introduction 23

lecturer whose main work focused on lexicography and grammar (*La llengua dels valencians*, The Language of the Valencians, 1967). In 1978, he founded the *Institut Interuniversitari de Filologia Valenciana*. He was also the target of many right-wing extremist threats and attacks on his life, which went unpunished. Vicent Andrés Estellés (1924–1993) is considered the most relevant Valencian poet in the twentieth century with widely known collections such as *El llibre de les meravelles* (The Book of Wonders, 1971). His poems have become symbols of the pro-Valencian movement.

2 Alacant is the native term. Alicante in Spanish.
3 Pompeu Fabra (1868–1948) was a Catalan engineer and linguist who brought about a thorough and highly influential reform of the orthographic norms of the Catalan language and enormously contributed to its standardization after centuries of total disarray in terms of spelling. His *Diccionari general de la llengua catalana* (General Dictionary of the Catalan language, 1931–1932) is considered a seminal work which established the basis for homogenizing orthography and recovering the unity of the language despite its dialectal variants.
4 Carles Salvador Gimeno (1893–1955) was a Valencian linguist, teacher and poet. A pivotal figure in promoting the new orthographical and grammatical rules of the Catalan language in the Valencian territory, he was one of the delegates in the conference that led to the signature of the *Normes de Castelló*. He also organized the language and literature courses in *Lo Rat Penat*. His production includes poetry, fiction and linguistic texts such as *Gramàtica valenciana* (Valencian Grammar, 1951).
5 Josep Giner Marco (1912–1996) was a Valencian linguist whose vast philological knowledge is widely recognized. A disciple of Pompeu Fabra at the University of Barcelona, he contributed to spreading the *Normes* and participated in various etymological, lexicographical and dialectal works as a language consultant.
6 Henceforth, all quotes from Catalan authors are my translation.
7 Joan Coromines (1905–1997) was a Catalan linguist specialized in Romance languages. Forced into exile after the Civil War, he became a professor at the University of Chicago, where he taught for 20 years. His enormous linguistic production includes the *Diccionari etimològic i complementari de la llengua catalana* and the *Onomasticon Cataloniae*.
8 Francesc de Borja Moll (1903–1991) was a linguist from Menorca (Balearic Islands). His most important work is the *Diccionari català-valencià-balear*, which he co-authored with Antoni Maria Alcover.
9 Joan Senent (1916–1975) was a Valencian publisher who opened several bookshops devoted to the promotion of the Catalan language. From 1969 to 1972 he directed the *Gorg* magazine, a monthly publication in Catalan which tackled social and cultural topics and which featured articles written by activists and intellectuals of the time.
10 Undermining age-old national cultures by reducing them to simple regional folkloric manifestations was one of the most explicit policies of cultural annihilation perpetrated by the Franco regime (Solé Sabaté & Villarroya Font, 1993; Santacana, 2013).
11 See https://themotheroffishes.com/
12 In this respect, Allensworth (1998, p. 11) makes a relevant distinction between *true* nation-states, such as Japan, Germany and Iceland, whose inhabitants "are members of a single, distinct nation with a sense of national purpose and destiny," and *Staatvolk* states, such as Spain, France and Russia, where one dominant ethnic group absorbs smaller ones and becomes "the heart and soul of the state" by imposing not only its language but also its myth system.
13 Collections of assorted folk materials had been put together by Joaquim Martí Gadea in 1891, Francesc Martínez Martínez in 1912 and 1920, and

24 *Introduction*

Josep Pasqual Tirado in 1930. Tirado is widely renowned for his *Tombatossals*, a tale based on a mythical giant of the same name that, according to the legend, founded Castelló de la Plana, the fourth largest city in the Valencian country.
14 Joan Amades (1890–1959) was a Catalan ethnologist and folklorist, as well as a passionate advocate of Esperanto. His *Costumari català* (A Collection of Catalan Customs, 1950–1956) is regarded as a seminal book in folklore studies.
15 Antoni Maria Alcover (1862–1932) was a cleric, linguist and folklorist from Mallorca (Balearic Islands). His most important work is the *Diccionari català-valencià-balear*, which he co-authored with Francesc de Borja Moll, and his collection of folktales, which he wrote under the pseudonym Jordi des Recó.
16 To put it simply, a legend may be defined as a traditional story considered to be true, while a folktale is a fantastic, fictional narrative with no historical base. The Grimm brothers explained the difference as follows: legends (*Sagen*) are "more historical" and folktales (*Märchen*) are "more poetic." Thus, the basic distinctive element is their different relation with the real world: the events in a legend are real and plausible though not historically accurate, while those in a folktale are assumed to be false (Albero Poveda, 2004, p. 128; Birx, 2010, p. 280–281).
17 The literary versions provided here maintain their original title. The list is not exhaustive.
18 A large part of the Iberian Peninsula was under Islamic rule for nearly eight centuries (between the years 711–1492). It was known as *Al-Andalus* or Muslim Spain.

References

Albero Poveda, J. (2004). *Les rondalles meravelloses i llegendes d'Enric Valor*. Publicacions de l'Abadia de Montserrat.
Albero Poveda, J. (2010). Velles històries, biografies de la memòria: Les rondalles valorianes a través dels seus personatges. In V. Cantó Doménech, V. Brotons Rico, & O. Pérez Silvestre (Eds.), *Enric Valor: El valor de les paraules* (pp. 71–82). Acadèmia Valenciana de la Llengua.
Allensworth, W. (1998). *The Russian question: Nationalism, modernization, and post-communist Russia*. Rowman & Littlefield.
À Punt Media (2018–2020). Catacric Catacrac [animated series]. Zootropo Studio. Retrieved from https://lacolla.apuntmedia.es/alacarta/catacric-catacrac
Babalola, E. T. (2012). Atrophization of minority languages: Indigenous folktales to the rescue. *International Journal of Linguistics*, 4(1), 158–173.
Barroso, L. E. (2013). *Narrative and the maintenance of Great Lakes Native American cultural identity* [Honors Thesis, Andrews University]. AU Digital Commons. https://digitalcommons.andrews.edu/honors/69
Beltran, R. (2007). *Rondalles populars valencianes: Antologia, catàleg i estudi dins la tradició del folklore universal*. Publicacions de la Universitat de València.
Birx, H. J. (2010). *21st century anthropology: A reference handbook, vol. 1*. Sage Publications.
Borja, J. (2017). Literatura popular valenciana: Postguerra, franquisme, normalització i renovació. In C. Oriol & E. Samper (Eds.), *Història de la literatura popular catalana* (pp. 405–452). Publicacions de la Universitat Rovira i Virgili.
Borja, J. (2020). *Enric Valor, memòries*. Institució Alfons el Magnànim.

Britannica, Editors of Encyclopedia. (n.d.a). Fairy tale. In *Encyclopedia Britannica*. Retrieved March 2, 2022, from https://www.britannica.com/art/fairy-tale

Britannica, Editors of Encyclopedia. (n.d.b). Norske folkeeventyr. In *Encyclopedia Britannica*. Retrieved April 20, 2022, from https://www.britannica.com/topic/Norske-folkeeventyr

Casanova, E. (2011). La riquesa lèxica de l'obra valoriana. In G. Lluch & J. M. Baldaquí (Eds.), *Nova reflexió sobre l'obra d'Enric Valor* (pp. 55–73). Institut Universitari de Filologia Valenciana.

Denecke, L. (2020). Brothers Grimm. In *Encyclopedia Britannica*. Retrieved April 12, 2022, from https://www.britannica.com/biography/Brothers-Grimm

Enciclopèdia Catalana. (n.d.). La Renaixença. In *Enciclopèdia Catalana*. Retrieved February 22, 2022, from https://www.enciclopedia.cat/ec-gec-0054881.xml

Ferrer Gironès, F. (1985). La persecució política de la llengua catalana: Història de les mesures preses contra el seu ús des de la Nova Planta fins avui. *Edicions, 62*.

Flood, A. (2016, January 20). Fairy tales much older than previously thought, say researchers. *The Guardian*. https://www.theguardian.com/books/2016/jan/20/fairytales-much-older-than-previously-thought-say-researchers

Giner, J. (1971). Preface. In E. Valor (Ed.), *Millorem el llenguatge* (pp. 5–8). Gorg.

Grimalt, J. A. (1978). La catalogació de les rondalles de mossèn Alcover com a introducció a llur estudi. *Randa, 7*, 5–30.

Iborra, J. (1980). Preface (Enric Valor: novel·la i societat). In E. Valor (Ed.), *Sense la terra promesa* (pp. 9–17). Prometeo.

Lexico. (n.d.). Folk tale. In *Lexico.com dictionary*. Retrieved February 10, 2022, from https://www.lexico.com/definition/folk_tale

Lluch, G. (2011). La vigència de les rondalles d'Enric Valor. *Serra d'Or, 621*, 44–47.

Lluch, G., & Serrano, R. (1995). *Noves lectures de les Rondalles Valencianes*. Tàndem Edicions.

Marín, I. (2017). Les primeres rondalles d'Enric Valor. *Revista Lletres Valencianes, 50*, 23–28.

Multilingual Folk Tale Database. (2014). *Aarne-Thompson-Uther classification of folk tales*. Retrieved March 7, 2022, from http://www.mftd.org/index.php?action=home

Montoya Abat, B. (1999). La contribució d'Enric Valor a la llengua i la literatura del País Valencià. In V. Salvador & H. van Lawick (Eds.), *Valoriana. Estudis sobre l'obra d'Enric Valor* (pp. 347–356). Publicacions de la Universitat Jaume I.

Oliag, N. (1998). Transcripció, intervenció, transformació (a propòsit de les rondalles d'Enric Valor). In M. Pérez Saldaña (Ed.), *Paraula de la terra* (pp. 187–196). Publicacions de la Universitat de València.

Oriol, C. (2011). Les rondalles d'Enric Valor en el marc de la rondallística catalana. In G. Lluch & J. M. Baldaquí (Eds.), *Nova reflexió sobre l'obra d'Enric Valor* (pp. 95–109). Institut Universitari de Filologia Valenciana.

Oriol, C., & Pujol, J. M. (2008). Index of Catalan folktales. Helsinki: Academia Scientiarum Fennica, FF Communications, *294*.

Rodríguez Almodóvar, A., & Lluch, G. (1999). Enric Valor i la cultura popular europea. In V. Salvador & H. van Lawick (Eds.), *Valoriana. Estudis sobre l'obra d'Enric Valor* (pp. 191–202). Publicacions de la Universitat Jaume I.

RondCat, Arxiu de Folklore (2014). *Catalan Folktales Search Engine*. Retrieved March 7, 2022, from http://rondcat.arxiudefolklore.cat/

Salvador, V. (2011). La novel.lística d'Enric Valor en el marc de la narrativa catalana. In G. Lluch & J. M. Baldaquí (Eds.), *Nova reflexió sobre l'obra d'Enric Valor* (pp. 112–124). Institut Universitari de Filologia Valenciana.

Sanchis Guarner, M. (1975). Preface. In E. Valor (Ed.), *Obra literària completa, vol. 1* (pp. 9–13). Gorg.

Sanchis Guarner, M. (2001). *Els valencians i la llengua autòctona durant els segles XVI, XVII i XVIII*. Publicacions de la Universitat de València.

Santacana, C. (2013). *Entre el malson i l'oblit: L'impacte del franquisme en la cultura a Catalunya i les Balears (1939–1960)*. Editorial Afers.

Seago, K. (2001). Shifting meanings: Translating Grimm's fairy tales as children's literature. In L. Desblache (Ed.), *Aspects of specialized translation* (pp. 171–180). La Maison du Dictionnaire.

Serrano, R. (1995). *Enric Valor: Converses amb un senyor escriptor*. Tàndem Edicions.

Serrano, R. (1999). Les rondalles d'Enric Valor i l'escola: una reflexió personal. In V. Salvador & H. van Lawick (Eds.), *Valoriana. Estudis sobre l'obra d'Enric Valor* (pp. 235–239). Publicacions de la Universitat Jaume I.

Smith, A. (1986). *The ethnic origins of nations*. Basil Blackwell.

Solé Sabaté, J. M., & Villarroya Font, J. (1993). *Cronologia de la repressió de la llengua i la cultura catalanes (1936–1975)*. Curial.

Stein, M. B. (2015). Aarne-Thompson index. In *The Oxford Companion to Fairy Tales*. Oxford University Press. Retrieved April 18, 2022, from https://www.oxfordreference.com/view/10.1093/acref/9780199689828.001.0001/acref-9780199689828-e-2

Thompson, S. (1955–1958). *Motif-index of folk-literature: A classification of narrative elements in folktales, ballads, myths, fables, mediaeval romances, exempla, fabliaux, jest-books, and local legends* (Vol. 6). Indiana University Press.

Thompson, S. (2021). Folk literature. In *Encyclopedia Britannica*. Retrieved March 18, 2022, from https://www.britannica.com/art/folk-literature

Uther, H. J. (2004). The types of international folktales: A classification and bibliography. Based on the system of Antti Aarne and Stith Thompson. *FF Communications*, 284–286. SuomalainenTiede Akatemia.

Valor, E. (1935, July 27). La importància de l'idioma. *El País Valencià*, 11, 2–3.

Valor, E. (1975). Preface. In *Obra literària completa, vol. 1* (pp. 21–27). Gorg.

Valor, E. (1999). Lectio Honoris Causa. In V. Salvador & H. van Lawick (Eds.), *Valoriana. Estudis sobre l'obra d'Enric Valor* (pp. 19–24). Publicacions de la Universitat Jaume I.

2 The Wood-Cutter of Fortaleny[1]
(A Story from the Tavernes Valley)

They say this really happened, and it did … a lovely little village, located in the middle of a wide and verdant plain in the Ribera de Xúquer.[2] It was surrounded by lush, leafy orchards with a wide variety of fruit trees that yielded wonderful fruits in season. At night, and especially in the long warm summers under the glorious dome of the stars, you could hear the secretive murmur of the great river in the distance rustling like dying wings through the poplar trees, tamarisks, willows and reeds. And by day you could see on the southwest horizon the hazy purple of the nearby peaks of the Corbera Mountains (then known as *Corbària*), about two and a half hours from the town.

At the time our tale begins, this place was a Roman possession: the lordly villa of a Patrician from Laci, surrounded by the well-kept cottages of hardworking local farmers who peacefully tilled the fertile soil under the protection of Rome. This placid community was made up of some 200 souls who worked for the Patrician. His name was Arènius (or Alènius, no one knows for sure). The town was then known as Fortalènium, which we nowadays call Fortaleny.

There was a kind of square in front of Arènius' villa, an open green where the little ones darted about and squealed like swallows, and the old ones enjoyed the sun and the fresh air and where the townsfolk met on celebration days. Leading south from the green was a narrow street with a sharp turn, and on that corner lived a baker who mostly made bread for the Patrician and, to a lesser extent, for the other folks of the village. They also brought him foods to be cooked in his oven. Sharing a wall with the baker lived the only wood-cutter in town, whose name was Paulus.

Paulus lived with his wife, was middle-aged, had no children and never would, undoubtedly by the will of God. Due to the vicissitudes of life after the Roman conquest, Paulus was a freedman, though he hadn't got an inch of land to his name. So, in spite of his wood-cutter's freedom, he and his wife could afford but little to eat and were often as hungry as Garronus—a sharp-boned Roman of Arènius' entourage who had fallen into disfavor with his lord.

DOI: 10.4324/9781003324232-2

What the wood-cutter loved was to go up into the mountains and chop his wood to sell; though in fact he had only two main customers: the old and scrawny Roman Patrician, who was always cold in that gentle clime, and the baker, who had to bake bread and who had no sons to go out and fetch his fire-wood.

***

It came about that the wood-cutter's wife, after so much deprivation, took to scrounging every penny they had and never bought cabbage, either for dinner or for supper; and this was a great misfortune for Paulus, as he loved a good cabbage to distraction. Night and day he dreamed of a nice, big plate of fragrant boiled cabbage, or of fried cauliflower.

Months and months went by.

"Have you cooked me cabbage today?"

"Ahhh, cabbage! You know we haven't got a garden," complained Floràlia, which was her name. "Where in the world am I supposed to get cabbage?"

"Peace, woman. Peace."

So in order to soothe his craving for cabbage, that day Paulus chopped away at the holly bushes and tree stumps as hard as ever he could.

But one day, at the height of the cabbage season, when Floràlia had hired out to weed the wheat fields a quarter of an hour from the village, Paulus pretended to be unwell and stayed at home. When she was gone, he rummaged through their valuables and managed to find a single copper coin. It shone like the morning sun. And what do you think he spent it on? Exactly right: a basket full of cabbages!

So his wife wouldn't find them when she came home, he hid them in the shed, beneath a few pine bough sheaves.

***

He got up early next morning as usual, before the first light, to chop wood. Floràlia was sleeping. He goes to the stable to fit out the donkey. He puts on the *bastum*, a kind of packsaddle with carrying rods on the sides, and ties on that an iron cooking pot, his work tools and his shoulder bag, with two cabbages and a loaf of bread. He leads the loaded donkey into the street and sets out along the footpath to Corbera. The great mountain range comes slowly into sight, like a mysterious realm in the vague early morning light. As the sun came up over the beaches of Cullera[3]—it then would have been called *Cullària* (or maybe something completely different)—Paulus skirted the Corbera castle, which at that time was fortified by means of low but almost impassable hills. The wood-cutter turns to the west and takes the road across the open meadow behind the castle that slowly rises toward the higher mountains. And when he reached the foot of the mountainside, far from the castle where no one could see him, he set about unpacking his things.

Morning turned to day in the midst of the woods. A breeze from the west pushed decorative clouds into the blue atmosphere and on toward the shining sea. The fresh forest smells, the sweet, forlorn whisper of the wind, rustling its delicate, invisible wings among the million silken needles on the branches of the pines.

Now Paulus felt all of this, but didn't know he felt it. The only thought in his head was for that basket of cabbages!

He chooses a round clearing among the rocks, picks up some pine and oak twigs and, with a handful of leaves and tinder and a flint, he makes a fire encircled by four flat stones. A little spring bubbled close by among the moss and rosemary plants. He fills the pot with water from the spring, chops up the cabbages and puts them in. Oh, those delectable leaves! He carefully stokes the fire with stems of rockrose till the water starts to boil and then, and then ... what a sweet perfume of boiling cabbage filled the air!

The wood-cutter's spirits were raised. An exquisite lunch awaited him. A marvelous *iantàculum*, as the Romans used to say.

While the cabbage was cooking, he'd tie together three neat bunches of wood—his whole load for the day—and would load them onto the packsaddle, one on each side and the other in the middle, as they still do today in the lands of Valencia. It was for the Patrician. Arènius never wanted anyone else to cut his wood, not even his closest servant, because Paulus was the cream of the crop when it came to picking the finest twigs, the driest stems of rockrose and rosemary and the deadest thorny broom that made the best kindling. And the baker? He was delighted. Paulus brought him long-burning firewood that gave the bread a delicate crust with a lovely smell of authentic mountain lavender.

So. Paulus leaves his concoction to simmer in his little hide-away, protected from prying eyes and hungry mouths, and goes off about 500 paces to work. He ties the donkey to an oak tree, takes off his cape, leaving only his knee-length tunic, and starts pulling up underbrush with a kind of pick that was used in Roman times, now and then chopping off a few pine branches with his axe.

Immersed in his work, he hears a sound like someone scraping their sandals in the pebbly dust. "Uh-oh, this could be trouble," he mutters, thinking about the cabbage. He straightens his agile axeman's body to its full medium-sized height and spies through beady, darting eyes like a lizard's, two glowing men, clad in the Roman fashion of the day, advancing calmly along the path nearby. One of them was tall and fair and had delicate features and the other one was stout and dark and as bald as a coot. He looked like a fisherman.

"Men from the sea!" Paulus said to himself, though he was sorely mistaken.

As they come nearer they cry out, "My good man, if you please!"

The wood-cutter leaves his tools and steps to the side of the path, adjusting his tunic and shaking the dust from his sandals.

"Friend and brother," said the bald, heavy-set stranger, "tell us, if you can, where we might find good wild mushrooms."

Surprised, and cautious, Paulus answered, "You're late, gentle travelers, very late. The season, as folks say, is well done now."

"Yes," insisted the older one, "but they told us at the castle that the air in the mountains is fresh and cool and there may still be some growing in the shadows higher up."

Paulus knew what he had to do. All he wanted was to get them away from the cabbage!

"I'll tell you how to get to a place where you might still find a few."

"Well then, tell us, brother," sweetly replied the younger one. His strangely majestic bearing left the woodcutter's flesh all tingling.

And it's true, there was something odd and commanding about that young man, almost otherworldly. All of a sudden, and without knowing why, Paulus wanted to be friends with him ... But beware! There was a pot full of tasty cabbage to consider.

"Look, kind sirs," the clever wood-cutter raised his arm and pointed, "look over there, toward the top of the hills. There are some wide clearings, close to the clouds, with a reddish soil that's some of the best in the world. If there aren't bushels of good mushrooms growing up there, there won't be any anywhere." And he closed his mouth and took on a distracted expression, as though he were still considering.

"Many thanks," said the strangers politely. And with no more ado they started the long, demanding climb. When they were finally out of sight, the wood-cutter breathed a sigh of relief.

**

Around mid-morning he was as hungry as a wolf. So he stopped chopping wood, left his axe and pick on the ground and made his way, with his mouth watering, to the boiling cabbage, which by now would be cooked. But only after squinting carefully all around the horizon to be sure he was alone.

At about 50 paces the aroma hit him. When he gets there, he takes off the lid and ... almost passes out from the shock. There wasn't even a single leaf of cabbage in the pot, only a thin, cloudy liquid with a few loose and stringy bits of green. He knew in a flash what had happened. Somebody had stolen his cabbage!

He had to sit down on the edge of a stone, his head in his hands, his legs atremble, his stomach empty and his heart in the dust. Who could it have been? The two strangers? No, it couldn't have been them; they didn't look like thieves, he thought. All the same, nobody else had been around ...

He couldn't figure it out; his head was spinning. At last, he got up and went over to where his donkey was tied by one leg, patiently grazing on a patch of tall grass, took the loaf of bread out of the shoulder bag and began to chomp away at it.

"I wonder if I can find something else to eat out here," he mumbled, looking all around. He managed to find a few pepperworts growing at the foot of a small boulder. They were already withered with the cold, but they were good!

And so that day that had promised such delight, his *iantàculum* turned out to be pepperworts and bread (still and all, in peace and good health).

He got back home at nightfall. It was cold and he found his wife in a foul temper. Instead of the usual *may the Lord bless you*, she greeted him with "I've lost the pot!"

Paulus only chuckled. "What do you mean, you've lost the pot? It was me, woman. I only wanted to boil myself some greens."

"Well, you could've let me know!"

* * *

The next day the wood-cutter took another pair of cabbages from his hoard (they were already starting to droop), put another loaf of bread in the shoulder bag and repeated what he'd done the day before. With stars in the morning sky, here he goes again, making his way up into the mountains. He gets to the very same spot; the weather is good; he starts a fire, fills the pot with water and puts in the two lovely cabbages, nicely chopped with his hatchet. The smoke rose up that morning like incense in praise of the pagan gods of Rome, suffusing the motionless air with a cabbagey aroma that made his stomach growl.

He walked about a thousand paces off, to the footpath that crosses the mountain from one side to the other. And what do you know? Around midmorning, when the sun was getting hot and Paulus was beginning to sweat from swinging his pick, there they were again—the two odd strangers from the day before.

"What's going on?" he thinks to himself. He abruptly ceases chopping wood, leans on the handle, his head tense and his eyes all squinting, waiting for the pair to come closer.

"Good morrow," they say.

"Good morrow," Paulus brusquely replies. "So, did you manage to find the mushrooms?" he adds, a little defiantly.

"What was there to find, my brother?" asks the older one in a friendly tone. "We walked a long, long way for nothing ... But we don't blame you for that."

"Well, I told you it was late for mushrooms," answers Paulus, somewhat calmer now.

And then the fair one speaks up: "You wouldn't know of another spot, where we could try our luck again?"

"The truth is, this is really the time of year for button mushrooms," says the wood-cutter with what might've been an ulterior motive. "If you'd like, you could go down toward the village ... Fortalènium. Down there, along the banks of the big river, there are lots of poplar trees and you'll find bunches of white mushrooms around the trunks of the old ones that'll make your mouth water." *Today it'll be a long walk*, he cynically said to himself.

"So which way should we go?"

Paulus gives them directions ... this way ... that way. They thank him and take their leave.

The wood-cutter returned to his strenuous exertions. But when his belly began to grumble he went to the pot and ... by Jupiter's fiery thunderbolt! There was nothing inside but boiling water, just the same as the day before.

"Now this is just too much!" he growled. He was mad!

And you can imagine how he felt. For the second day in a row he only had bread and the miserable pepperwort to eat and a few straggling sprouts he could find along the edges of an open field.

Still grumbling to himself, he goes back home at nightfall, has supper in ill-tempered silence and goes to bed without a word of explanation to his wife, who all the time was saying, "Paulus, you're acting so strange. What in the world is going on?"

The following day he went out, as usual, at the break of dawn. He took along the "*bàstum*," the shoulder bag with a loaf of bread, tools to cut wood, the pot and, of course, another pair of cabbages. Today he was feeling tired (after so much disappointment) and he rode out on the donkey, something he seldom did, as he loved to go on foot.

On that third day (the third day is always decisive) up in the mountains, sun well up, blue sky polished like a mirror, after he lights the fire, instead of going off to cut wood, Paulus goes about 200 paces from the pot and hides in a little ravine. And then, around the same time as before, the two fellows we already know show up.

Paulus was horrified! He couldn't understand what was happening. At first he wanted to attack them, but he glanced at the younger one and suddenly started to tremble from head to foot. And this Paulus was no coward! He had more nerve than a wildcat!

"Good morrow, brother!" they say.

"Good morrow, if the gods be willing, and as long as we have food to eat and no one eats for another," Paulus replies, with a glint of malice in his eyes.

The visitors ignored the wood-cutter's defiant tone. There he was, swarthy from a lifetime of work in the open air, eyebrows wrinkled together in a frown, axe in hand ... with an odd mixture of anger and confusion on his face. The younger of the strangers smiled sweetly, and Paulus didn't know how, but the axe fell from his hands. The stout bald one also smiled, but his face was more like an animal's. He said in a firm and manly voice,

"We've come to thank you, kind wood-cutter. Yesterday, at last, we found some mushrooms, though not the good wild ones, and we've got some here in this bag."

Saying which, he took a small sack from beneath his robe and handed it to Paulus. He opened it and saw that it was full of sweet-smelling button mushrooms from the poplars. A very fine thing indeed. This was food fit for a Patrician, or maybe even better, and poor old Paulus had never found any for himself as they were much sought-after and very scarce. Still and all, he paid them little heed; he was still upset just thinking about those cabbages. The only thing he wanted was cabbage, cabbage and more cabbage! Because for a long time now, his wife hadn't cooked him any.

"Many thanks," he said at last, handing them back the bag. "It's not that I don't appreciate this, but the truth is, they're not that much to my liking." ...*What I want is what's boiling over there in that pot*, he almost blurted out, though he bit his tongue and held it back.

The three of them stood there a while in silence.

"So today you don't want to look for wild mushrooms?" Paulus finally asked, with a rush of anger.

"No. Today we've come to bid you farewell," replied the older one. "We're leaving the region. Off to see more of the world,"

"Well then, so long," said Paulus heatedly. But he thought to himself, full of resentment, *Good riddance, you pesky outlanders*.

The strangers set off up the path, as though they intended to cross the mountain, and were soon out of sight among the thick foliage of the woods. He calculated they'd be going in the opposite direction from where his pot of cabbage was boiling and so, reassured, he went back to chopping away at the gnarled roots of junipers, holly and rosemary bushes. But not more than ten minutes passed before he jumped up in the air with a terrible thought in his mind, "But what if they turned aside?"

He throws down his tools and runs to hide behind the boulders that surrounded the clearing where he'd made his fire. And *oh ye gods of Rome and of Greece and of Fortalènium*! What does he see? He couldn't believe his very own eyes! Those two outlanders, sitting with their robes above their knees, had—to judge from the sweet perfume that met his nose—taken off the lid of the pot of cabbages.

Howling like a wolf, Paulus leapt from his hiding-place, axe in hand, and rushed forward to do them ill. "Ah-hah! I've caught you this time!"

The strangers stood up and the younger one pierced him with those portentous eyes. Paulus stopped dead in his tracks, stunned, five or six paces away, as though both of his feet were nailed to the ground.

And then the older one, in a melodious but commanding tone of voice, said to him familiarly, "Paulus, wood-cutter of Fortalènium: your heart has been hard and you have not had the courtesy to invite us to partake with you this tasty meal of boiled cabbages. And as you prove to be so selfish, my Lord here present has decided to give you a timely lesson ..."

"Pray tell me who you are!" pleaded the wood-cutter, dropping his axe to the ground.

"Strange that you know us not," replied the older one, "since, although you have to hide it from the world, you and your wife Floràlia are Christians. Know well, then, that you have the honor and the glory to witness before you *Christus* in the flesh and the humble fisherman *Petrus*, who died before a handful of Christian martyrs."

Being a good Christian—in spite of his love for cabbage—Paulus recognized them and fell to his knees.

"Stand up, stand up," says Christ. "Your sins have not been grave, even if you have yielded inordinately to the temptation of cabbage ... beginning with the theft of that copper coin." He smiled, indulgent, and continued, "We know full well that you sent us astray on purpose ... but you have borne the test of the loss of your cabbages without an excess of disgrace."

"We could see," laughed Saint Peter, "that raising your axe was an empty threat."

Full of fear and trembling, Paulus said nothing.

"And so," added Christ with a joyful voice, "I shall grant you whatever it is you think you need."

The wood-cutter's emotions were changing so fast he didn't know what was happening.

"Ask away. Ask now while you can," kindly insisted Saint Peter.

And then the peasant's nerves began to calm down. He thought for a while, and finally he looked the Lord straight in the eye (oh yes, he was a bold one!). "I want five things, my Lord."

"So be it. What are they?"

"First, a sack with a string around the neck so I can close it. Anything I say will have to go in and can't come out unless I want it to."

"Granted."

"Second, a hammer that nobody can steal from me."

"Go on."

"Third, a fig tree in my yard that will yield figs during all the year and, if anyone climbs up it, they won't be able to come down unless I let them."

"Done."

"And number four, a pair of dice that will always let me win."

"Take care now, wood-cutter," interrupted Saint Peter, thinking that Paulus was taking advantage of the Lord's good will. "If you ask for so much, you'll end up with the power of a Patrician but the knowledge of a peasant, and the sin of pride will get you into Hell."

"Never mind, Peter. I've given him it, but not as he asks. He needn't have a pair of dice; but whenever he plays at dice he'll win. And so shall it be."

And the shameless Paulus continues: "Fifth and last, Lord, that no one may make me get up from whatever chair I sit in."

"Is that all, then?" asks Saint Peter impatiently.

"Well ... all," stutters Paulus, "uh ... not quite all. Now if God be willing, I'd like to have 700 years to enjoy my gifts."

"All right. Everything granted," says Jesus, "but be sure to use them wisely and keep in mind the salvation of your soul."

And with that they blessed him and disappeared and he never saw them again.

It had all happened so quickly that Paulus wasn't sure if he had dreamt it. But then he looked down at his feet and saw the new white sack woven of a strong, thick fabric and at his side he saw a hammer with a sturdy handle and a head forged of shining iron, and he knew it had all been real. And next he looked at the pot and found the cabbages there, all nicely cooked and waiting. So he sat himself down and, with a rough-hewn fork made of a rosemary stalk he contentedly savored the very best *iantàculum* he'd ever had in his wood-cutter's life. And maybe even better than any enjoyed by the Patrician Arènius, who was so refined that his tastes had been jaded by exquisite, over-spiced foods.

That night Paulus went back heavy-laden to Fortalènium and had to recount all of the incredible and marvelous events of the day to his wife.

***

The following spring, which wasn't long in arriving, a fig tree sprouted in Paulus' yard and grew and grew like it would never stop.

Floràlia didn't want her husband to make use of the gift of winning at dice; but he made a few trial runs on the sly and in no time had won an *úncia*.[4] On feast days he gambled with his neighbors, but not for much, since all of them were poor. On the other hand, if a Roman soldier stopped in Fortalènium—as often happened—on his way to Corbera castle, the wood-cutter would fleece him. Those days he was making good money, but to cover it up (and also because he dearly loved to work in the cool mountain air) he kept on cutting wood for Arènius and the baker. Little by little, Paulus and Floràlia left behind their lives of deprivation and began to take on a healthy glow.

But before summer came, the weather started turning foul. The olives fell unripe from the trees; the grape leaves withered on the vines; the leaves of the fruit trees turned yellow and dry and a plague attacked the grains and turned them black and hard like coal. Those were bad times for the *coloni* and the *liberti* and the *servi*.[5]

Fortalènium went from bad to worse. You could hardly see a tray of bread; people ate whatever they could—greens, boiled pepperwort, carrots instead of bread. At the same time, Floràlia saw through her window trays of bread going from the baker's to the Patrician's villa. And these were the only ones to be seen because, of course, Arènius, no matter what the circumstances, would never lack for flour.

Then one day, the wood-cutter had an idea. What about the sack?

The village was still; the villagers were out in the fields; the crickets whirred in the trees. Paulus hadn't gone out for wood and was lurking just outside the baker's door. In his hands he carried the sack the Lord had given him. It happened in a flash: one of Arènius' maidservants exits the bakery with a tray of a dozen loaves on her head, covered with a kitchen cloth. Paulus steps from behind the door, opens the sack and whispers, "Loaves, enter here!"

Suddenly the tray felt lighter on the maidservant's head, but she only gripped it down harder and continued on her way. It must have been the wind. Still, when she left the street, she noticed that the tray was as light as a feather. She takes it off her head, removes the towel and sees that the bread was gone.

"Oh no! Oh no! My master will kill me!" she cries.

There was much ado after that in the village, but the mystery was never solved.

The following days, Floràlia and Paulus ate bread to their hearts' content, even if they did feel an occasional pang of remorse.

***

Not long after, all of the regions of the Roman Empire were invaded by the raucous hullaballoo of festivals. They had begun in the big cities and moved to the mid-sized ones, and then to the towns and finally arrived at the villages and hamlets like Fortalènium. A great event had occurred in Rome, and now its echoes and effects were reaching the Ribera de Xúquer with a joyful explosion of festivities. The Emperor Constantine had accepted Christianity and granted Christians the freedom to practice their faith in public. Christianity hadn't yet reached all of our lands, but it was established in the important cities and towns and their surroundings. In Fortalènium, located in a populated area and close to modern cities and towns, most of the inhabitants were Christians. The year was 313.

The celebration in the village went on for days since Arènius, though not of the faith, was a gentle and kind-hearted man. Paulus left off chopping wood for quite some time, travelling instead from town to town and playing at dice, as gambling was a part of the general festivities. True, it was a very bad year, but the generous dispensations of the Emperor had brought the region back to life and every home was joyful again. The people forgot their cares and there was optimism everywhere. Business was on the rise and the peasants even started in to battle the plagues with whatever means they had which, needless to say, were not numerous.

And so it was that Paulus found an atmosphere propitious for gambling and everywhere he went he raised a tumult, an uproar, a scandal. No doubt about it! Every time he threw the dice there were so many black dots that it looked like a flock of starlings. But what was he to do? He couldn't lose, even if he wanted to. In three or four days he managed to bring home half of the *peculis*[6] in the whole region.

Soon it got out that Paulus was rich, from the brand new clothes he and Floràlia bought and the satisfaction that shone in their faces. Arènius bade the wood-cutter to his villa and said he would make him a citizen of Rome if he paid a special tribute of 20 silver *sestercis*.[7] Paulus thanked him and hastily brought him the money. Arènius congratulated him and, content with the wood-cutter's good fortune, sent off the parchment with the request and the money to the Roman prefect.

In order to encourage the spread of the Christian faith and to commemorate the Emperor's decree, they began to build a little church, to which Paulus made a donation of ten *uncies*. When the church was finished, the tunic he bought to wear to the first Mass sparkled and shone like the sun. That day, too, Floràlia was so well-dressed she looked like a Patrician's wife.

Needless to say, from that time on, there was never a shortage of cabbages on Paulus and Floràlia's table.

* * *

And what do you think happened next? Paulus stopped aging. He simply stayed in his forties, just the age he was when he ran into Saint Peter and the Lord back in the days when he was crazy for cabbages.

The years went by and, as had to happen, Floràlia passed away. Generation after generation came into the world and lived and grew and died with a persistent monotony that Paulus found appalling. He always stayed the same.

This should have made the townsfolk wonder, but they were a forgetful lot and they just got used to him being there, unchanged. And so he became a kind of institution: the village wood-cutter who never failed to give free wood to the poor. Yes, he just loved to use his axe! He had a nice fortune stashed away, owned his own lands and always had the best donkey in the area. And sometimes, when the spirit moved him, he still went round from town to town to give the dice a roll.

Though he provided them all with good lives, his many wives grew old and died in time. So every 30 or 40 years he'd marry another woman about his age, or maybe a little younger, who would make a good match.

And he trained each one: when cabbages were in season they had them every night for dinner—boiled or fried, leaves or flowers—and sometimes, too, for lunch. And as time went by the story of the two strangers and the pot in the woods faded out of memory ...

So Paulus the wood-cutter peacefully lived the 700 years the Lord had granted him.

* * *

Fortalènium had seen the many changes that occur in 700 years of history, and now it was a Muslim town with its own minaret, even though the poorer inhabitants—the peasants who worked the land—still maintained their faith in Christ, and their customs and native tongue were rooted in the past. The names, though, had altered. Paulus was now Ben Paulo and Fortalènium was called Fortalénio. Needless to say however, most of the villagers still lived from the hard-won bounty of the earth, the patient, demanding labor of cultivating the soil in the midst of a lovely profusion of plants and the comforting silence of centuries.

As Ben Paulo approached the end of those years that the Lord had permitted him, he suddenly began to grow visibly old. And so, in 1013 his hair was gray, his arms and legs were spindly and he tired very quickly when he wielded the axe and pick. This had never happened before. But he still loved to go up into the majestic mountains, especially those spots behind the beautiful Corbera castle, which held so many distant and ineffable memories for him.

That winter had been hard. One afternoon Ben Paulo caught a chill and went to bed and called Sahida, his current wife, to his side. At midnight he had a burning fever that left him undone. "Ay, Sahida!" he moaned. He was afraid. "I can't breathe, Sahida. I've never had anything like this before ... I'm not feeling well at all ... I think I'm going to die."

Weeping, Sahida prepared him cup after cup of herbal tea and laid mustard plasters on his chest. And from time to time she rested on some cushions by his side. Later, in the early morning, and exhausted from hearing her husband's labored breathing, she fell into a deep sleep. And soon, at daybreak, something mysterious happened. By the flickering light of a burning lamp, Ben Paulo sees a terrible woman come in: bony flesh, sallow cheeks and eyes alight with a diabolic gleam. She was wrapped in a sheet. Terrified and feverish, he thought, "This must be Death."

"Have you come for me?" he asked with an effort, though the answer was clear.

"Yes, I've come for you. Who else would it be?" answers Death with a horrendous grin.

"Ai, my poor wife. It'll be such a shock for her."

"Don't fret, Ben Paulo. I wouldn't be so inhumane. I've sent her into a slumber she won't wake up from till I've taken you away. Then she'll only see your body, lying calmly in the bed, as though you were asleep. This way it will be easier for her."

And then Ben Paulo looked through the window and saw that the sun had risen. Death noticed his stare. "What's that you're looking at?"

"Oh nothing. It's nothing." But Death also looked through the window into the yard.

"Ah, I see. The fig tree is full of fruit. It pains you to leave it?"

"Yes," confessed Ben Paulo, "They're so delicious now."

"Hmmm. They do look good," Death admitted, walking over to the half-opened window. And then she added, "Listen, I don't want to be a bother. While you're getting ready to die, I think I'll just pop out and have a taste."

Still breathing heavily, Ben Paulo smiled, "Oh yes, do. And have as many as you'd like."

So Death, wrapped in her winding sheet and carrying, as usual, her devilish scythe, climbed out through the window. And there she is, at the top of that beautiful, leafy fig tree that never ceased to bear fruit and that looked even now as though it were summer, every wide leaf like a juicy, fresh umbrella and every honey-sweet fig as heavy as an ounce.

But as soon as she reached the first limb, Death noticed something ugly—ugly indeed!—taking hold of her. All of sudden she felt very, very heavy, as if her feet were shackled to the thick boughs. Unable to climb any farther, she started right in to pick the figs and gulp them down so fast she hardly had time to chew. They were delicious!

Then she heard the wood-cutter's voice. "All right. I'm ready to die, my lady," followed by an odd little laugh.

Dutiful Death, hearing that Ben Paulo was prepared to die, started back down the tree. But what was her surprise when she found that she couldn't move an inch! She strains, she grunts, she shouts, she cries, she drops her scythe—and even the half-eaten fig in her hand.

She saw Ben Paulo's grinning face at the open window. He was suddenly healthy again. "You've dropped your fig," he called with a laugh.

"It's me that has a fig for a brain, to let you trick me so," she complained. "You cursed wood-cutter, what bewitchment is this?"

Ben Paulo's only answer was, "Could you please be quiet now? I really need to get some sleep."

At that moment Sahida woke up. She was amazed to hear her husband's forceful, happy voice again. "What's going on, Ben Paulo? By Allah the all-powerful, you're well again."

He wasn't just well; he looked once more like a 40-year-old. "I am, I am," said Ben Paulo, clearing his throat with a laugh. "Come, have a look out here."

Sahida looked into the yard. "Why ... it's Death!" she cried out, horrified.

"Don't be frightened, my lovely wife. She came to get me and I trapped her up there in the fig tree. She won't come down for a thousand years, unless I say so."

Sahida went out to spread the news and during that morning everyone in the village came to their house to see the monster.

"Have no fear, my brothers and sisters," proclaimed the sly wood-cutter. "Now all of us are safe. Enjoy! Eat and drink to your hearts' content!"

* * *

Things went on this way for a number of months. But such an unnatural state of affairs couldn't last forever. With Death imprisoned in a fig tree, everything everywhere was changed. The ill didn't die, fights broke out for the pettiest of reasons and many people were injured. The sick and infirm suffered greatly, especially those with incurable diseases. Many of these ended up going mad and crying out for Death to take them. What can I say? The ills of the world were spreading fast and finally reached Fortalénio, and the good-natured, carefree Ben Paulo began to lose his nerve.

Every day he went into the courtyard to have a little chat with Death. She was also feeling desperate and had lately lost her appetite for figs. "Ben Paulo," she constantly begged, "please let me down so the cycle of renewal through life and death can go on."

So one day Ben Paulo said, "OK. I'll set you free ... The world isn't going very well ... But you'll have to promise that you won't take me away..."

Death thought it over. "Well, I haven't got the power to let you live forever. How about another 700 years?"

The wood-cutter found this offer reasonable and accepted. "Come down," he said, and Death was able to move again.

She hurried to the ground and picked up her now somewhat rusted scythe from the dust and fallen leaves. She wrapped herself up in the winding sheet and disappeared from the place in a flash.

It was the 1st of January, 1013.

***

To cut a long story short, in 1713 Ben Paulo was called Pauet. After more than 1,400 years of life, he was still cutting wood. He was still rich, too. His money never ran out and he lived in the same village where he had been born in Roman times. But that village was no longer known as Fortalèniun (nor Beniarení as the Moors had called it during some time), nor Fortalénio as the Mozarabs called it, nor any other ugly-sounding name to the wood-cutter's ear. At that time it was called, as it still is today, Fortaleny, in the lovely and lilting Valencian tongue that was spoken throughout the Ribera.

Pauet was a well-loved, spry old man who still enjoyed the occasional game of dice. He lived in a tidy little house beside the same bakery as ever with his present wife, who came from the town of Albalat and was nearly 70. During this second reprieve that Death had granted him he hadn't remained in his forties but had, as the years went by, very slowly aged.

This year the winter was cold and rainy. Pauet, who couldn't stay still for long and always had to be out and about, got his feet wet walking through the puddles in the roads and caught a cold that just wouldn't stop.

"Marieta," he said one morning to his wife, "my head is pounding and I'm aching all over. I feel like something the cat dragged in."

"You stay in bed and I'll fix you a soup with mallow roots and buds."

Pauet, the wood-cutter of Fortaleny, smiled strangely. "All well and good, Marieta. But there's nothing to be done."

"Oh my Lord!" she exclaimed. "What in God's name are you saying?" She still didn't know her husband's history.

Pauet remembered that on that day it was exactly 700 years since he had freed Death from the fig tree. It was all over now! "Don't be too upset, Marieta, but I have to die today."

She started to bawl but Pauet only smiled. "Don't you cry, woman. I'm good friends with our Lord ... Now, now ... let me tell you the story." Which he did, to his wife's ever growing amazement. "And after all that," he said, coming to the end, "the Lord granted me 700 years of life in the very same year that Constantine gave Christians the freedom to publicly practice their faith. And then, 700 years after that, I cheated Death, as I've just described, and she gave me 700 more years, and they're up today. Do you see it now?"

"Oh, don't make me suffer so, Pauet," she cried. "It can't be true. You don't look like you're going to die. You just got your feet wet on the way from playing dice."

"My feet?" laughed Pauet. "All right. You'll see."

And so it was, that very same night they heard three slow, terrifying knocks at the door. "Whoever you are, come in," he said.

The bedroom door swung open and there, on the threshold, was Death, bony and sallow as ever, and Marieta, by the will of the Lord, fell into a deep sleep.

***

This time Pauet didn't try to argue or delay. To tell you the truth, after 1,440 years of life, he was a tad fed up.

"Let's go, whenever you say the word," he said to Death.

"Well, the bad news is that I've got orders to send you to Hell," the emaciated one replied. "And it makes me sad. You're so cheeky and clever that I was getting fond of you. That said, you'll be allowed to take along whatever you'd like on the journey."

The wood-cutter quickly stood up and grabbed the sack and the hammer with magic powers that he always kept nearby in a closet. And that very moment he felt a tremendous pain. It was so sudden, though, he hardly suffered at all. He felt himself being carried through the air and into a deep, deep chasm, one he had seen before, up on Simat Mountain. After a while they entered a gigantic cave, at the end of which there opened a flaming door. Four highly grotesque and mischievous demons came out to greet him. And at that moment, Death disappeared.

Pauet had his sack and hammer. The demons were shrieking like, well, demons. They take him into the chamber of fire and start in to torment him with red-hot skewers. But as soon as they touch him, he lets out a scream and flails all around with his hammer and lays them every one out on the ground. And then he says, "All right. Now I want to have a word with the Head Demon."

"Here I am," says the Devil, stepping out of a brightly-lit cavern. He was elegantly dressed, with a cape of fire, gilded horns and a long, pointed beard like a goat. "What a pretty picture," says Pauet. "Into the sack! Now!"

"What the ...?" The Head Demon feels himself being pushed by an irresistible wind right into the sack, where he couldn't move an inch or see a thing. Pauet closes the sack with the cord and ties it tight and commences to beat it with the hammer. Unmercifully.

"Hey! Hey!" yells Satan. "This is too much! You'll break my horns and all. Leave off with the hammer!"

The other demons rushed to help, but as soon as they touched the hammer they fell right down on the ground! The wood-cutter guffawed: "Don't be fools! This hammer is blessed. You'll never be able to take it from my grasp," and bam! bam! he kept on pounding the Head Demon.

"Throw him out! Throw him out! Get him out of Hell and let him go wherever he wants," the Devil ordered.

Hearing these words, Pauet stops pounding. He opens up the sack and out limps the Devil, his head all full of bruises and lumps, and he sets the victorious wood-cutter free.

In no time Pauet found himself somewhere far from the fiery cave at the top of a mountain on a dark and freezing night. The hammer and the sack were gone. He had dropped them in the waters of Acheron. The stars in the sky seemed very close.

"Well, if they don't want me in Hell," he says to himself, "I'll go to Heaven. It can't be far." He was shivering like a puppy. "Brrrr, it's cold!"

Something had to be done.

He stared and stared at the black dome of night until, at last, he spied to the east a kind of glowing cloud where the stars were thickest. "Hmmm. I wonder if Heaven is over there." It suddenly crossed his mind to jump up, and ... look! He was floating like a balloon, as light as a feather. And so, without a care in the world, he skipped and glided his way toward the empty vastness.

The mist began to take shape. As he got closer Pauet made out a swarm of sparkling clouds. When he finally arrived, he found that they were shining gates made of ivory and gems. And above it all glowed the mystical triangle of the Trinity, like burning coals.

Pauet rejoiced, "This must be Heaven!"

He stepped up and knocked assertively at the gate. He heard a sweet, harmonious music inside. *What lovely aubades*, he thought, enchanted. *How I'd love for Marieta to hear them.*

No one answered, so he knocked again, this time even harder. A small window, like a spy-hole, opened and he heard a voice: "Ah, so you're here at last!"

As we know, it had been more than a thousand years, but Pauet recognized the deep, firm voice of Saint Peter.

"It's Pauet, the wood-cutter of Fortaleny."

"I know, I know, and only too well. I'm afraid your case isn't clear. Wait here while I go and check the books."

Pauet felt a terrible chill. If he hadn't known he was already dead, he'd have thought he was going to freeze to death.

Finally Saint Peter came back. "Look here, Pauet. You've got hundreds of games of dice, a stolen tray of bread, cheating Death ... Too much mischief! I'm sorry, but you're going to have to spend a good number of years in Purgatory to cleanse you of your sins."

"Have I been that bad?" asked Pauet, surprised.

"Yes, you have. I've read of families ruined, the beating Arènius gave his servant for the stolen bread ..."

"But ... I didn't know anything about all that," the wood-cutter protested.

"Of course you didn't ... You gambled, you took the money and left. But there were lots of poor fellows who fell out with their wives for losing the family's funds, and two who hung themselves from an olive tree because they couldn't bear the poverty you caused them ... The gates are closed! Away with you!"

Then Pauet got angry. "So why did the Lord grant me the power to win?"

"To put it to good use, you ingrate!"

"The good use was to gamble and win, not to gamble and lose."

During this conversation with the saint, Pauet had been trying to get a look through the spy-hole to see what Heaven was like. And what a coincidence: at that very moment he saw, in an immense hall, a long procession of angels and archangels and seraphim and a host of blessed souls celebrating one of those festivals of chants and hallelujahs that are probably held on a fairly regular basis in a place like Paradise. All of them were singing a melodious hymn that filled their hearts with a complete and definitive joy.

"Saint Peter, just let me have a look," Pauet begged "and after that I'll go straight down to Purgatory."

The Saint took pity on the cabbage-loving wood-cutter and opened the gate a crack so he could see inside.

Peering over Saint Peter's shoulder from the threshold, Pauet took in a marvelous sight. And then, among the brilliant multitude that trailed the angels he spotted, with his keen woodsman's eye, his first wife, whom he had loved more than anything in the world.

"Floràlia!" he shouts.
"What's the matter?"
"It's my wife, from Fortalènium."
"She can't hear you," says the saint. "They're making too much noise. And anyway, there's no time to lose, Pauet. It's off to Purgatory for you and we'll talk again in one or 200 years, when your soul has been shriven."
"Can't I just say good-bye to Floràlia?!"
"Well, all right. You wait here and I'll go get her."

Saint Peter, unsuspecting, gets up from his chair—upholstered in a purple velvet that must have cost a fortune—and goes toward the joyful procession to find Floràlia and bring her back to say good-bye to her husband. But when he had taken ten or twelve steps he hears a thundering belly-laugh behind him. Recalling the power the Lord had given him, Pauet had sat down in the poor saint's chair.

Peter looked back and slapped his forehead with his hand. "Oh my goodness! I'd completely forgotten!"

"So, Saint Peter, you can't make me get up," the wood-cutter crowed. "I'll sit here in your chair forever and forever."

***

And so it was Pauet went to heaven after all. Since no one could make him stand up against his will—and the word of Christ can't be taken back—Saint Peter had to forgive the wood-cutter's sins (it was the easiest solution) so he could remain in glory for all of time to come ... and give Peter back his chair!

Notes

1 The consonant combination "ny" is pronounced like the "gn" in "poignant."
2 A region in the province of Valencia, through which runs the Xúquer River. It lies about 30 miles to the south of the capital city.
3 The consonant combination "ll" represents an approximant lateral palatal sound, phonetically represented as /ʎ/."
4 A bronze coin minted during the Roman Republic.
5 Plural forms of *colonus*, tenant farmer; *libertus*, freedman and *servus*, servant or serf.
6 Plural of *peculio*, a small fortune (excluding property) whose management is conceded by the head of a household to a son or servant.
7 Plural of *sestertius*, a large brass coin used during the Roman Empire.

3 The Spinster Sisters of the Penya Roja

(A Story from Castalla)

Once upon a time there was a very little house perched high at the top of the Penya Roja. It can still be seen today, a whitish dot on the crest of that colossal mountain. But it's uninhabited now; the walls are falling down from the wind and the snow and the rain; and the roof has disappeared.

The Penya Roja is a massive, elevated peak and is not at all easy to climb. It's surrounded by sudden, steep drops into black and daunting ravines and it often lies for days, and even weeks, beneath a thick pall of clouds that rise up loaded with moisture from the Mediterranean Sea.

Even though the summit is so high and foreboding, many centuries ago two aged sisters lived in the house, which was built on a flat ledge. The only thing they owned was that poor plot of mountain land and its house, a few white goats, a grey-bearded ram and three or four apple trees that grew nearby. During most of the year they made cheese with the milk from the goats and they sold whatever baby goats were born. In the autumn and winter they picked the apples and packed them in straw in baskets to sell to the landowners and townsfolk of Tibi, a quiet village at the foot of the western side of the mountain. The summers were nice so far up in the mountains. But now that they were old, the sisters were fearful of the winters, when the ground was covered with snow or hailstones, and of the springs, with their thunderstorms and lightning.

Now these two sisters—who had once of course been young—had the names of flowers: one was called Lily and the other was Rose.

Poor Lily had always been somewhat uncomely. Rose, on the other hand, had been in her youth as lovely as a princess in a fairy-tale: dark, rich hair, rosy cheeks, snow-white teeth and a smile like a ray of sunlight. Now though, all that was left was a memory. They were two little wrinkled old ladies, both of them ugly, with hair on their lips, noses like the beak of a gull and skin as dry as parchment.

Lily had always been jealous of her sister, but she kept her feelings hidden all their lives, tempered no doubt by sisterly affection; and they got on well together, with no unseemly shouting or fights.

* * *

One year the news went round that the son of the king would be travelling through the mountains, including the Penya Roja. The prince was handsome and soft-hearted, easy to enamor and had an uncommon love of the countryside. It was said that he often went out hunting to relieve a certain unshakeable sadness, which his closest friends at court believed to be caused by the fact that he had reached the age to want to find a feminine heart to beat in harmony with his own.

Like most uncomely women, Lily was very clever. And ever since she caught wind of the news, she couldn't stop turning over plans in her mind. One cold February night, with snow and hail coming down all day and the wind howling in the chimney, the sisters were sitting by the fire. Lily revealed her plan to her less intellectual sister.

"Rose, I have an idea."

"What idea?"

"An idea that could make you the envy of the Kingdom of Valencia."

"Oh Lily, dear. Don't be silly ... You're making fun of me."

"No Rose. This is serious. You know I've always been a deeper thinker than you. Just hear me out and you'll see."

"I'm listening, I'm listening," she said, both innocent and incredulous.

Lily's ugly face was grave, and she pronounced her words like an oracle: "I'm going to marry you off to the prince."

Hearing such foolishness, Rose broke out in a belly-laugh. She was sure her sister had lost her mind.

But Lily was adamant. "Stop laughing and pay attention. I can get you married to the prince as sure as these mountains will still be covered with snow and ice in the morning."

"Whooooh, whooooh," moaned the northwest wind in the chimney, as though it wished to agree.

"Have you forgotten," objected Rose, "that I turned 79 the day before yesterday?"

Lily paid her no heed and went on with her plan: "Word is that the king's son is hunting up in these mountains. There's been another light snow, so they're bound to be out tomorrow following the trails of rabbits and hares. And since we have some of the nicest bushes in the region just outside our cottage, it's a sure thing that one track or another will lead them by here. And when that happens I'll go out to speak to him, and ... well, you just leave it all to me. From this moment on, do everything I say. Go on to bed now and put your thumb in your mouth and keep it there till I come in to get you in the morning with the prince."

"But why? What kind of nonsense is this about sucking my thumb?"

"Don't ask questions and believe! If your thumb stays wet all night, it'll swell up and be as firm and soft as when you were just 15 and you had the skin of a baby."

Rose wasn't convinced. "What? Maybe if my face looked pretty ... But only my thumb?"

But Lily only smiled a mysterious smile. "All right! Off to bed with us both. Good night. And don't forget to do as I say."

So Lily, quite content, went to her bedroom and Rose, perplexed and intrigued by her sister's plan, went to hers.

* * *

The next day Lily opened her west-facing window that overlooked the valley to check the weather that the luck of her family depended upon. She was pleased to see the sky had cleared and the sun was shining. It was a beautiful day and the fields were covered with a thick layer of snow. "Perfect snow for the prince to follow rabbit tracks!" she happily exclaimed.

Then she went to her sister's room to see how the thumb was coming along. "Good morning, Rose. Let's see that thumb."

Rose stuck out her thumb from the thick blanket that covered her so that Lily could examine it under the light coming in through the window. She was delighted to see that, after a whole night in her sister's mouth, it looked exactly like a young girl's finger. It was adorable. It could have belonged to a 15- or 16-year-old princess. It also made a terrible contrast with the poor old woman's wrinkled face.

"You're such a devil, Lily."

"Just keep your mouth shut and believe and we'll be rich. You'll live like a queen, and I'll be able to go down to live in Tibi and won't have to spend the rest of my days doing all the hard work we have on this cold mountain."

Then Lily got a hammer and some nails and boarded up the window, leaving Rose's bedroom as dark as a winter's night.

Rose was perplexed. "Why are you doing that?"

"Look," explained Lily, "if I can get the prince to come in here, he mustn't see anything but your thumb. That's why I'm closing off the window. If he sees that face of yours, all of our hopes will be dashed. So when he comes in, you be sure to keep yourself covered from head to foot."

Lily prepared their breakfast over a good, indispensable fire in the kitchen outside. She also heated some milk and made a few things more, in case her plans worked out. Then she took the food into Rose's room and they had their breakfast together. Afterward she ordered, "OK, suck your thumb again!"

Then she went out with a staff in her hand to take the Valencian goats and the ram out to pasture.

And everything happened just as she had planned. The king's son was lodging at the Sant Francés farmstead, on the Salviar Heights, about an hour's ride on horseback from there. That day the prince had gone out hunting in the mountains with his entourage and, not long after she left the cottage, Lily noticed in the distance the sounds of hunting horns as the party approached the Penya Roja. The dogs were barking and yelping as the hunters from the palace slowly came into view through the oak trees and hollies.

Lily walked out a good way from the cottage, followed by the goats, beating away at the underbrush to make the snow fall off so the animals could nibble the leaves. Then she heard the cornets and galloping horses coming closer, and she almost dropped dead with a mixture of amazement and fear when she saw the splendor of the youthful nobles with their servants and pages and, in their midst, the king's son, more dashing and gallant than all the rest.

The prince rides up to Lily and her goats, halts and then dismounts. The old woman drops to her knees on the snow while the goats and the ram, skittish with the cold and this unexpected intrusion, begin to make their way toward the little corral behind the cottage.

"Rise, my good woman," says the son of the king in a strong and melodious voice. "Do you live here in this house?"

"Yes, my prince."

It's true that Lily was ugly, but she knew how to make herself at least look friendly. As she rose in obedience to the prince, he noticed a certain charm in her bearing.

"It would please me, lord," she spoke up boldly, "to offer you a cup of warm milk ..."

"Come," said the prince to his companions, "let us see the dwelling-place of this kind and sociable subject, who desires to refresh us with milk from her goats."

Of course this was exactly what Lily had hoped for. She led the prince and his small following to the front of her modest home.

Now the poetic effect of this beautiful landscape scene was not lost on the king's son. His heart was filled with wonder. And in truth, it was a spectacle worthy of an artist's brush: the milling huntsmen, dressed in their bright attire; the powerful steeds decked out with the finest saddles and glittering bridles; the surging and clamorous dogs ... all of this before that isolated cottage set among the breathtaking peaks of the Penya Roja. From a height of 4,000 feet the young nobleman marveled at the blue expanse of the sea in the distance. The eyrie was surrounded by a complex medley of mountains: steep rocky cliff-sides, snow-covered summits and dizzying ravines, virgin forests dark with shadows ... and at his feet, the spotless white covering of snow, like a magic carpet that turned the holly, rosemary and thorny broom on the roof of the cottage into a marvelous filigree of lacework that covered over the ugly face of poverty. And off in the broad, flat lands that stretched toward the sea, the deep green stains of the warm orchards and groves of Sant Joan and Mutxamel and Campello.

His heart was beating strongly with the presentiment of some new adventure.

"Do you live here alone?" he asked as he entered the cottage, followed by two of his company.

"No, my lord. With my grand-daughter."

"Ah!" The prince's heart beat faster. "And what is her name?"

"Rose, my lord ... She's only a child—15 years old." She pronounced these words with an innocent smile that touched the hearts of her listeners.

"By the banner of King Jaume!"[1] the prince exclaimed. "She must be as beautiful as her name. And what of her parents?"

"Please sire, honor this, your house, and sit," said the cunning old spinster.

The king's son sat down beside the hearth, where a warming fire of oak boughs was crackling; and the others sat down too, while Lily brought them walnuts, almonds, bread and a delicious soft cheese, along with cups of warm milk, all of which was welcome fare on a morning with such a cold north wind. She also bade them taste some sweet-smelling apples from Beneixama, red as the setting sun. In short, she treated her guests with the greatest deference.

"But what about your grand-daughter's parents?" the prince insisted.

"My lord, her parents are dead," she answered in a moving tone of voice and wiped away a crocodile tear with the corner of her embroidered apron.

"Oh!" The prince seemed affected.

"Yes," continued Lily with a compelling sincerity, "it's such a sad story ... It pains me to remember."

"Don't do it then," said the prince. "I will not have you sad on my account."

"Enough to know, my lord, that our side of the family are humble commoners. But on her father's side ..."

The king's son pricked up his ears, "Yes?"

"She carries royal blood ...from the House of Granada."

At this point one of his attendants, a close adviser, spoke up. "My lord, they may be Moors."

At this, the prince appeared to be upset.

"I know what you are thinking," said the quick-witted spinster, "but the girl is a Christian and her father was too... That was why it happened ..." And here she fought back a sob. "My daughter was so pretty, so graceful, and her name was Lily, like mine."

"Ah ... so they were Christians," said the prince, relieved. "But please tell Rose to come out so we can meet her."

"Oh my! Oh my! It's delicate ... You see, her mother ... the customs of the East. I promised her, my lord, and you *are* so young and handsome ..."

The prince's heart was moved. He stared at the fire in the hearth in silence.

After so much delay and frustration, he suddenly blurted out, "Lily, my good woman, I want to see her, if only for an instant."

"I fear, dear prince, that it cannot be. Do as you will with me. Perhaps, under force ..."

"No, no. Never!" interjected the noble lord.

"Well ..." the wily old woman seemed to reconsider, "I could just let you enter her room—she's still abed. She must not show her face, not even a hand ... but a finger, yes, a finger. That's what they made me promise. No one must see more than a finger before she marries."

By now the prince's heart was racing.

"I shall see the finger! Blessed be God! That will be enough! And you say she is beautiful?"

"My lord, as beautiful as her mother, as you will see."

Now the prince was at that dangerous age, between 18 and 20, when a young man can fall in love with the shadow of a pretty woman, with a beam of moonlight, with a phantom ...

Meanwhile, Rose had overheard everything from her bed. She was amazed at how easily her sister could lie and get them into this mischief. But since, if it worked out, the result would favor her, she decided to go along with the ruse and play her role. And so, while the conversation went on outside her door, Rose ate three morsels of cod that Lily had given her after breakfast to make her voice sound smooth and soft. Then she chewed a mouthful of quince to fill the room with a delicate, nuptial aroma.

So. The prince went in first, followed by Lily, who carried an oil lamp with a couple of burning wicks, and then the two attendants. He felt his way in the dark to the bed.

"Dearest Rose," he said in his finest voice, mustering all of his royal courtesy, "I, prince and heir to this kingdom, respectfully salute you."

Covered from head to foot, Rose answered his greeting with two small, silly words. Yet they were spoken in such a mellifluous tone (she had had a beautiful voice as a girl) that they pierced the prince's heart.

"If you please, my lady, might you reveal to me your lovely physiognomy?"

"Oh! Oh my dear!" Rose whined. To tell the truth, she was also good at this game.

Lily interrupted. "Rose! This is the son of the king!"

"Oh, oh, oh," Rose complained, pretending to be shy. But in the end, she allowed him to see her thumb.

By the light of the lamp, the youth beheld that plump, firm, pinkish and appealing thumb and fell to his knees, his heart racing wildly. At this point Lily was sweating profusely. To prevent any mistake that could cost them their lives or land them in a dungeon, she politely requested that they retire from the chamber. And not a moment too soon. As they left, Rose began to sniffle, as though showing her thumb were the most shameful thing she'd ever done in her life.

When they returned to the kitchen, the king's son said, "Lily, you must not deny me. I want to marry your grand-daughter—and as soon as possible. She has noble blood (aside from your words, I can tell by her skin), she is a Christian, and I shall never find anyone else with so sweet a voice. What's more, I am certain there's no other lady in all the realm as lovely as she."

"Ah, my lord prince ... nothing would make me happier," said the old maid slowly. "But no ... no. The poor girl would die. Didn't you see how upset she was—how she almost cried just showing you her thumb? How can such an innocent and timid girl get married? No, no. I'm sure she could never do it."

But the prince was vehement. "What can we do then, Lily? If you deprive me of this joy, then I'm the one who'll die. Of melancholy. This is a most exquisite adventure, in the most marvelous location in the realm, and I want it to last for the rest of my life."

"Well then, my lord and prince," said the diabolical spinster, "let it be so. But with one condition."

"What is it?"

"On her wedding-day she may wear whatever gowns you wish. But she has to be completely covered—except for her thumb, of course, since that you've already seen."

"Done!" he agreed at once, too full of joy to contain himself. "The two of us shall be wed!"

And so it came to pass. The prince refused to leave the region until everything was arranged, so he lodged at the Sant Francés farmstead in the Carrasqueta Mountains. From there he sent out his men to search the realm for the finest and most luxurious dresses and the most expensive jewelry—gold and precious gems—for Rose, and a matching wardrobe for Lily, as well as for his entourage and, of course, for himself, in preparation for the grand event. And during the rest of the week Lily was the only person allowed into her sister's room and was to dress her when the memorable day arrived.

For reasons that are easy to comprehend, the king's son chose not to set foot near the cottage. At the same time, though, he sent a contingent of guards, who camped outside in tents, to watch over the damsel who would soon be ascended to royal princess. The prince's two closest counselors often visited Lily, alone or accompanied by servants, to bring exquisite gifts, jewels, gems and all of the other accessories needed to celebrate an event of the kind that was now in the offing. But no one, absolutely no one, attempted or was allowed to see the girl that everyone believed to be Lily's beautiful grand-daughter.

In a week's time everything was ready. That day the sun shone merrily, melting away the snow; and a noisy, chattering congregation gathered before the humble cottage. Rose, all bundled up like a mummy, followed by the prince and his retinue of counselors and courtiers, and Lily, so elegantly arrayed that she looked like a venerable noblewoman—all made a joyous procession that lasted for hours, descending through ravines and over hills to the flatland below and then through every village and town to the royal palace in Valencia. The king and queen, after hearing the descriptions the prince had sent them, were waiting anxiously and curious to see their future daughter-in-law.

I need not recount the details of that princely wedding, which was without a doubt as sumptuous and exciting as such celebrations always are, with the usual open-mouthed onlookers. But when it was over, the time came for the prince to be alone with his wife.

At that moment Lily, protesting that she was old and poor, and a simple soul, said she wasn't fit to be a member of the court and wished only to go back home. In addition, she asked the kind-hearted prince to swear that he would never go to visit her again. The which he did, with tears in his eyes, and they parted.

Thus assured, she went straight out to sell the gems, rings, bracelets and other costly articles she had no further use for and, with a big purse full of gold and silver coins, she returned to Tibi. And though she made an effort not to be too showy, the townspeople wondered at her wealth. You see, with the help of the ingenuous prince, there had been no news of the business at the cottage, so no one had an inkling of her successful plot. It was only known throughout the realm that the prince had married a foreign princess. Even the king and queen, who were aged and no longer directed the working of the realm, believed all that their credulous son (who believed it himself) had told them.

***

Meanwhile, there was a great uproar at the royal palace. The prince, whom we know was smitten with love, was determined to see Rose's face on their wedding night, in spite of her whining protests. You can imagine what their perfumed bed chamber would be like in the palace of a kingdom as wealthy as Valencia. And certain it is that the prince almost fell over dead with the shock when he got a glimpse of poor old Rose's wrinkled and leathery face.

At first, the impression left him speechless. Then he sat down in a satin-covered armchair and wept for his dead illusions and shattered royal dignity. Then came an attack of rage and he almost killed the old woman. In the end, he grabbed her by the nape of the neck, opened the window and threw her out to fall like a sack of stones on the ground below.

But fate, or accident, or maybe some evil spirit intervened. She fell instead on the well-kept hedge of garden flowers that surrounded the palace, and her life was spared. Still and all, she was very badly shaken by the fall and too weak to get to her feet. There she lay, gaily dressed in white, adorned with orange blossoms, ribbons and laces, with a face to make an angry man laugh.

She lifted her voice in a bitter lament. "Oh, woe is me! Aii, my husband doesn't love me. Oh to be back at the Penya Roja!"

But she had fallen at the back of the palace and no one heard her. The guards were all at the main entrance and were drowsy from the generous libations of the wedding feast.

At that very moment, though, five students floated by in a boat on the river. They were out serenading to the delicate strains of guitar chords and a violin. They heard her cries during a pause. And being young, they thought at once that this would be a chance for some adventure. True, Rose's voice wasn't the most appealing, but she hadn't stopped eating the occasional morsel of cod, which left it at least passable. So they moored their boat, leapt over the wall that surrounded the palace grounds and sought out the poor old thing.

"What ails thee, good woman?" they asked, holding back their laughter.

"Oh, my children, my husband doesn't love me."

"And who, pray tell, is your husband"

"The son of the king."

The students had heard about the marriage and were amazed, but of course they didn't know how the prince had been fooled so miserably into marrying this aged woman. Now two of their number, who had come from a far-away country in the East to study in Valencia, had magic powers. "Shall we put a spell on her?" they proposed.

The other three applauded. "Yes, yes! Put a spell on her. A wonderful idea!"

"By my magic powers," said one of the Oriental youths, "may this poor old woman be as young and beautiful as ... a 15-year-old girl!"

"And by my powers," said the other one, "if she tells anyone, anytime, anywhere in the world what we've done here tonight, may she become old and ugly again."

There was a sudden **Boom**! and Rose was not only a pretty girl but just as lovely as when she had been 15.

Content with their good deed, and thinking how surprised the prince would be when he saw her, the students went back to their boat—but not without throwing a pebble at the window of the room where the prince was weeping disconsolately.

Still lying on the flowers, Rose started in to cry even louder than before. "Oh cruel, cruel fate! Made so beautiful by God and my husband doesn't love me!"

The prince heard this, of course, but it sounded at first like rain. He opened the window to see what it was, looked down and saw his wife. But now, in the moonlight of Valencia—known by all for its special glow—he noticed that she wasn't as ugly as he thought. No, on the contrary, she was very pretty indeed!

"My God!" he cried, more confused than ever. "Is this a dream? Why she's as lovely as the sun! What's the matter with me? Can I do nothing right?"

He raced down the stairs of the palace to the grounds, took her in his arms and covered her face with kisses and abundant tears of remorse.

"Don't cry, my prince," murmured the graceful, seductive girl. "I've read about the kind of thing that happened to you in tales of princes and princesses like us ... Some evil witch must have cast a spell and blurred your sight so you couldn't see me as I really am."

And the king's son loved her even more, as she proved to be so understanding and forgave him.

***

They lived very happily from that moment on, and one fine day they had a little prince, as pretty as an angel. There were celebrations throughout the realm. In Tibi, Lily heard the news along with everyone else and she was speechless. Up until then, in her evil heart she supposed that the prince would have discovered the ruse and had her sister killed, or at least imprisoned for life in some dark dungeon. As for herself, she was sure that the prince wouldn't break his promise not to try to find her. But imagine how she felt when she heard that Princess Rose—her spinster sister—had had a son!

"This is impossible. It must be a lie," she muttered like a witch to herself, as she paced back and forth in her house in Tibi. "And at her age! Why, she should be dead!" She felt like she was going mad.

To find out if the story was true (and also because she was now more jealous of her sister than ever), she gathered some money and set out for Valencia. She took a room in an inn and waited until Sunday, when the prince and princess attended High Mass at the cathedral. As they approached the entrance, Lily saw her sister at last, but just as she had been at the age of 16.

Her dried-up, wrinkled body shook from head to foot. She was green with an envy she couldn't control. She didn't care what had happened, or why. She only thought that if her sister had turned young she had to find out how. And if Rose didn't want to tell her, she'd be capable of scratching out her eyes with the same fingernails that at this moment were digging into her own flesh.

And so, one fine day she decided to take a chance and went to the palace to see the princess. "Tell her only, please," she said to the guard, "that Lily is here from Tibi."

When Rose heard this, she was filled with joy. She had been sad that her sister didn't want to visit her. When Lily was ushered into her chamber she excused her ladies-in-waiting so they could talk alone.

"Welcome, dear sister." She embraced her warmly. "I'm so pleased to see you again."

"How did you get so young?" Lily asked, without a word of greeting (for we know that was the only reason she had come).

Rose was surprised and hurt. In a flash she remembered the second Oriental student and his spell. So she said, carefully measuring her words, "Look, this is what I did. I found a tanner and asked him to inflate my body through my ankle like a hide to make leather."

Lily didn't even say good-bye. Urged on by her enormous envy, she rushed out like a shot and found the first tannery she could. She took out the purse full of coins and demanded, "Tanner, inflate me right now!"

"But ... what if you explode?"

"This is gold! Do as I say."

The tanner, a chubby self-satisfied man, acquiesced to her irresistible argument. Able craftsman that he was, he hung her by one leg above his tanning table, made an incision in her ankle, inserted the nozzle of his bellows and began to pump in air.

The old woman's skin began to smooth out, the wrinkles disappeared and Lily, in spite of the trembling that wracked her body, felt herself lighter, as though she could fly.

"Bring me a mirror!" she ordered.

The tanner closed the incision with a clasp, left the bellows on the table and brought the mirror. Lily could see that she was inflated and that her wrinkles were gone, but she was still old—no wrinkles, true, but as ugly as ever.

She was furious. "More air!" she shouted.

"Take care, madam! Your skin isn't what it used to be," warned the tanner.

"Pump in more air and I'll give you another purse of doubloons!"

So the tanner went on with the bellows and, all of a sudden something horrible occurred: she exploded with a noise like a thunderclap! The workshop was covered with bits of skin and bloody flesh and flute-shaped fragments of bone that seriously injured the rash and greedy tanner. And nothing was left of the spinster of the mountain but the many little pieces they gathered together for her burial.

Note

1 A reference to *Jaume el Conqueridor*, also known as *Jaume I d'Aragó* (1208–1276). Highly revered as the architect of the Reconquest, he was also an important figure in the development of Catalan, encouraging literature written in that language.

4 The Castle of the Sun
(A Story from Bèlgida)

In olden times there was a little kingdom, highly desired by its neighbors, nestled among the Aitana, Serrella, Benicadell and Mariola mountains. An area containing the delightful Seta valley, the ravines of Penàguila, the meadows of Alcoi, the Cocentaina plain and the tiny Travadell and Perputxent vales is enclosed by these intricately sculpted mountains. Every dip in the land has its own little stream; every ravine has its spring; and every hillside is covered with a blanket of Holm oaks and pines. All of this formed the kingdom in question.

In those days the region was rife with castles large and small, like those in Penàguila, Alcoleja, Penella, Cocentaina, Beniarrés ... but one ruled over the rest. Today it is gone, except for a few lonely ruins at the foot of a tall hill that still is crowned with what were once its watch towers. It was called the fortress of Benillup and was the home of Abd Allah ibn Malik, the Moorish king who reigned in that God-given land of hamlets and villages, farmhouses and flour mills, smithies, tanneries, carpenters and laborers and all the rest that makes up a vibrant, industrious community. Abd Allah had converted to Christianity many years before; he was now quite old and had only one wife and a son, called Muhammad.

Mudjàhid and Hayran, neighboring kings, coveted Abd Allah's fertile lands. So when he died, one day in March, they both made a sojourn to the castle—each one (by coincidence) taking a different road—accompanied by two trains of warriors. Abd Allah's widow, a Christian named Margarita de Bell-Puig,[1] greeted them with honors and lodged them for some days in the castle. But she insisted that her son Muhammad would inherit the land and roundly and indignantly refused to cede the domain of Benillup to either of the two pretenders. They, however, could not be convinced, and at the royal banquet that was held on their last day there, the following tense exchange took place.

MUDJÀHID (who came from Dénia): "Mine is the right of succession to the throne of Benillup, as I have always been the protector of our late friend Abd Allah ibn Malik."

HAYRAN (who came from the south): "Mudjàhid, you already have enough with your coasts and the islands you have conquered, not to mention the

DOI: 10.4324/9781003324232-4

realm you have inherited. It is I who need wet and fertile lands, since much of the kingdom of Múrcia, where my subjects live, is dry."

MARGARITA DE BELL-PUIG: "By the natural right of birth and inheritance, the kingdom of Benillup must be for my only son Muhammad. So dismiss the idea from your crowned heads."

MUHAMMAD: "I do not acknowledge your imagined rights to my kingdom, even though, it is true, my father enjoyed your royal protection from the incursions of the Christian kings. My loyal subjects also wish it so."

MUDJÀHID: "In this you are mistaken. If you be Christian (and you are), then how can you defend those subjects, most of whom are Muslims, against the Christian incursions? Betrayal may easily, though inadvertently, find a place in your heart."

On hearing these words Muhammad's face went pale as wax with anger. He jumped to his feet, his hand on his sword.

"Halt!" It was the voice of a very aged banquet guest who looked so frail and ashen that he might at any moment turn to dust. "I propose a solution by which Allah can make His judgment known."

"And what is that?"

The one who had raised his voice was a magistrate in the kingdom, a prudent man who was known and respected throughout the land. His name was Sulayman ibn Abú.

"Let the three who pretend to the throne of Benillup have jousts with horse and lance in the fashion of Christian knights. He who triumphs shall reign here in peace forever."

Hayran and Mudjàhid consented to the magistrate's plan. But Muhammad objected: "How will I, the legitimate heir of Abd Allah, be seen if I am treated the same as a pretender from beyond the borders of our kingdom? Would it not be unjust?"

"If you are defeated in the joust," proposed the magistrate, "you will be given a second opportunity. You may reclaim possession of the realm by giving the victor the sum of 10,000 silver dirhems[2] within a period not exceeding ten days."

The kings of Dénia and Múrcia found this proposal acceptable.

Mindful of the threats of those two powerful monarchs, Margarita de Bell-Puig and her son finally acceded to the magistrate Sulayman's verdict, or solution. Thus, it was agreed that the lists would be constructed on an open field not far from the castle and, in the month of May, when the weather in that mountainous region was certain to be favorable, in the presence of witnesses and adherents from all three contending sides, and with Làbib al-Almiri, the king of Tortosa, as Marshal of the Field, the famous joust would be held.

The preparations began at once. And by the tenth of May the carpenters, blacksmiths, craftsmen and laborers—come from all the nearby hamlets and villages (Billeneta, Gorga, Benimarfull, Benilloba, Almudaina and Benillup itself)—had constructed an enclosed field of contest fit for the joust, with high walls made of planks, a platform for the judges and witnesses and other important personages, and wooden benches for any other curious onlookers from the Moorish population. All at the expense of the Lady Bell-Puig.

The 15th of May arrived. Mudjàhid of Dénia and Hayran of Múrcia, who had both returned to their respective kingdoms after agreeing the terms of Sulayman's proposition, came once more to the castle. As before, they were accompanied by their retinues, this time so numerous that, with the exception of the most important guests, they had to be lodged in tents on an empty tract of land between the castle and the village. It was around 12 o'clock on a glorious morning. Hayran and Mudjàhid were invited to climb to the top of the watch tower, from where they could admire the extensive mountain ranges and delightful valleys that stretched out for miles into the distance on every side. In those Arcadian days, the Almudaina Mountain, on which stood the great castle of Benillup, was covered over with a sweet-smelling forest of Holm oaks, junipers and pines. To the west, shining in violet tones, were the oak woods of Alcoi, the small peak known as the Ull del Moro and the Cint Ravine. To the south and southeast the rugged crests of Serrella, the towering summit of Aitana and the dark mountainsides of the Penàguila range closed off the horizon. The Penya Cadiella, highly coveted by powerful rulers in years to come, rose to the north like a rocky, impassable curtain.

This panorama stirred a much stronger yearning in Hayran's heart than in Mudjàhid's. For Hayran could not help comparing the dry, sparsely populated lands of Múrcia (apart from the then limited fertile fields of Segura) with the wonderful forests, streams and lakes of this territory, with its lovely sun-drenched summers, snowy winters and showery springs. The crops were rich and abundant, the olive and almond groves copious, the fruit trees in flower or heavy with a wealth of ripened fruit. This fruitful land was marvelous.

Just before sunset the Knight Marshal, the king of Tortosa, arrived in a splendid carriage, accompanied by a small entourage of courtiers and armed knights.

Noble dame that she was, Margarita de Bell-Puig spared not the slightest expense. The celebration, the Muslim and Christian victuals and the festive proceedings in the castle and surroundings were simply exquisite. And, after three days of games and entertainments, the moment of truth arrived. The formidable Muhammad, his fiery eyes behind the upraised beaver of his helm, rode out of the castle with a determined martial air. Armor shining in the bright morning sun, he held his buckler on his left arm and an imposing lance in his right hand. From their respective camps Hayran, not so tall as Muhammad but brimming with strength at his some 40-odd years, and Mudjàhid, lighter than Muhammad, tall, with aquiline features and a wiry, agile body, proceeded to the lists. Both were worthy opponents. Many of their followers, as well as Muhammad's subjects, were eager to witness this joust in which the fate of their small kingdom—and their own—would be decided.

And so took place that glorious day in May, under a cloudless blue sky, one of the most renowned and shortest jousts in the history of those lands.

The tribune was full and the Sergeant Marshals had taken their places, presided over by the prudent king of Tortosa, Làbib al-Amirí, who was seated beside the delicate Lady Margarita. The contenders drew lots and luck determined that Muhammad jousted first against Mudjàhid. Due to the proximity of their kingdoms, these two had closer ties. They carried out a proper and ceremonious joust, but without much passion; for in truth, the king of Dénia's affection for Muhammad was stronger than his desire for greater lands. Only their pride as knights compelled them to compete with a certain level of intensity. Thus, on the sixth pass Mudjàhid was toppled by Muhammad, who was consequently declared the winner of the first match.

The second match pitted Muhammad, now somewhat spent, against Hayran, who was seething with anger and ambition. Each one takes his place; the signal is given; they charge; and Muhammad is clamorously thrust from his saddle by a powerful impact from Hayran's lance. How could it be? Muhammad's subjects, alarmed by the rapid defeat of their prince, raise a heart-rending tumult.

Muhammad's men rushed to assist their lord, but only his pride was wounded. The members of Hayran's retinue cried out in victory and shouted insults, as though they already felt they were masters of the realm. And meanwhile, the widow Margarita de Bell-Puig had to be attended by Làbib al-Almirí; she had fainted away as soon as she saw her son hit the ground.

When all of the formal ceremonies of the joust had been completed, everyone returned to the castle, or their camps, where the feasting and festivities continued and the transmission of the crown was discussed. For the truth of the matter was, neither Margarita de Bell-Puig nor her brave and hapless son Muhammad would be able at that moment to produce the 10,000 silver dirhems that the magistrate Sulayman ibn Abú had determined should be the price to redeem the kingdom. What could be done?

Later that night, under a starry sky, Margarita and her son retired to a discrete closet where they could speak beyond the hearing of servants and guests. Through the windows they saw the torch-lit camps, they heard voices and shouts and, from Hayran's men, chants of victory and joy accompanied by the sweet music of lutes and guitars, all of which dampened their spirits and weighed down keenly on their hearts.

Margarita had tears in her eyes as they searched for a solution to their quandary.

"We could sell all of the wheat reserves, the olive oil in the amphoras and all of the farming tools to pay the 10,000 dirhems," she suggested.

"But to whom, mother? ... No, that won't solve the problem. Maybe it would be better to let Hayran go back to his lands without paying him; and then we could find some strong allies and go to war ... But that would be a blow to my dignity, since I freely accepted Sulayman's verdict. If we had objected at the time ... we could have waged war honorably. Now it's too late."

Margarita was disconsolate.

60   The Castle of the Sun

A deep sense of hopelessness overtook Muhammad. He bade his mother good-night; but instead of retiring, he went down a secret stairway to an exit from the castle. He wanted to walk in the cool night air and take counsel from the silent company of the stars. After a few minutes, though, he noticed footsteps behind him. Fearing that he might be murdered by one of Hayran's henchmen, he spun around, his dagger drawn, and saw a shadow— it must have been a man, his face was hard to make out—approaching with a small torch in his hand.

"Hail, sayyid[3] Muhammad."

"Hail! Who are you?"

"I am called the Man of the Sun," said the stranger, giving a slight, respectful bow.

He was closer now and Muhammad could see his face in the torchlight. He was tall, and his clothing was Moorish. Though the fabrics were black, they seemed to have an expensive sheen. A few precious gems shone from his turban. His face, though completely dark, had the traits of the Caucasian race. And the whites of his eyes stood out strongly from his energetic, sculpted features. He had neither beard nor moustache.

Muhammad was curious. "What do you wish of me?" he asked.

"I bring you your salvation."

"How?"

"I have the 10,000 dirhems and can lend them to you so that you may redeem your crown."

"Who are you and why are you here in my kingdom?"

"I am a jewel merchant."

"And what must I do for you in return?"

"I only ask that you pay me back the 10,000 dirhems."

"When?"

"A year from now."

"And where?"

"It is far. You will have to go on foot, alone and unarmed. It will take you a couple of months to get there: the Castle of the Sun. That is where I get my name. You will find it by going toward the western horizon."

All this time, the Man of the Sun had held the torch. They were standing in a small clearing among the pine trees, close to the edge of a ravine. From it rose the murmur of a stream in the darkness. As Muhammad failed to open his mouth for a full minute, the swarthy stranger spoke: "You must decide, sayyid. My people are awaiting me."

Muhammad was unsure. "Why do you come to my aid?"

"Do not inquire ... if you seek your salvation."

"I shall need some time to think."

"Impossible. I must be on my way. Yes or no?"

Considering his dilemma and thinking this help must be sent from heaven, Muhammad accepted the loan. Then the Man of the Sun leaned the torch against a rock, took a small velvet pouch from his tunic and handed it to Muhammad. Being so little, it couldn't contain much. The prince opened it and took out the only thing inside—no more nor less than two large precious gems that shone like stars in the torchlight.

"These," explained the Man of the Sun, "are the In-xa-Allah diamond and the Siriac sapphire. Any knowledgeable Jew will give you the 10,000 dirhems for them. I expect you to live up to your royal promise."

Muhammad returned the precious stones to the pouch.

"I give you my word as king, or as future king," he solemnly swore, "that I shall pay you back the 10,000 dirhems, or the gems themselves, in one year's time at the Castle of the Sun."

With that, he placed the gems in his tunic.

Satisfied, the Man of the Sun picked up his torch, gave Muhammad a curt nod and an enigmatic smile, put out the flame and disappeared into the night.

Within the allotted time Muhammad went on horseback to Dénia, accompanied by his faithful servant Abú Yacub and two armed men. There he sought out the famous jeweler and money lender Ismaïl, and left the diamond and sapphire in pawn for 10,000 silver dirhems.

Five days later he was back at Benillup, and the following morning, in the grand hall of the castle, witnessed by l'Abib al-Amirí, Mudjàhid, the magistrate Sulayman ibn Abú and the Marshals of the joust, Muhammad and his mother delivered into Hayran's hands the 10,000 dirhems to recover the crown. A parchment was signed recognizing the undisputed sovereignty of Muhammad and his descendants, in peace and independence, *per in aeternum*. It was mid-morning. Soon the news spread throughout the realm and festivities were held from Banyeres to the strait of Orxa, and from Agres to the mountain passes of the Aitana range. Those who were camped at the castle also celebrated with equestrian exhibitions that cost those warlike followers of Mohammed more than one good tumble or painful contusion. By mid-afternoon, when the air turned cool and a few ribbons of mist adorned the sunny peaks, all of the guests departed in a joyful procession ... each one to his own home and hearth, and God in them all.

* * *

Bad news and stays for paying debts fly like the wind. And so slipped by six months of the year the Man of the Sun had given Muhammad to return the 10,000 dirhems that had saved the realm of Benillup. In the meantime, harvests had been gathered, everything that wasn't indispensable had been sold, and Muhammad and Margarita had put together enough money to repay the debt, plus interest, which came to 500 dirhems. The prince went again to Dénia and recovered the two gemstones in order to give them back to the mysterious Man of the Sun as he had promised.

An unarmed knight on foot would raise suspicions, if not the downright scorn of the population. Under such circumstances, and in those remote times, the conditions imposed by his savior were tantamount to a sentence of death. And so, when he had the gems in his possession, Muhammad decided that the safest way to travel unarmed would be to disguise himself as an impoverished muezzin, whom no one would suspect of carrying riches, and in this guise undertake the long journey on foot, as agreed, to the Castle of the Sun.

One fine morning, two months from the deadline of the stay, Muhammad set out for the western border of the little kingdom, wearing his disguise and accompanied by his aged servant, Abú Yacub. He rode on horseback and carried a small rucksack filled with 30 gold coins to cover the expenses of his long pilgrimage and any unforeseen emergency. He kept the Siriac sapphire and the In-xa-Allah diamond in the small velvet pouch, hanging from a string around his neck. Abú Yacub followed on foot.

They took the path heading down by the village of Benimarfull, turned left at the bevy of white ravines that lead down like steps to the Cocentaina plain, which they crossed along one side, and took the westward road through the highlands of Polop. At nightfall they reached the Banyeres mountain pass, the western limit of the realm of Benillup. With tears in his eyes, Abú Yacub bade farewell to his master, who dismounted, put the rucksack on his shoulders and handed him the reins of the horse so he could ride it back to the castle stables. Abú Yacub embraced Muhammad, got clumsily into the saddle and set off for Benillup.

"God be with you, sayyid."

"Farewell, faithful Abú Yacub."

The light tapping of horseshoes quickly faded away at Muhammad's back and, as the sun was setting, he found himself alone with a cold night approaching, treading on frozen earth and surrounded by brooding mountains with forests blanketed by snow and frost.

After an hour's hike in the darkness, he saw a large village ahead. As is often the case in these highlands, it nestled around a hill that was crowned with a castle. The gates were still open so he entered and found lodging at an inn. He asked at supper whether anyone knew the way to the Castle of the Sun, but all replied that they had never even heard of such a place.

The next day he was lucky with the weather. After the innkeeper woke him, he went out to continue his journey and found the air had warmed and a wind was blowing from the east. It was something of a bother, but it thawed out the ground and was blowing patches of snow off of the mountains.

"A good sign!" Muhammad told himself. "The hand of God is protecting me."

He was, as we know, disguised as a muezzin; but beneath his Moor's clothing he carried a rosary, for he was a follower of Christ. He bore no weapons, as the agreement stipulated, though he did have a sturdy staff with which to ward off any animal or defend himself against some evil-doer.

***

Indefatigable, Muhammad had been travelling for more than a month, always asking about the Castle of the Sun at the inns where he lodged some evenings (the villages were getting farther and farther apart) and receiving not a jot of information from man, woman or child. When he slept in the rough he built a fire to scare off wild animals such as foxes, deer and wolves.

And so, one dark night, far from any human habitation, in the middle of an immense plain that could discourage even the heartiest traveler, the weather playing havoc—sudden rains, then clear skies and hurricane winds—Muhammad had, as they say, reached the end of his tether. And, to top it off, he had found out nothing at all from anyone about the Castle of the Sun. He was almost ready to give up. "My God," he thought, "if I don't find the Castle of the Sun I won't be able to return the jewels on time, and the Man of the Sun will think that I am not an honorable king." And now he was in a deserted place with no one to ask.

Sunk in this quandary, chilled painfully by the wind, he suddenly saw what seemed to be a slice of the moon above the black and almost invisible horizon. It had a faint, reddish glow and must be, he thought, (as he was fond of astronomy) some unknown celestial body. But no ... for as he advanced the light grew larger and larger, till at last he could see that it came from a window. And when he approaches he finds an unusual house, narrow and tall, squeezed in among three gigantic trees—one on each side except for the front, with the door.

The rain was getting heavier. Muhammad walked up to the building and knocked on the wooden door with his staff. In an instant he heard a strong, masculine voice from within: "Is he who knocks a Christian?"

"Yes," answered Muhammad. He was surprised, as this was Muslim territory.

"Slide your rosary beneath the door," ordered the voice.

Muhammad obeyed.

The door was opened and he entered. Inside he finds a friendly hermit, short and hale, with dark eyes and a long black beard. He returns the rosary, invites Muhammad to sit by the fire, helps him dry his clothes, gives him a plate of warm food and, only after all of these preliminaries, asks his name and the purpose of his journey.

"I am Muhammad of Benillup. I come disguised as a muezzin for safety's sake, in search of the Castle of the Sun."

"And I am Bartomeu, hermit of this chapel and your servant, brother. And ... pray tell, who directed you this way?"

"No one; perhaps it was I myself, as I lost my way in the dark and rain."

"Or perhaps it was the hand of the Lord," observed the hermit. "You have been lucky, Muhammad of Benillup, for this is an isolated, lonely spot and there is no other house for leagues around."

"You are right. God must have guided me ... Too often we forget. I had even run out of food."

They remained a moment in silence. Outside, the pattering of the rain, inside, the snug crackle of burning firewood. The sounds were soft and soothing.

And then, as though it had suddenly struck him, Bartomeu asked, "Did you say you were searching for a castle?"

"Yes. The Castle of the Sun."

"And you are very eager to find it, no?"

"Yes I am."

Bartomeu knitted his brows. "Ah, Muhammad, the truth is I know nothing of the castle you seek. I am very sorry. But I can give you bread, and a couple of slices of salted beef, and some walnuts. And you may stay here as long as you like. But the Castle of the Sun ... still and all ... I have a brother, also a hermit, who may be able to help you. He lives close to a main thoroughfare, where you often hear folks talking about strange, far-away places."

Muhammad spent that night at the hermitage. The next day, stocked with bread, salted beef and walnuts, he gave the friendly hermit a gold coin as alms and set out westward, always westward, in search of Bartomeu's brother, whose name was Efraïm.

For five days he made his way across unplanted fields, unforgiving marshes and leafy oak woods with almost impassable underbrush, till he came at last to a very wide salt flat that reflected so much sunlight he had to squint to see. He found a few trees whose foliage blocked the reflections and sat down in the shade to eat a good slice of beef with bread and walnuts. Then he drank deeply from the water he carried in a canteen and lay down to nap.

The cool late-afternoon air awoke him. He got to his feet, stamped a few times on the ground and started on his way again, guided by the bright northern star in the sky. The footing on the salt flats was easy. Reflecting the fading light, they didn't hurt his eyes as they had before and helped him find his way in the darkness. After about three hours the ground began to rise; the salt flats gave out and he found himself once more among the harsh bushes of a hillside. Climbing patiently, he reached the top and saw, on the other side, a wide expanse of land with a copse of tall, leafy trees, out of which shone a light. Muhammad wondered if he had taken the wrong way, but suddenly—as though in reply—he felt a sense of relief. Under a sliver of moon that had risen above the horizon, he made out a white band between himself and the dense trees and saw that the light came from a house.

"The main thoroughfare!" he said, satisfied.

He followed the road, approached the trees and knocked on the door of the house. There was a light coming from the window beside it.

"Is he who knocks a Christian?"

"Yes! And is he who asks Efraïm?" answered Muhammad as he slipped his rosary beneath the door.

Efraïm opened the door at once. He resembled his brother Bartomeu, but was taller. "How do you know my name?"

"Your brother Bartomeu told me it."

"Come in. Come in."

Muhammad introduced himself and spent the rest of the night there as in the previous hermitage. He rose the next morning, heard Mass, and afterwards told Efraïm that he was searching for the Castle of the Sun, but didn't know where it was.

"I have heard people passing on the thoroughfare speak of the place, but I do not know its location."

Muhammad's heart fell again. Would he ever be able to find it? His discouragement showed in his face.

"What ails you?" Efraïm was worried for him. "You look so sad. Don't be down-hearted. We have another brother three day's journey from here, to the northwest, and he will surely be able to help you."

Muhammad was skeptical. "So he won't be like his brothers?"

Efraïm broke out in a pleasant, ringing laugh. "No ... he's not the same. No one knows exactly what it is or where it comes from; but the truth is he makes birds talk. The hermitage he lives in is as big as a church, at the foot of the Gredos Mountains. At nightfall, one of each kind of bird that lives in the mountains and plains and valleys of the region fly there to sleep. One of those birds must have seen the Castle of the Sun you're looking for and can tell you where it lies."

Muhammad thanked him profusely, kissed his hand and gave him a gold coin as alms and in repayment for a small amount of food. And then he took his leave, but not without first ascertaining the way to the third brother's house. His name was Jeremies.

It took him two days to get there. When he was still an hour away he could clearly make out the third hermitage, large as it was, at the edge of the foothills of the Gredos range. He had to hike down a steep incline and then back up again. After a half an hour he could see the building's red roof tiles, wide and ordered, and its grey walls covered with ivy at the corners.

He got there at twilight.

Jeremies came out greet him. He was a good bit older than his brothers, taller and more slender, with a white beard. And like them he had a friendly air and a gleam of warm intelligence in his eyes.

As soon as he saw Muhammad he exclaimed, "You must be my brothers' visitor, come in search of me."

"True." Muhammad was amazed. "I am that visitor, and I bring you regards from Bartomeu and Efraïm."

"Please come in!"

The hermitage looked larger on the inside, probably a church. They went through a low door on the right to the living quarters, where Jeremies dwelt alone. The nave was lit by two lanterns, and as they walked Muhammad could see the small chapels with their saints and, from ceiling to floor on the walls, hundreds of wooden perches that must have been for the birds to sleep on at night.

They sit down by the fire; Muhammad tells Jeremies his name and after supper inquires about the Castle of the Sun.

And could you believe it? Muhammad's heart dropped to his feet when he heard Jeremies say with a smile, "I don't know where this Castle of the Sun is."

"But, your brothers ..."

"You didn't let me finish, young Muhammad. Don't forget about the birds."

"And tonight too?"

"Yes, as always. I never lack their company."

He rose and led Muhammad into the hermitage where, in the light of the two lamps and a large torch that Jeremies lit, Muhammad could admire the most surprising spectacle in the world. The walls were lined with birds of all kinds and colors, every one sitting silently on its perch.

Jeremies pointed to a large black bird, fatter if possible than a raven, perched above the main altar. "Do you see that one up there?"

"Yes."

"I don't know him as well as the others. He started coming a few days ago ... We'll begin by asking all of the important ones and then ask him if they don't know."

Followed by the astonished prince, Jeremies went round the room, questioning the birds one by one.

"Bird of yellow feathers," he said to a kind of oriole that opened its eyes as the torch approached, "do you know the location of the Castle of the Sun?"

"No," answered the oriole in a high, sibilant voice. "I only fly to the banks of streams and giant fig trees. I know nothing of castles."

As he listened, Muhammad's hair stood on end.

"Bird of green feathers," said Jeremies to a handsome duck that was so fat it bent the perch where it was resting, "have you ever seen the Castle of the Sun?"

"I'm sorry, but I only have eyes for lakes and ponds."

And thus they asked more than ten birds, chosen completely at random, till they finally came to the one above the altar.

"He may know more than all the rest about castles," suggested Jeremies, "for he must be able to fly very high and far ... Bird of black feathers, do you know, by chance, where the Castle of the Sun may be?"

The lugubrious bird spread its huge raven's wings and opened its black and reddish beak. It was a terrifying sight.

"I certainly do indeed," it answered in a firm, baritone voice.

Muhammad was more amazed with every passing second by the sights and sounds of this magical world he had stumbled into. And though he found it frightening, he worked up the courage to ask: "Master Raven ..."

The ill-tempered bird broke in, "I am not a raven! Know that I am the Shadow of the Sun ... And if you wish I can lead you tomorrow to the castle you seek. But you must trust in me and follow me closely."

Muhammad was delighted. They agreed to set out at first light the following day.

Then the big black bird stopped talking, closed its eyes and fell into a deep slumber. Jeremies and Muhammad went back to the living quarters, where Muhammad slept very snugly in a small bedroom with a four-poster bed with a thin straw mattress. The anxious prince rose before sunrise and, looking through the window, watched the countryside define itself in the early morning light, studded with crystals of frost that shimmered like tiny white stars.

Jeremies was already in the kitchen when Muhammad walked in. While they had a friendly breakfast together, a beam of reddish light came in through a window.

"I fear I must be off," said the prince reluctantly, "for my time is short."

After their meal, the hermit gave him bread and victuals for a few days and water from a pure, cool spring among the trees beside the hermitage, filtered down from a mossy hill. Muhammad gave him the time-honored gold coin as alms and repayment and the two of them went in search of the Black Bird, or the Shadow of the Sun, as he called himself.

Muhammad was surprised to see that the birds had left the hermitage, but relieved when they found the large raven sitting on his perch above the main altar.

As soon as they entered, the Shadow of the Sun fluttered down to their feet and said, "You must follow me, muezzin. On my own, I can fly to the Castle of the Sun in an hour. It lies behind the high mountains to the north. But as we shall have to adopt your pedestrian pace, it will take us a week or more to get there."

"I am most grateful, Shadow of the Sun," replied Muhammad. "How can I repay my debt to you? ... Mayhap you needn't go to so much trouble. If you tell me the way to the castle, then certainly I can find it on my own."

"Easy to say!" replied the bird, "but I have no doubt that you could never find it on your own. There are plains, rivers, rapids and dangerous ravines; there are large expanses of thorny bushes where you'd lose your way and be lost for months or die with your clothing and your flesh in tatters ... No, no; much better for me to take the trouble to guide you there."

"And what can I do to repay you for giving so much aid to a complete stranger?"

"Nothing at all. We birds also like to do a good deed from time to time."

And so they departed. The Black Bird led the way on foot—hop, hop—(he was relentless) while Muhammad had to lengthen his stride to keep up behind. And even so, it took them days. They spent their nights in caves the raven was familiar with; they ate beside hidden springs that the bird knew by heart; they passed through rocky culverts; they skirted large expanses of thorny bushes mixed with intricate vines and, when they topped the high mountain range the Black Bird had pointed out from the hermitage,

Muhammad was greeted by the sight of a lovely green valley, across which stood a sunny hill crowned with a castle of moderate dimensions.

"Do you see it?" asked the Shadow of the Sun.

"Indeed I do," replied the chuckling prince. "And a fine location it is, atop the hill with all of the valley at its feet. Nothing to block the sunlight from dawn to dusk."

"Yes, yes ... true," agreed the Black Bird, though with a tinge of bitterness that surprised Muhammad. "Look," continued the winged one, "there's a spring ahead surrounded by big oaks, and the hills will serve as protection. What do you say we spend the night? And tomorrow we can go to the castle; for though it seems near enough, it is still some hours away on foot."

Muhammad wished to continue hiking, but he deferred to the bird out of courtesy. They walked to the spring, started a good fire and supped. Afterwards, with the whispering crowns of the trees for a coverlet, they went to sleep. Or at least the prince did.

The early morning light and the cool air it brought, now that the fire was out, woke Muhammad from a pleasant dream of the lands of his beloved Benillup and of the delicate Margarita. And when he opened his eyes and looked around, he was all alone! What was happening? Where was that Black Bird, the Shadow of the Sun?

"Well," he said to himself, "I'm sorry he's gone, but I no longer need him to get to the castle."

The unusual bird had vanished without so much as a fare-thee-well.

Muhammad had a bite to eat and took a long, deep drink of the pure spring water coming from beneath a rock and set off. Taking his time and enjoying the caress of the sun, sweet now with the coolness of the season, he came at last to the foot of the castle hill. But it wasn't quite what he had expected. Not that it wasn't a proper fortress, with four good towers, solid walls, well-made embrasures and stout doors reinforced with iron fittings. But it had no moat; and you could hear no voices of soldiers or guards; and before the main entrance, sustained by a pair of Roman columns, there was a kind of latticework bower that would be more typical of a sprawling farmhouse than a fortress. (This structure, devoid now of grape or vine, was supported by the columns and the castle wall and must have been a lovely sight in summer, lending the building a homely rural air.)

Muhammad was surprised to find the place so quiet. He thought it might be uninhabited and was about to knock at the portal with his staff when he sees, sitting atop the latticework, a bird that he recalled from his own lands—a magpie, about the size of a pigeon and very chatty. But this one, to his surprise, had a high-pitched, lilting voice rather than the magpie's low forceful tone. Still, he paid it little heed. Knock! Knock! And the portal opens ... there stands the Man of the Sun in person! Meanwhile the magpie flies off unnoticed and disappears into an embrasure of one of the towers.

"Come in, Muhammad, come in. I've been expecting you!"

Muhammad bowed and went in through the half-opened doors.

As we've already seen, the prince was a clever, quick-witted fellow, and he noticed at once that the Man of the Sun was upset. They first walked into the armory; and from there they followed a rough-hewn stairway to the first floor, where they entered a sparsely decorated main hall. At one end there was a dais, and on it four ladies.

"Prince Muhammad, this is my wife, and these, my daughters."

Muhammad greeted them with immaculate courtesy, and no small surprise. For though he hadn't seen the Man of the Sun very well in the flickering light that evening in Benillup, he had assumed from his clothes and bearing that he was a Muslim. But no—the four ladies here wore no veils and they looked at him freely, as Christian women would. Were they, perhaps, Muslims who had adopted Western customs?

His wife had a wicked face; the two elder daughters looked like eagles, but were less than owls; and the youngest, who was standing, as she had just arrived, was very pretty indeed and had a friendly air about her. It was she who, on her father's orders, took the prince to his chamber so he could put away his things (rucksack, cape and staff) and rest from his long journey.

That night they gave him a good enough supper; but to Muhammad, who hadn't partaken of cooked food in months, it simply seemed divine. And yet, in spite of the cordiality a good meal always produces, this one was more like a candle-lit funeral, since the host's obvious ill humor cast a shadow over all.

One thing had surprised Muhammad on first seeing the ladies, and he confirmed that impression here. The Man of the Sun, as he had noted in Benillup, had very dark skin; but the women, though brunettes, were much fairer.

The supper over, a few wordless and apparently resentful servants brought out an aromatic coffee from Arabia. Muhammad, to fill the uncomfortable silence, spoke up: "My lord Man of the Sun, you must be aware that I have come to fulfill my promise, that is, to return the two gems you lent me in order to pay the 10,000 silver dirhems and redeem the crown of Benillup."

"Well, you cannot do so," he spit out angrily, "for seven hours have passed since the deadline we agreed."

"What?"

"You heard me."

"But sir, a few hours, when it was a journey of months? And where is the proof of this delay you claim? I fear you go too far."

The servants had all withdrawn, and the ladies remained silent.

The Man of the Sun fumed on, "I am more powerful than you might think from the appearance of my castle. That is my secret. I shall send word out to all of the kingdoms of Al-Andalus,[4] including Benillup, to make it known that Muhammad keeps not his royal promises."

A tremor ran through Muhammad's body and a spark of anger kindled in his heart.

"Sir," he answered with a controlled dignity, "I have kept a careful count of every moon and am confident that I have complied with my word."

The Man of the Sun made no reply. He clapped his hands twice and a servant appeared. "Bring us Prince Muhammad's rucksack."

The servant turned on his heels, went to the prince's chamber and fetched the rucksack to the dining hall.

"Pay me, if you please!" ordered the Man of the Sun sternly.

"There is nothing in this bag, sayyid. You can tell your man to take it back to my room."

Then he took out the pouch that hung from his neck and handed it over to his disagreeable creditor. "Here they are—the In-xa-Allah diamond and the Siriac sapphire."

When the Man of the Sun took them out of the pouch, his daughters' eyes lit up with joy.

"Oh, oh!"

"They're back at last!"

"Well," admitted the Castilian in a rough voice, "your debt is settled. But in penalty for your late repayment you will remain a year in one of the castle cells."

Muhammad turned yellow and green with indignation. He thought about his own physical prowess and was tempted to give the scoundrel the punishment he deserved.

And as though he had read his mind, the Man of the Sun called in two sturdy servants, naked from the waist up, who grasped Muhammad firmly by the arms.

"You will pay for this insult and injury, Man of the Sun!" Muhammad cried with a slow-burning anger. But, keeping his dignity, he made no effort to free himself.

The daughters were frightened; their mother, though, gave an evil laugh.

"You do not wish to be locked up?" inquired the Man of the Sun.

"Of course not. I have repaid my debt and I wish to return to Benillup ... At some point my mother, who is now the indisputable queen, will send out someone to find me, and I assure you that you will suffer. We have powerful friends."

The Man of the Sun thought this over and, after a short while made the following proposition: "Well and good. If you do not wish to rest and be well-fed in a cell, neither too hot nor too cold, you may win your freedom by performing some tasks, under your honor as a king."

"Ah, then ... you acknowledge that I have such!"

The Castilian was silent.

But Muhammad agreed (what was he to do?) to submit to the tasks without knowing what this enigmatic and warped character had in store for him.

"Release him!" he ordered the servants, and Muhammad was freed from their steely grip.

"You shall hear the tasks."

"I am listening."

"First: I shall give you a basket. You will get up early in the morning and go to a field of my choosing, not very far from the castle. There you will construct a wall eight feet high enclosing an area of 500 square feet. Inside you will dig a flower bed and plant it with roses and carnations, and on the night of the same day you will bring me the basket filled with the flowers you have grown."

Muhammad felt his anger rising, but he managed to control it.

"And what else?" he asked.

"You will know the second task when you have completed the first."

They left the dining hall—the women had not uttered a word—and after getting the basket from a servant, Muhammad returned to his chamber chafing with anger and impatience. Wasting no time, he undressed, got into bed and put out the lamp.

His brain was churning with thoughts. The task was obviously impossible. How could he escape from this dilemma? What was the mystery surrounding this place? And what were the real intentions of the evil guardian, or whatever he was, of the Castle of the Sun? And then he thought of the youngest daughter's face and called to mind the slender form of the magpie he had seen on the latticework at the castle entrance. Without knowing why, he had a strange feeling that the bird and the girl may be one and the same.

And his feeling was correct.

***

Muhammad now found himself in a perilous situation, much more perilous than he could have imagined. In truth, as he slowly came to realize, he had fallen into the hands of a pair of sorcerers, the Man of the Sun and his wife. These two charlatans had nothing more than the castle, their three daughters and a few dark-skinned servants. The castle's location was lovely, but the terrain surrounding it, due to the harsh climate, was barely good for a sparse crop of rye or barley and was, in reality, a wasteland. The servants hunted; the villagers in the distant hamlets on the castle grounds worked the land and paid out shares to the Man of the Sun ... Taken all together, it was very little. But the couple had a talisman—a small ivory cross made by the devil himself, with an owl hanging upside down—which they obtained from God knows where. And with this cross they could work transformations. For example, they could make fine cloths out of ivy leaves, turn the pebbles of reddish quartz you could find on the castle hill into rubies and other such bewitchments. And thus they maintained the castle and managed to cobble together a handful of dirhems. Also, using the power of the talisman, the husband and wife could turn themselves into any type of bird. The Man of the Sun often took the form of that large raven we saw above the altar of Jeremies' hermitage, after having followed the prince in secret during most of his journey. The foundation of their lives and power was, then, that small ivory cross encrusted with a few precious gems, which they jealously guarded in a wooden box in their bedchamber.

In the form of birds—herons, ravens, eagles and smaller ones like greenfinches and goldfinches—the Man and Woman of the Sun had travelled far and wide and knew many of the secrets of the Muslim kingdoms. The man had seen the realm of Benillup on several occasions and had fallen in love with it. On seeing it for the first time, disguised as a peaceful crow, he flew back to the Castle of the Sun to describe the beauty of those fertile eastern lands to his wife. Then and there they decided to use their evil arts to conquer it. Disguised as different types of birds (once, as a goldfinch, he was able to sit calmly in the trees around Benillup castle and even dared to perch on a windowsill), he had heard Margarida and the prince talk and talk and had learned of Muhammad's dignified character. He knew that the prince was a man of extreme honor, a faithful slave to his word ... and this knowledge led him to conceive a diabolical plan to make the kingdom his own.

"That land," he wistfully said to his wife, "all of it ... it's just too good! I'm sick and tired of this Castle of the Sun and its poverty. There we shall be well-respected, famous monarchs, with thousands of subjects, hundreds of thousands of acres of cropland and olive and almond orchards, hundreds of farmhouses, dozens of streams and springs, rolling fields that lighten the heart to see them ... That'll be the life! Then we can leave off the miserable spells and enchantments and cast the talisman into a gutter."

"And our girls," added his wife enthusiastically, "will live like what they really are but cannot now be: three beautiful princesses."

They had often repeated this pleasant conversation in the intervening years, as they did tonight while Muhammad slept.

"You'll see," said the confident Man of the Sun, gesturing excitedly as he undressed. "The plan will work out perfectly. He won't be able keep his word, and the dishonor of breaking his royal promise will mean Muhammad's abdication. He will have to give up the throne of Benillup, and then it will be ours."

But they hadn't counted on Miriam's kinder intentions. Nor did they know that their youngest daughter had been spying on them for years and had discovered the source of their magic powers—and sometimes even made use of the talisman herself! What? It was impossible! Miriam, that sweet young girl from beyond the Gredos Mountains, why she was a mischievous little minx! How many years did it take her to discover her parents' secret? Those parents who wanted more than anything to avoid the life of a miserable sorcerer for their daughters ... But the fact is that Miriam knew where the ivory cross was hidden and she used it as much, or more, than they did; even if, till now, it was only for innocent games and transformations.

So, that very night, when her parents were sleeping, or at least closeted away in their chamber, and all of the servants (as well as her witless sisters) had retired, Miriam took the talisman from its hiding-place beneath her blouse and rubbed it and said,

> By the horns of the goat
> by the beard of the ram
> to walk beneath this door
> an ant I am!

And she turned into one of those ants with a big, shiny head like a black needle. All of her clothing shrunk and was invisible. Muhammad was asleep, and as soon as she passed beneath the door she turned into a girl again. She leaned over the prince and whispered; "Muhammad, Muhammad."

"Who is it?" he asked, half awake.

"It's Miriam ... I come to tell you that you must beware. My parents seek only your destruction."

All of this was said in darkness.

"And what can we do?"

"You must agree to all of the impossible tasks my father sets you," Miriam replied, "and I shall help you to succeed. Rest easy about tomorrow ... I shall be in the field at the appointed hour and will aid you in building the wall and planting and picking the flowers."

He didn't know why, but Muhammad felt that he could trust this young girl. Then he asked, "But why do you wish to help me when we've only just met?"

"Because you are good and noble and trusting. And now ... good-bye!"

She pronounced the magic spell again, so low that Muhammad thought she was murmuring a prayer, and turned into an ant in the darkness and left the bed chamber.

The morning light crept in next day through the open window, waking Muhammad. He rose, got dressed, took up the basket and went to the dining hall, where a servant was waiting to give him breakfast. He ate some meat and nuts, drank some water and left the castle. There seemed to be no other living soul than the servant, who carried the basket with food for the coming day.

"Where is this field where I have to dig the flower bed?" Muhammad asked when they got outside.

"Don't worry. I shall lead you," answered the servant. He was, like all the others, dark-skinned, strong and naked from the waist up.

Walking steadily, they soon reached the place the Man of the Sun had chosen. It was below a gently sloping hill with a lovely view of a stream surrounded by woods. But it couldn't be seen from the castle. When they got there they found beside a small hedge, an axe, a hatchet and a hammer that the evil lord of the castle had obviously sent beforehand.

The servant pointed out the emplacement of the flower bed the Man of the Sun had ordered, made a low bow to Muhammad and returned to the castle. Then the prince looked carefully all around and spied, sitting on a branch of a birch tree and plainly visible, a very pretty magpie. He heard it cry out, "Do you see me?"

"I do! You must be my friend Miriam. I remember seeing you in this guise on the latticework outside of the castle."

The magpie flew down to his feet and suddenly took on human form. "I've come to help you, Muhammad."

"How?"

"You know full well that you cannot build a wall, plant a flower bed and pick its flowers in a single day."

"Yes, only too well."

"All right. Now you'll see."

Miriam took up the hatchet and began to cut stakes. "You go down to the stream and get some reeds to use to tie the gate."

And so it was. Miriam cut more than 500 stakes in the woods and the prince made lashes from the reeds to hold them together. Afterwards, Muhammad beat in the stakes with the hammer and they made a structure that surrounded 500 square feet, as the lord of the castle had demanded. Inside it the ground was covered with thorny vines and brambles.

It was almost eleven by the sun and they were tired out from the work, so they sat down beside the field in the pleasant shade of a chestnut tree.

"Why are we going to all this trouble?" Muhammad asked.

Miriam gaily confessed, "Thanks to my parents' talisman, I have magic powers. Here it is. It is called the talisman of transformations. The first thing I do when I take it is, turn a small piece of wood into an ivory cross that looks just like it ... but it has no powers, of course. Then I leave it in the jewelry box where they keep the real one so they won't suspect a thing."

This was happy news to Muhammad.

Miriam continued, "The talisman only has the power of transformation. Tasks have to be carried out; hard work is rewarded ... You pronounce a few magic spells, rub the cross three times against your left palm and the miracle is produced."

Muhammad examined that rare and precious object in wonder. He saw the owl hanging upside down. It was made of delicate filigree.

"And how did they obtain it?"

"My father has always taken the side of evil against good. I believe, when he was young, he befriended a wicked sorcerer who was being pursued. He died shortly after and left the magic cross and the knowledge to use it to my father."

Miriam had also brought some food (she only used the magic for special occasions when it was really needed), and they had lunch together. Sitting with their legs stretched out on the cool, silky grass, they ate with relish, enjoying each other's company. They drank from time to time from the crystalline water of a spring nearby. Afterwards, they filled the basket with brambles and thorny stems. And that was when Miriam had to intone the appropriate spell. First she lit a fire with a flintstone and some tinder she had in a pocket of her skirt. Then she cast in two pinches of salt and a cinnamon-colored perfume that made a blue smoke. She had to ask much of the talisman and that required a complicated ceremony. She knelt down on the ground and Muhammad did the same (thinking the whole time that it would not be easy to extract himself from this dilemma). And then she pronounced the following invocation:

Owl with eyes as round as a plate:
heed my prayers and guard my fate!
You sleep by day
and you live by night,
transform what I point to
in your sight.

And Muhammad enounced a solemn, "Amen!"

Then the maiden closed her eyes, brought her hands together and raised her face to the sky. Muhammad would have sworn that at that moment he felt a soft push of air, like a thick bunch of invisible wool had flown by between them. It could have been the muffled flight of an eagle owl or a duke owl. Had it woken up to help them?

Miriam spoke as though in dream:

May the fence turn into a wall;
brambles and thorns—
carnations and roses all!

She got to her feet, her face alight with a smile, "I have seen the Duke Owl with Round Eyes. You will be safe."

Muhammad let out a cry; "Oh Saint Mary of Benillup!" looking at the basket by his feet. "It's full of flowers!"

Then he turned and, instead of the fence of stakes held together with reeds there stood a well-made, solid stone wall. And inside it, a garden full of carnations and roses.

"You're wonderful!" he exclaimed, full of joy.

But Miriam was gone; he only saw a small magpie flying toward the castle. So Muhammad slowly made his way back. When he got there he went up the stairs to the main hall, where he handed the basket full of roses and carnations to the pair of magicians. Their three daughters were there, as well, Miriam feigning complete ignorance of the affair.

The couple were wide-eyed with amazement. They had been sure that Muhammad would never be able to accomplish the outlandish task they had set him. They were seething with hardly contained anger.

"Good, Muhammad. Very good," said the hypocritical Man of the Sun. "You have carried out your task and kept your royal word ... for now." And then he added, "Tonight, at supper, I shall give you your second task."

And so that night, the six of them at table, Miriam did all she could, pretending to be distracted, to avoid Muhammad's eyes. But all the while she was listening attentively to hear the details of the second task.

After the meal the Man of the Sun commanded: "Tomorrow, Prince Muhammad, you will pull up all of the roses and carnations and plant the garden with Muscat vines, and you will bring me half a bushel of grapes in the evening."

They gave him an empty harvest basket, which he took upstairs to his room.

The next day everything went the same. Muhammad got up, took the harvest basket and went down to the dining room. The same dark-skinned servant as the day before was there, and he gave him breakfast and food for lunch, though he didn't go along since Muhammad now knew the way to the plot of land.

When he got there, even though the sun was just peeking over the horizon, he saw the Man of the Sun examining the wall and the flowers.

"Good morrow!"

"Good morrow!"

Not another word was spoken.

Muhammad found a hoe and some pruning shears on the grass beside the garden. He sat down beneath the birch tree and waited for the bird (which was really Miriam) to show up, which she did as soon as her father had gone back to the castle.

She took on human form and they greeted each other fondly. "This time we won't have to do so much. We'll cut 500 blackthorn stakes and plant them like the shoots of grapevines.

They prepared the stakes with the shears and had them all in the ground by the middle of the day. A little hole in the earth with the hoe for each one. And soon enough they were all standing perfectly in order.

Miriam pronounced the magic spell and the stakes turned into vines, heavy with sweet Muscat grapes, and the roses and carnations disappeared.

That night Muhammad gave the couple the basket, filled with delicious-looking grapes. They picked up a bunch at random and took a bite.

"This is good!" the wife exclaimed. She was astonished.

"This young man is a marvel!" said the Man of the Sun sarcastically. But in his heart his rage was boiling. He could hardly keep the steam from hissing out through his gritted teeth.

The two older sisters wolfed down grapes like they had never tasted them before. Poor dim-witted things. Miriam, however, ate only three.

When the rest of the company had retired to their chambers, the Man of the Sun and his wife remained alone. "This false muezzin Muhammad knows more than we do," he said. "No use giving him a third task."

"Let's kill him," proposed his wife. No beating about the bush.

"All right. But first I want to torture him and force him to sign over the throne of Benillup to us."

"How will we do that?"

"Tell the servants to prepare a large cauldron of boiling water. We'll bring him down and threaten to scald him to death unless he abdicates the realm in our favor."

"He's a tough one," observed his wife.

"But he'll soften up," said the sinister Man of the Sun.

They prepared to carry out their terrible plan.

But of course, they didn't imagine that their youngest daughter, instead of going straight to bed, would turn herself into an ant, go back into the kitchen, hide in a crack between two tiles and overhear every scandalous word her parents said. Her tiny heart grew warm with pity and love for Muhammad.

The Man of the Sun and his wife gave the servants their orders and went to their bedroom, but they didn't undress. No, they waited until midnight and tiptoed to the prince's chamber, so as not to awaken their daughters, to take him downstairs to the boiling cauldron. But in the meantime, Miriam, as an ant, scuttles to Muhammad's room, turns back into a woman, awakens the prince and says, "Do as I say. I'll wait for you as a magpie at the entrance to the castle."

Muhammad throws on his clothes and rushes out to find the bird waiting on the ground. He follows it in silence down a secret stairway to the stables. Remaining in the guise of a bird, Miriam tells him, "Stay right here. I'll be back in a jiffy." And she flies away. While he's waiting in the stable, Muhammad sees three handsome horses.

Miriam goes up to her bedroom and spits three times through the window; then she flies straight back to the stables, turns into a human and says, "You take the black horse and I'll ride the white one. But first we'll tie some sacks around their hooves to silence them."

"And what about the gray horse?" asks Muhammad. "He looks very strong and fast."

"He is. But he's still untamed. He'll only let my parents ride him."

"What a pity."

Then they muffle the other two horses' hooves.

Meanwhile, up in the castle, the Woman of the Sun and her husband were getting anxious as midnight approached. She was worried. "What if he tries to get away?"

"Don't fret, woman. He has the honor of a king!"

"See here. If we don't go get him right away, I think I'll have a fit. My nerves are killing me. If the girls are asleep, let's take him downstairs now."

The Man of the Sun agreed.

So, they tiptoe up to their daughters' bedrooms. They softly knock at the first door—no reply. They softly knock at the second door—no reply. They knock at Miriam's door and hear a tiny voice inside, "Who is it?"

They look at each other in surprise and whisper, "This one hasn't yet gone to sleep."

The kitchen was nearby and the business of boiling Muhammad would be rather noisy, so they wanted to be sure their daughters were sleeping like angels. They should, under no circumstances, be aware of the crime that was going to ensure their future as high princesses.

A few minutes later they hurried back and knocked again at Miriam's door. "Daughter dear!"

And the second spot of saliva answered, "What is it?" (in a very low voice—it was drying up).

"Time to go to sleep," said the Man of the Sun, rubbing his hands together nervously.

The third spot of saliva could hardly answer: "Uuuu," it said.

"She's asleep."

And thus they were delayed.

So now they go to Muhammad's chamber with two swarthy servants and knock at the door. But no one is inside. The rucksack and the staff were lying in a corner. Frightened to the bone, they run downstairs again to Miriam's room, throw the door open and discover in the half-light that her bed is disheveled and empty.

"That evil little vixen!" curses her father, beside himself with rage.

He leaves his wife in tears and runs in search of the talisman. Little does he know that he finds the counterfeit. He intones a spell—and nothing happens! Then he goes down to the stables.

"What luck!" he exclaims, relieved. "They've left the fastest horse behind. Now I can catch them."

He leaps on the horse with an ease you wouldn't expect for his age and gallops out of the castle like a shooting star.

Now while all this bustle was going on, Miriam and Muhammad had made their way south under the cover of darkness, toward Jeremies' hermitage, which was, as we know, several days' journey away on the other side of the Gredos Mountains. And as the sun slowly rose, they were able to ride faster and faster. With the full light of day they could see the mountains ahead. But when Miriam looked over her shoulder she made out a small black shape in movement in the distance and she knew it was her father on the racing steed.

She was filled with despair. "All is lost," she thought. But then she remembered, "I have the real talisman. That means he can do us no harm with his magic. Let's turn off here to the left and hide in these woods."

Muhammad obeys. But even though they take a path lined on both sides with leafy branches, they soon hear behind them (the path has so many bends there's nothing to see) the clop-clop-clop of the hooves of the Man of the Sun's horse.

At that moment they come to a glade. "Let's stop here," suggests Miriam.

They do; and she begins to mumble spells and invocations, as fast as she can, with the shiny talisman in her hand. Muhammad was only able to make out "goat ... owl ... eyes as round as a plate."

Finally Miriam whispers breathlessly, "It's done. You will be a hermit and I'll be the Virgin Mary! The horses will be the hermitage and the bells!"

As quick as a wink they change: a hermitage with ancient walls covered with ivy, all quite rustic, and a very nice altar inside where Miriam stood as a figure of the Virgin, that didn't resemble her at all. Muhammad, in the form of an old hermit, was sitting in the sun on a rock beside the door.

The Man of the Sun rides up, all out of breath, and dismounts.

"Have you seen a man and a woman go by here on horseback?"

"No, my lord ... But we are going to celebrate Mass. If you'd like to join in ..."

"No!" bays the Man of the Sun. "I don't go to Mass; I'm a Muslim. A fig for your Mass!"

He rides off furiously the way he came, almost killing the poor gray horse in his rage. And when he reaches the Castle of the Sun he tells the whole story to his viper of a wife, who listens to it all with mounting disgust.

"You miserable fool!" She spits out the words. ""Don't you know there's no hermitage in those woods? The building, the bells, the hermit ... it was them!"

"Of course," blurts out the Man of the Sun, "Miriam must have the real talisman, because the one in the jewelry box is a useless fake. If only I could turn into a raven ... I'd peck them back here with my beak!"

"Stop your silly dreaming and go feed the horse," she hissed.

The Man of the Sun fed the gray horse oats and, after an hours' rest, they set out again in pursuit of the fugitives.

By this time Miriam and Muhammad were deep in the Gredos Mountains and coming close to Jeremies' hermitage. They crossed a gorge and came to a wide valley with springs and good crops, all surrounded by high snow-capped peaks, where they gave the horses a rest to catch their breath and drank from a pure stream that mirrored the rising morning sun.

They hadn't had time for breakfast, so they also paused for a bite to eat. But at that moment they heard a faint sound of horse's hooves coming from the gorge.

"It's my father again," exclaims Miriam. And she kneels down, takes out the talisman and recites her magic spells.

Afterwards she says, "The horses will turn into a fence; I'll be the garden plot planted with cabbages and you'll be the gardener."

In another wink of an eye Muhammad finds himself inside a garden fence with cabbages at his feet and a hoe in his hand.

Miriam's father arrives, his face going black with frustration and rage. "Gardener, gardener, have you by chance seen a pair of fast horses go by here, ridden by a lad and a lass?"

"No, I haven't seen or heard a soul ... But would you like a cabbage?"

"No, we have cabbages galore at home, you stupid peasant."

He goes back again to the Castle of the Sun, and his shrew of a wife gives him another good tongue-lashing.

"You block-headed idiot! The gardener must have been Muhammad, and the fence and the cabbages ... it was them! Get out of my sight, you useless fool. This time I'll go myself."

Though stinging from this well-deserved dressing-down, the Man of the Sun was, in fact, glad of his wife's decision. He was tireder than a field-hand at the end of the day. He drank himself a king-sized glass of wine to calm his nerves and lay down to sleep like a baby for hours on end.

Meanwhile, his wife had to wait for the horse to renew its strength with a generous serving of barley and carrots. By that time, though, it was midnight and she wouldn't be able to go out in search of Miriam and Muhammad till the following morning, as she'd only waste her time in the dark. And when she finally did go out, she loaded on so much weight that the otherwise speedy horse was hindered in its pace. She took along a very big bow and, instead of arrows, some unlit torches with long handles made of thick cane. The couple had invented them. The torches' heads were an infernal mixture of resin, sulfur and birch wood charcoal—a secret of the Orient they had managed to discover. When they were shot from a tautened bow, the friction of the air ignited a terrible flame, so hot that it would set fire to anything it touched. But they were extremely heavy, and she only took three.

"I'll show them, that pesky pair!" she said to herself, over and over again.

She rode over hills and plains, rivers and streams; she crossed the Gredos Mountains and in no time at all passed close by Jeremies' hermitage. More than a woman, she looked like a banshee on horseback, flying enraged toward her victims. Then she came to that immense plateau it had taken Muhammad weeks to cross and, with the piercing vision of her beady eyes, she spied something moving close to the horizon. She made out a couple of figures and exulted, "It's them. They won't get away this time!"

Soon enough, Miriam and Muhammad stopped to catch their breath in a dense copse of Holm oaks. And then they saw her coming their way.

"It's not my father now. It's my mother. And that's even worse," said Miriam.

Muhammad was mute. He could only marvel at how this tender girl was protecting him, when it should have been he, a knight, who protected her. But what was he to do? The times and circumstances were changing in this unpredictable life.

Hidden now behind the oak trunks, Miriam knelt to the ground and repeated the pagan spells: "Goat, owl, eyes as round as a plate" and rubbed the beautiful talisman. "Done! There will be a wide river between her and us. The horses will be the flowing water; you will be the fish; and I shall be the river banks."

Her mother was getting close. **Boom!**—there was a muffled clap in the air. And the river appeared, full of the murmur of cool running water that would only last as long as it took for their salvation.

"I know it's you!" cried the irate woman. "Your disguises and transformations will be of no avail!"

And she starts to shoot those fiery artifacts. Zzzz, zzzz, zzzz! There were three, as we have seen. And since the Woman of the Sun didn't know where the fugitives' weak points were, she heaved three times on the bow and sent three burning torches in three different directions into the calmly flowing water. But then, suddenly feeling astonished by what she had done to her own daughter, she left the river, thinking to herself, "I must have roasted them like some Sant Llorenço."[5]

A half an hour later a profound silence reigned in the place. Little by little, the spell wore off. The river, the fish and river banks disappeared and Miriam and Muhammad and their horses returned to their original forms. The steeds, having been the river, were covered with burns, but they weren't so bad that they couldn't go on. And soon the two youths saw a pastor's hut, where they asked for sawdust and oil to soothe the horses' wounds, which they received. The animals were greatly calmed when they felt the unction on their skin.

* * *

And that was the final danger they faced on their journey home. The Man and the Woman of the Sun understood that, with the marvelous talisman in their power, the prince and Miriam would get back safe and sound to the kingdom of Benillup. So they gave up their evil ambitions at last. It was about time!

After a few days, Miriam and Muhammad came to the Banyeres Pass. Though it was summer, the air at those heights was fresh and cool, like a splendid spring day. Miriam was deeply struck by the landscape of the realm of Benillup, especially the many small, aromatic plants and flowers—chamomile, thyme, broom, poppies, morning glory, hawkweed—sprinkled throughout the fields and meadows. And as soon as they crossed into Muhammad's lands, in little more than an hour, he got down from his horse and walked to a clear-flowing spring of very cool water beside the Barxell River, running beneath the sunny slopes of the Mariola Mountains. Miriam, too, dismounted, and they both drank. It was then that Muhammad, reverently, delicately, but filled with eager emotion, asked her to be his wife and future queen of Benillup. It was around mid-morning.

Needless to say, Miriam was in love with young Muhammad, as all of her efforts to keep him safe had proved. She realized, sadly, that her parents were not worthy of her love and determined, from that moment on, to devote herself completely to this youth who had asked for her hand in marriage. Of course she said yes, and promised then and there to convert to Christianity; for Allah is always Allah, and all beliefs of people of good will are joined on His exalted throne.

On the rest of their journey, Muhammad proudly showed his fiancée the singular beauties and attractions of his mountainous lands. For Miriam, every smallest detail, even the most humble, was lovely, sheathed as it all was in the magic power of pure and trusting love.

After crossing the lands of Alcoi, and then Penella, with its brooding castle, and the many white vales of Benilloba, strewn with pebbles and oleander, they came at last in sight of the fortress of Benillup. There was a warm noon-day sun. The first person to spy them was the faithful Abú Yacub, who had spent long months in the watch tower built atop the high hill next to the fortress. He let out a sudden shout, raising a commotion in the small court. The muezzin started to chant from his minaret, the townsfolk gathered outside the castle, the chapel bell pealed, and the joyous uproar echoed as far as the ravine of the nearby Almudaina Mountain ... Happiness invaded everyone's hearts, and especially the heart of Margarita de Bell-Puig, who had recovered her son and gained a beautiful and valiant daughter-in-law.

Not long afterwards, with memorable pomp and circumstance, they celebrated Miriam's conversion to Christianity and the two of them were married. And one of the wedding guests was the aged and nosy magistrate Sulayman ibn Abú.

The years went by, and Margarita grew old surrounded by her children and grandchildren, and when she died she was mourned as a good queen and loving mother. The virtuous husband and wife assumed the once-disputed throne and reigned for many years over that peaceful and light-filled realm. And as long as they lived, for better or for worse, they heard nothing more of those strange inhabitants of the distant Castle of the Sun.

Notes

1 The final combination "ig" preceded by a vowel is pronounced as the "tch" in "catch."
2 A silver coin used in Muslim countries.
3 From Arabic: a name denoting someone believed to be a descendent of the prophet Muhammad, equivalent to the English "liege lord" or "master."
4 Name of the area of the Iberian Peninsula under Muslim rule from roughly 711 until the Christian *Reconquista* in 1492. At its height it covered most of today's countries of Portugal and Spain, excepting the northwest of the peninsula, and a part of present-day southern France.
5 Saint Laurence (225–258) was one of the seven deacons of Rome under Pope Sixtus II. He was martyred in 258 by the Roman Emperor Valerian, slowly burned to death on a gridiron over smoldering coals.

5 King Astoret

(A Story from Bèlgida)

They say that … many, many years in the past there was a majestic castle at the heart of the Safra Mountains. Today, you can still find lovely forests of white pines, rich with the balsamic smell of their sap, in the region; so in those distant times the place must have been a veritable paradise. In addition, the castle was bordered by pleasant paths and tree-shaded walkways with well-kept flower beds and stretches of fertile land where a great variety of crops was grown.

The castle was inhabited by a king named Astoret and his small but elegant court. He was a handsome young man with fair skin and blue eyes, and his heart was kind, though at times his behavior was whimsical and impetuous. For you see, he was an orphan and had been brought up by his guardian and tutor, the courtier Baltasar del Seny,[1] who had somewhat spoiled him as a child.

In his teens he became very fond of the noble sport of the hunt, which had been beneficial for his growth. But then, in his early 20s that fondness became an overriding passion. Baltasar del Seny did all he could to teach the youth to love the animals and plants and magnificent landscapes of the region. And above all to respect the breeding times of the birds and hares and badgers and other denizens of the woods as though they were sacred.

And King Astoret was wont to obey that norm.

One year, however, at the height of summer, he heard that a badger had gnawed down a field of fine ripe wheat that was close to the castle, located to the north in a place where the farmers were under the protection of the fortress. Now the king had not gone out to hunt for several months, and his barely contained desire to do so now took the form of a great indignation over the destruction wrought by the badger. And so, against Baltasar's advice, he prepared a hunting party to search the forest for signs of the beast.

At mid-afternoon, the sun still high, he rode out in the company of four young courtiers and a pair of servants who were skilled trackers, and they sought out any traces of the badger's retreat from the wheat field.

It didn't take them long. When the badger heard the barking of the dogs and the hoofbeats of the horses, it scurried out of a clump of bushes and the

DOI: 10.4324/9781003324232-5

king spurred his horse so furiously in chase that he was soon out of sight of the rest of the company.

The badger was strong and plump and ran like the wind through the underbrush beneath the pines. Still, after a half hour's chase, and all alone, the king managed to corner it against the face of a cliff, where it had no escape.

And then something amazing happened. The badger was immobile; the king aimed his crossbow and at that moment heard a voice coming from he knew not where: "King Astoret, do not slay the badger. If you do, you will regret it."

But the king, overcoming his surprise and still furious after the lengthy race, blurted out: "Be you badger or be you demon, now you will die!" He released the arrow and mortally pierced the animal's furry flesh. In that instant the badger exploded with a loud bang, and in its place appeared a tall, wrinkled old hag with a face like a sour crabapple.

She spoke in a threatening voice: "You have shown, King Astoret, that you have a heart of stone, and I have decided to punish you. On this very day you will fall in love with a beautiful damsel you will see in your dreams, but you will never ever meet her in the flesh."

Then the witch, sorceress, evil fairy, or whatever she was, vanished in a flash; while King Astoret stood there motionless, not understanding what he had seen.

Soon he heard his companions approaching.

"Where's the badger? What happened, sire?"

Astoret was at a loss. "I don't know," he stuttered, "it disappeared."

That night, when he had been asleep in his sumptuous bed for around two hours, he saw her in a fleeting but very sweet dream: a young woman of maybe 18 years, with olive skin and delicate features, a slender figure and soft, wavy hair that fell to her shoulders.

King Astoret rose the next morning with a strong desire to see her again, even though he knew it must be practically impossible. "She probably doesn't even exist," he told himself. "It must be a spell, cast by that evil old woman."

But the dream kept coming back for quite some time, though not every night. And Astoret began to suspect that it was somehow real.

He got accustomed to the young lady's face, and needed to see it. He grew surly and distant, and only found respite in the joy of his occasional dreams which, however, were always brief.

Maybe it was an evil trap, or it might have been fate, which leads our mortal lives through winding and surprising pathways. Whatever it was, he felt a vague apprehension, for his forebears, and even his father, had persecuted witches in the region; and this could be a spell cast on him out of revenge.

It was his custom to take long horse rides through the woods and to stroll through the castle gardens, almost always in the company of his counselor

Baltasar. But since he had started having the dreams, he preferred to go out alone in order not to be distracted from his thoughts about that mysterious lady and his imaginary fancies.

He soon lost all appetite and turned sullen and melancholy. The knights and ladies of his small court were all perplexed by his behavior and attempted to lighten his mood with excursions, parties and dances. But all to no avail.

"What is it that ails you, my lord?"

At last, the faithful Baltasar del Seny, walking with him one morning outside the castle, managed to wrest the secret from his heart.

The old man listened thoughtfully, and when Astoret had finished, said, "Yes, this could be a wicked act of revenge, an ugly trap. Who knows? Your ancestors did hunt down those shadowy inhabitants of the forest and lords of the night. But you ..."

And then he asked, "Can you not give me some idea as to where I might seek out this young maiden?"

"I can tell you no more," answered Astoret. "She smiles at me; at times she even sings me a beautiful song—always the same one. She stares at me with her lovely, dark eyes ... But she doesn't tell me who she is, nor who sends her to my dreams, nor anything else to clear up the mystery."

"Tonight, my liege," requested Baltasar, "do me a favor. Ask her in the dream, if you can, what her name is. This, and nothing else."

The king agreed. As soon as he finished his supper he retired to his chamber, nervous with anticipation, and quickly went to bed and straight to sleep from the strength of his yearning. Luckily, at midnight the girl appeared again in his dreams. She was smiling, as always, but this time with a hint of sadness. She sang that melodious song, with its echoes of distant lands, different people and far horizons.

In his dreams until now, the young man had been unable to speak a word, as though he were enchanted. But after the urging of his venerable counselor, he made an effort and managed to say (without waking up—you see what a serious case this was!): "Permit me to know your name, who you are and where I can go to find you."

But a look of fright crossed her face and she suddenly disappeared.

The king was sorely disappointed and woke up on the spot. It took him God knows how long to get back to sleep again. He rose the next morning pale and bleary-eyed, with no appetite for food and more discouraged than ever. What had become of his youthful impulse and happiness and strength? The courtiers, the other inhabitants of the castle, the servants: they were all taken aback to see their lord like this.

After breakfast, Baltasar invited him once more to the kind of walk they had used to take. It was a quiet morning and the sun was partially covered with thin white clouds, like a bride's veil.

"What happened last night, my liege?" asked the courtier nervously. He could see from Astoret's demeanor that things had not gone well.

The young king recounted his dream, without leaving out a single detail.

"But I told you," said Baltasar in a delicate reproach, "not to ask for anything but her name. You must tread very softly and slowly with such apparitions as this."

The king assured him that the next chance he had he would do as Baltasar said.

A night went by, then two, then three ... and no sign of the lovely apparition. The king began to think that he had lost her forever; but then, on the fourth night—Mother of God what joy!—she appeared again, glowing with beauty and charm.

He didn't even let her start to sing: "Tell me your name!"

She smiled at him and answered, "My name is Margarida Blanca," and she straightway started to fade into the distance.

The next day though, King Astoret awoke impatient and excited. He called for Baltasar and told him the beautiful damsel's name. Now she seemed less distant and mysterious.

"Fine!" del Seny beamed. "Now we have an important clue."

And that same day he sent out four messengers on horseback to the four quarters of the world, to inquire in all towns large and small if anyone knew an attractive maiden by the name of Margarida Blanca.

But it just so happened that the witch of Safra—her name was Safranera—who often roamed the castle grounds dressed as a beggar or even, at times, in the guise of a tawny owl like the ones that sometimes hooted at night on the battlements or the window ledges of the fortress, caught wind of this development. So she decided to make herself invisible and follow the servant who rode to the north.

Safranera couldn't be certain that her curse would be completely successful, as King Astoret might count on the help of friends with magic powers or beneficent fairies. She knew she had to be careful.

And in effect, the servant who went northward crossed three valleys and the four mountain ranges that separated La Safra from La Vall de la Terra Blanca, where Margarida lived, on the outskirts of the village of Agullent. He was also the one who met most hardships along the way.

Ever mounted in his saddle, he pulled Safranera along in his wake, as they say; but he never did see her, flying on a new broomstick she was breaking in on this journey beyond her usual forest haunts. And of course, those times when the messenger asked after Margarida Blanca and received a negative reply, the witch did nothing. But when he reached Agullent and the answer was *yes* and he was directed to the modest house where she lived, the witch whispered a spell in his ear so that he couldn't hear what was said to him.

"Do you know a fair maiden by the name of Margarida Blanca?"

But instead of their reply, what he heard was, "No, not at all. No one by that name in Agullent."

"Much obliged," the poor fellow answered.

And so he rode right out of the place he was seeking and never knew a thing.

In a couple of months all four riders returned to the castle, exhausted and weak as a wilted leaf of lettuce, without any word of Margarida.

News of this failure spread through the castle like wild fire. The ladies, above all, had their doubts: "A mysterious maiden? It must all be a dream."

"Yes, in the end it'll turn out to be a wild goose chase!"

"And all of us beating our heads against a wall."

"The king will get what he deserves."

"That's another kettle of fish!"

The place was rife with gossip.

And of course, after the useless searches almost everyone believed that Margarida Blanca was nothing more than a figment of the febrile imagination of a deluded king. Except for the faithful Baltasar.

* * *

The elder courtiers, in effect the king's counselors, now began to meet without him in order to discuss the problem freely.

"The king is going downhill fast."

"Nothing good can come of this."

Some proposed a solution: "We should find him someone to marry. There are lots of beautiful princesses in the neighboring kingdoms ... If he marries he'll surely forget about those phantoms that are tormenting him."

But del Seny shook his head. "I think," he said, "before doing that, we need to get to the bottom of this mystery that's hounding the king. These dreams he has have been repeated so often they've taken on an air of reality. The king's mind is perfectly clear ... So we're obliged to make at least one more effort to solve this conundrum. I propose that we visit Jeremies, the astrologer."

They were all convinced by his reasoning and agreed that Astoret and Baltasar del Seny would make the visit together.

This astrologer was a very prestigious figure. His full name was Jeremies de Camara and he lived not far from the Salines Lagoon, on a high black mountain to the east of the lake. It was called Mount Camara, from which the astrologer took his surname.

The following day the king and his counselor, accompanied by two trusted archers, set off on horseback. It was a ride of several hours. The weather was disagreeable: black clouds reared their threatening heads to the east and a bothersome humid wind was blowing in from all directions. The usual combination in the latter days of autumn.

They reached the lagoon by midday. Its quiet mirror reflected the dark Salines Mountains and the unsettling face of the sky. They stopped for some lunch beside a forest of enormous umbrella pines, known as the Plaça[2] Pines, close to the foot of Mount Camara. There they left the archers in a rude stone hut to await their return from the mountain. The king and counselor carefully made their way up treacherous goat paths to Jeremies' cave, located high on the mountainside.

The astrologer heard their approach—the sound of human voices and the clatter of horseshoes—and stepped out of the sizeable cave that was his home. Baltasar gave him a friendly wave from a distance and Jeremies, recognizing his lord and king, proffered a deep bow.

They reach the cave and dismount. After a ceremonious greeting, they shelter the horses in a corner of the cave and make themselves comfortable farther inside.

King Astoret had only seen this famous but prudent man, who looked into the past and the future with complete integrity through his occult science, a few times in his life. He stared at the astrologer with hope in his eyes. Tall and slender, still strong and with a white beard that reached his waist, Jeremies' friendly and respectable air produced a feeling of security and trust.

He invited the visitors to sit down by the hearth, where a great fire was burning. Its smoke went up through a chimney in the rock. At the sound of a powerful thunderclap that echoed through the surrounding mountains, Jeremies said with a smile, "Thunder in winter, cold and snow in the mountains!"

It was almost night and the storm, growing fiercer, began to hurl down sleet and hail on Mount Camara. It pelted the open entrance of the cave.

"My Lord King," continued the astrologer, "if your purpose is to consult me about some mystery, then you have chosen a propitious time. On a stormy night like this I shall be able to serve you to great effect, for the fury of nature often affords the revelation of many hidden secrets."

Needless to say, this information raised the visitors' hopes.

"Even though we cannot see the stars?" asked the king.

"Much better thus, as the lightning is like bits of stars that come down to visit us."

Jeremies refreshed them with a simple but tasty evening meal: very tender roasted meat, a local red wine, newly-baked bread and toasted walnuts and almonds.

Nervous and sickly, Astoret was somewhat impatient with the astrologer's lack of haste. But he held his tongue. And at last the old man asked them for the nature of their visit, and the king unburdened himself with a brief, but precise description.

Then the sorcerer, without a word, went to a recess in the cave and fetched a few small sacks of white and pink powders, some flasks filled with thick, smoky liquids, a small silver pan and an iron stand. Of course, it was all magic paraphernalia. Close to the entrance to the cave, in a spot protected from the falling sleet, he piled some dried twigs on the ground, lit them and placed the iron stand and the pan above the flames. Then he poured in some of the mysterious liquids from the flasks.

Outside, from the cloudy sky, came the occasional peal of thunder; the mouth of the cave lit up with the bluish glow of the lightning.

"Sirs," said Jeremies, "come closer, if you please. Now stare at the opening of the cave which, you see, because of the darkness outside, resembles a curtain of black cloth."

They did as they were told, and stared into that darkness. Then, Jeremies threw two full pouches of the powders into the pan, where the liquids were bubbling noisily, and fell to his knees murmuring an unintelligible incantation.

There was another flash of lightning, very bright this time, and for a moment the three of them, astonished, their hair standing on end, saw a window appear in the black opening of the cave. It framed the face and torso of a young woman.

"Margarida Blanca!" exclaimed the king.

Then the lightning faded out and the image vanished.

Jeremies slowly got to his feet and the three of them returned to their seats by the fire.

"Gentlemen," resumed the astrologer, "as you have seen, the veil of mystery covering the king's dreams has been pulled back, but only a little and not enough. The only thing that is clear in this, my Lord, is that you have been bewitched, enchanted. That is, you are under the power of a spell."

"But is she a real woman?" wondered Baltasar del Seny.

"I should say she is, good sir! And genteel to a fault, more than enough to make a fine wife for a king ... However, she is not wealthy ... The eave above the window we saw, with mildewed tiles worn down by the weather and the years, indicate a house of the poor ..."

He ceased talking and seemed to be lost in thought.

"And now ..." said the king at a loss.

"Now the problem is mine, my Lord. It is I who must seek her out, from here; though they say that he who sends another never goes. I shall send, and I shall go, I promise you."

Astoret felt hopeful.

Bundled up in blankets and lying on mattresses of ram's fur, he and Baltasar slept soundly through the night. The next morning they said farewell, left a small purse of gold coins in the alms box and rode back to the castle.

And it was odd: in the midst of the hunting season, the king observed the animals—partridges, thrushes, hares, rabbits and even eagles and hawks—with tenderness. He was struck with admiration for their beauty and grace, their marvelous, effortless flight, and felt no urge, as before, to shoot them. *Well,* thought Baltasar, *now that he's suffered for love, his heart has become softer for all of God's creatures.*

***

When they had gone, Jeremies thought about his friend, the fairy of the lagoon, whose name, naturally, was Salina. The first thing he had done that morning was read through a parchment scroll that contained all manner of spells and conjurations for every eventuality: tight spots, conflicts, joys and sorrows, revenge, favors, mysteries, deaths, births, weddings. And when he found the ones he needed to consult for the case in hand he left the cave—the weather had cleared—and picked a few bunches of rare herbs: great mullein, shrubby gromwell, fraxinella. Though blasted by the harsh weather, they were still usable. He tied together a good sheaf and set it alight at the entrance of the cave to invoke the aid of the fairy. The subtle aroma of the smoke would reach her in a few minutes on the wings of the breeze.

Later that evening he received Salina's visit. Her age was indeterminate, but it was clear at first sight that she had a kind heart. Jeremies was happy to see her and, as was the custom, told her in verse what he needed.

> *Salina, fairy of the lake,*
> *who lives alone where the waters break,*
> *the king, Astoret,*
> *is sorely distraught.*
> *He requires your aid*
> *for his life to be remade.*
> *Provide him, if you please,*
> *The grace of your remedies.*

The fairy made a graceful bow and responded in kind:

> *Good Jeremies,*
> *trusting and pure,*
> *you who love your liege*
> *may henceforth rest assured.*
> *Say with what he is besieged*
> *and we shall find a cure.*

The ritual ceremony completed, they sat down by the hearth and the astrologer divulged the monarch's complaint and the occurrences at the castle.

The fairy asked him some questions about the details of the apparition, both in Astoret's dreams and on the night of the storm. And then she said, "Jeremies, we must admit that the situation is grave. We are faced with the evil arts and designs of a wicked, if somewhat crack-pot person: the witch Safranera. She is very powerful, and she must have a grudge against that youthful, self-indulgent king ... But you needn't worry. Leave it in my hands."

They then spoke long of many things, and after being pleasantly entertained by her comrade in marvels, she returned to the lagoon. Jeremies watched from the mouth of the cave until her graceful white figure faded out of sight in the growing darkness of the evening.

The very next day Salina took on the form of a poor beggar woman and in no time at all—maybe she rode on a great big dragonfly—she went to La Vall de la Terra Blanca and the village where Margarida lived. There, she went from door to door as an old woman asking for alms.

The day was cold; the sky was cloudy and grey.

It just so happened that when Salina came to Margarida's house, the girl was all alone, as her parents had gone to the market in Ontinyent to sell some of the poultry they raised. She was staring out of the well-known window at a few swirling snowflakes that were just beginning to fall. Salina saw that she was eating a pomegranate.

"Good morning, Margarida Blanca!" she said.

"Hey, you know my name?"

"Yes, they told me it in the village. They said you are generous with the poor."

Margarida was a kind-hearted girl, but she also laughed a lot and liked to have fun.

"If you can answer me a riddle, I'll go down and give you a plate of warm food," she proposed to the counterfeit beggar.

"Fine, my lovely lady."

And so she asked: "What is as white as the snow and as scarlet as a pomegranate?"

Salina broke out in a hearty laugh. "Oh, my dear girl, that's an easy one. It's King Astoret!"

Margarida was deeply moved. "And what is he like?"

The fairy gave her a description.

"Oh yes, he must be the fine young man that has been coming to me in my dreams. One night he asked me who I was, where I lived … And it frightened me so—I thought it must be magic—that I woke up right away," the girl told her.

"Yes, Margarida," answered Salina, "he must be the one."

"All right, my good woman, I'll come right down."

Margarida went downstairs and opened the door and showed her into the kitchen. There were still some embers in the fire, so Margarida put on some dried olive branches to bring it back to life, and soon the old woman was enjoying a nice warm plate of boiled beans. When she had finished, the girl implored, "Now tell me about the king."

"Oh, he lives in a lovely castle, but it's very far away, many, many leagues from here. And Astoret is bewitched."

"That doesn't matter. Tell me how to get there."

"Well, that's not possible now, and I'll tell you why. The castle is located in the Safra Mountains. And in those lands, in the summer, they have a big harvest and they thresh the grain on the castle's threshing-floor. Now according to the stars, the next big harvest will yield more than a thousand bushels of grain, but the stalks may well be so tough that no one will be able to cut them. The threshers, with nine mules and nine threshing stones, will try and try, but it will be useless. When they become desperate, you must show up, take hold of the nine sets of reins and get to work. It's the only way to break the spell on the unfortunate king."

"With heart and soul!" interjected Margarida.

"You'll have to thresh and thresh tirelessly," continued Salina, "both day and night ... It will be no easy task. On the ninth day, if you can last that long, the threshing will be done and the spell will be broken. The king will become his old, happy self again, now so long forgotten, and will ask you to marry him."

Margarida Blanca was amazed. She couldn't believe what was happening. But because she saw a gleam of sincerity in Salina's eyes, she never for a moment doubted that it was true ... After the strange dreams she'd recently been having she was willing to believe something marvelous could happen.

"Still and all, good Margarida," warned Salina, "Don't think it will all be a bed of roses. The task before you will be daunting and painful and you must steel yourself if you hope to succeed."

Margarida said that she was ready, come what may. And the fairy described the long journey to the castle.

They said farewell and Salina left the house and began to tread the fine carpet of newly-fallen snow. Margarida went up to watch her from the window, but the beggar woman had disappeared.

**

She was so sweet and affectionate that of course her parents loved her tremendously. Margarida had half of the winter, all of the spring and the beginning of summer to convince them to let her go in search of King Astoret. At first they were against it, but little by little they came to understand it was their daughter's destiny. And so, with tears in their eyes and their hearts in a knot they bade her farewell one sunny July morning, and she set off on the way to the Albaida Pass, as the mysterious Salina had instructed her.

What a powerful force love is! Deep down inside the determined girl was afraid, even if she had gone many times with her parents to sow and reap fruit in those fields and to search for mushrooms and pick thyme and sage and pennyroyal in the mountains and was therefore familiar with the terrain. The idea of leaving her native village so far behind on a journey into the unknown put her courage to the test.

Carrying a bundle in her hand, she walked the road along those round wooded hills that border the Agullent Mountains. She heard a thousand mysterious hisses and other sounds coming from the forest. Sometimes they chilled her spine. She was wearing a simple white dress, cotton stockings, pretty Catalan sandals with their ribbons crossed and tied above her ankles: and her hair was done up in two braids, one on each side of her head. She was such a graceful, good-looking girl!

And that time of day—shhh!—the fields echoed with the voices of the laborers and the sweet tinkling of sheep bells among the flocks. A July day: small cumulous clouds above the high mountains, a polished sky.

She made her way with a hopeful heart, and after a few hours she found herself alone on the mountain pass, from which, in the distance, she could see a series of tall, blue-tinted mountain ranges. The sight made her spirits drop. *Oh Lord, how will I get over those big barriers?* she thought.

She started down the mountain toward a green plain with cultivated fields and olive groves. The pleasant aspect calmed her down.

There was a strange house set on a curve in the road; it was very narrow and taller than any house she'd ever seen before. The roof tiles, windows and door were quite pretty. A small oven jutted out on the right and at the very front a well, with a tiny roof, a pail and cord and pulley to collect rain water. A great oak tree before the door gave cooling shade.

Margarida went to the door and knocked: a hoarse woman's voice said from within: "Whoever you are, come in!"

She opened the heavy door, lined with iron plates, and saw in the midst of the entranceway, with its brown clay floor, a slender old woman as tall as a pole, with a wrinkled, clever and pleasing face. In spite of her outlandish appearance, wearing a black bodice and a full-length woolen skirt with pleats, she seemed very nice.

"Good day, good lady"

"Good day to you, my girl ... Come in, come in!"

The house was clean and neat, and similar in design to houses in this region: the hearth was close to the entrance; next to the hearth was the opening of the oven, two long stone benches on either side; in the middle of the room a table for meals, three low chairs and two very tall ones, all five with strong wooden frames and wicker seats, and farther in a room with an extraordinarily long bed, and then the pantry. Behind the house there was probably a small courtyard with stacks of firewood and cages for hens and rabbits.

The place was checkered with light and shadow.

Margarida couldn't contain herself: "What a nice house you have!"

The old lady invited her to sit, gave her a glass of cool water from the well and said that her name was Marieta. It hardly compared with her unusual stature.[3]

"My name is Margarida Blanca," answered the girl.

"Fine, fine! And what brings you here?" asked Marieta. Without awaiting a reply she continued, "Whatever it is, I'm happy to see you, because I'm often alone. And seeing a young lady like yourself brings back memories of my long-lost youth ...It comforts me ... But tell me about your journey. From the bundle you're carrying, it must be a long one."

"It is, ma'am. I'm searching for King Astoret."

Marieta drew a deep breath. "My dear girl! It's such a long way, and dangerous!"

"Will I have to cross those mountain ranges you can see to the southeast?"

"No, no. Not at all! I'll tell you how to get there. Don't go east, or even southeast. You have to go south; that's where the king's castle is ... . But now, let's have some lunch."

"Good idea," said the girl, "I'm famished."

They sat at the table and Margarida ate from the food she was carrying. But Marieta gave her water and fruit, some delicious local apricots.

During the meal, Margarida couldn't help looking at the odd old lady. Without being obvious, of course. *How tall she is!* she thought. *If this house didn't have such high ceilings...*

Marieta said she could stay for the night.

"You have a long journey ahead of you and it would be better to take it in stages, one day at a time," she explained. "In any case, you may be in danger here. I have only one son, but he's a real piece of work! The West Wind!"

Margarida was amazed. "Oh my Lord!"

"Now don't you worry, dear. He never stays long; always going out to blow and blow to keep these plains and mountains dry. He'll rest a few hours and be off to blow some more!"

"What could your son do to me?"

"What could he do? He's stronger than an ox and has a temper like a tornado. The little time he's here he wants to be left alone—no visitors. Oh, he's set in his ways, that boy. But I can hide you in the pantry; he never goes in there. And when he leaves, you can sleep in my bed. I'm old and tough and I can stretch out on one of the benches in the kitchen."

Margarida tried to say no, but in the end she accepted.

That night they had a quiet supper, after which Marieta went outside to look for her son. She saw that the boughs of the pines were beginning to sway and went back in.

"Hurry! Into the pantry with you. My boy's on the way!"

It was dark inside, and Margarida breathed in all of the appetizing smells of preserves, sausages, cured ham and aromatic herbs.

She wasn't there for long, a couple of hours at most. And through the door she could hear everything.

"Good evening, mother!" The house shook, and so did Margarida, with fright.

"Hello, you rascal!"

"What's this? I smell the scent of a human," he said in a huff.

"Don't get upset. Some travelers came by and I gave them a drink of water."

"I'm starving!"

After supper, she heard him say, "Mother, give me an olive branch to pick my teeth."

And at last, he decided to leave. "So long, ma! I'm going out to blow all night. The pines are full of worms and I want to sweep them out to sea and drown them."

The door slammed shut with a bang and Marieta knocked at the pantry door. "You can come out now, Margarida Blanca!"

What a relief! She came out, still shaking, and whether she wanted or not, had to lie down and sleep in the old lady's extra-long bed.

The next day they went outside and, as promised, Marieta told her how to get to the king's castle. "From here you go down to the Cocentaina plain, to the left of Mount Mariola. You'll see the village at the foot of a high castle. You'll get there around midday and you can drink the clear, cool water from the wonderful fountain they have there after your lunch. Then you go straight south up a long hill and you'll find the mouth of a great big ravine on your left. You have to get through it before nightfall, because some wolf could come down from the Carrascal Mountains and gobble you up. The other end of the ravine gives onto a broad stretch of land and there you'll see a house just like mine. It belongs to Roseta, mother of the East Wind. She'll take you in and will tell you how to get to the third house."

Grateful, Margarida gave her a kiss like she'd give her own grandma and started to leave. But Marieta went on, "Here, take this hazelnut. If you ever find yourself in a tight spot, break it open and it'll give you aid."

The girl thanked her, placed the hazelnut in the pocket of her blouse and said farewell.

She walked all day. After having lunch beside the fountain in Cocentaina, she found the deep long ravine, and close to nightfall she made her way to the stretch of land Marieta had described. It was filled with planted fields and the crops were still green, as the harvests are late at those altitudes. And not far along she saw, beside the road, an odd tall house.

"That must be it," she murmured to herself.

She approached the door and knocked.

"Whoever you are, come in!"

She opens the door and sees another old woman, Roseta, who is also extremely tall and has a kindly face. She was pudgier than Marieta.

And here things went pretty much the same.

"My name is Margarida Blanca."

"And where are you off to?"

"To King Astoret's home."

"My darling girl! It's a long and hard journey! Look—"

And all of a sudden she leaps up out of her chair and says in a tizzy, "Hide, Margarida. It's my son!"

She put the girl into a large vat and covered it with the lid, careful to leave a small crack with a bit of wood so she could breathe.

In a moment Margarida heard the East Wind's voice: "I smell the flesh of a human!"

"Nonsense. You're just hungry for your supper."

But in a couple of hours the coast was clear. The winds never hang around for long, and before midnight the East Wind was on his way—though not without asking for a cherry tree branch to clean his teeth before leaving.

Margarida climbed out of the vat, had supper and lay herself down to sleep in the mistress's bed till the sun was well up the following day.

Over breakfast Roseta gave her directions for the day's journey. She had to keep on going south and she would see a village with two small castles on the right, which she needn't enter. After that she had to cross a wide valley. The laborers in the fields would direct her to the foot of the Lloma Llarga, a mountain in the Castalla range. There she would find the house of the North Wind.

Margarida thanked her and took away an almond Roseta gave her with these parting words: "If you ever find yourself in danger, my girl, break this open and you'll get help."

"Good-bye, good-bye."

Walking slowly under a blazing sun, Margarida was fatigued when she reached the foot of Lloma Llarga, where she immediately saw the North Wind's elongated house.

What can I say? The North Wind's mother, Hermenegildeta, also received her warmly and, before her son came home, hid her in a small cellar. The wind had supper, complained about the smell of human flesh, picked his teeth with a juniper branch and was off again.

"You can come out now, dear girl," said Hermenegildeta affectionately.

They slept through the night; they woke up and had breakfast; and at the doorway the old lady told Margarida where she had to go next: a steep road up and over the Dels Guills Pass, so high it sometimes touches the clouds. Before she left, Hermenegildeta gave her a walnut with the same advice at the others.

Margarida spent the day getting over the Del Guills Pass under a glaring sun. The road seemed interminable. She was going down the other side as night came on, and she came to the source of the Petrer River. It was surrounded by frightening steep hills, rough-looking and lonely. But then her heart rose when she spied, not too far away, another house of a mother of the Winds.

She spent the night there, with the mother of the Southwest Wind, who told her the next day where she should go to finish her journey and reach the castle.

"If you shake a leg, Margarida," she said, "you can get there before the evening ... I have no gift for you, since I know my sisters have already given you the talismans you'll need."

Needless to say, Margarida was also scared in that house when the Southwest Wind showed up and she heard his curses, the clatter of supper and how he asked for a thick carob tree branch to clean his teeth.

As Margarida made her way across the Elda and Petrer valleys, the July sun was beating down with a vengeance. She stopped for lunch on the other side of Monòver, then a small, cheerful hamlet at the top of a low hill, and after that she crossed a wide stretch of barren land and dry river beds until at last she reached the pine woods of Safra. There she met some muleteers.

"How much farther to the castle?"

"You can be there by nightfall," one of them replied.

But they were doubtful, for she looked so exhausted that they figured she would have to stop somewhere to rest in the shade.

When she had climbed the lower slopes of Mount Safra she was worn out; her feet were almost bleeding and her mouth was dry. But there was no spring in sight and her food was all used up. She sat down in the shade of a strawberry tree.

"What if I crack open the hazelnut?" she murmured. "I can't go any farther. And what will happen when I have to work all night on the threshing floor?"

So she places the hazelnut on a flat rock and strikes it with the edge of a smaller one.

She didn't expect what happened next! A whitish smoke came forth from the broken shell and turned into the figure of a woman with a very white face, very white hands, a very white dress, transparent ears and hair so fair it seemed like threads of gold. She held a glass that was filled with a pure white liquid.

"Do not fear, Margarida. You have called for me and here I am. I come at the behest of Salina, the fairy of the lagoon. Drink this glass of hazelnut milk and you will be able to thresh the grain for nine days without the need to sleep, or eat, or drink, or cool yourself from the heat."

Margarida, who by now was hardly surprised by anything, said only "Thank-you very much," and drank the whole glass. It was sweet.

"One thing," warned the apparition, "you have to drive the mules and the threshing stones as fast as ever you can, because if you haven't cut all the hay, ground the chaff and thrown away the stalks by midnight on the ninth day, all will be lost."

And with that, both woman and glass, which Margarida had handed her back, disappeared.

The final leg of the journey was easy for the girl. When she got to her feet, she found herself even more rested than when she had left Agullent. She was strong and light of foot again!

The way led into the mountains. They were lonely and dry; but there were majestic pines; and the aromas of the wild plants grew more and more pungent and bracing. In some places the underbrush formed a carpet of lavender and purple and violet bluebells.

When the sun was on the western horizon, she came to a fertile expanse of land at a bend in the road and, on the other side of that, sitting atop a low hill, was the king's castle! So many towers and turrets, walls and battlements, crenels and windows! And what a marvelous drawbridge, spanning a dark, imposing moat. And the gardens and parks that stretched as far as the eye could see. The setting sun tinted it all with the splendor of a striking golden hue.

Margarida's heart beat wildly.

And then, what does she do? Well, for fear of being seen she crouches down before a clump of pines to observe the movements of all the folks walking in and out of the castle. And then she noticed the chants of the threshers on the threshing floor, which wasn't far away, and the voices of the guards as they made their rounds, and the hoofbeats of the horses, the barking of dogs and the cries and laughter of women and children. From where she was kneeling, there must have been less than 400 paces to the fortress. And she strained her eyes to see if Astoret might appear in one of the windows, or outside taking a walk, even if—as she had only viewed him in her dreams—it would have been hard to distinguish his figure from those who might be with him.

But the vision she yearned for was nowhere to be seen. For it turns out that ever since Salina had gone to Margarida's house, that is, in the midst of winter, Astoret had had no more of those dreams that he hoped for every night. And as you can imagine, he had no desire to speak with anyone or to leave the palace. He was inconsolable. Nothing and no one could move him.

***

The lovely damsel remained where she was until it had grown dark. The castle had fallen silent; its windows were closed and not a light could be seen. Now and then, from the towers and walls, the cries of sentries could be heard, shouting their reports, and even the metallic footsteps of the soldiers as they made their rounds in the cool evening air.

Margarida worked up her nerve and slowly approached the threshing floor. In the starlight she made out some dark figures beneath a large oak tree. It was the threshers, who were lying down next to the grain spread over the ground. They seemed to be covered with sacks. On the threshing floor, their reins left free, were nine mules that silently lowered their muzzles to the straw and chewed peacefully away in great mouthfuls. She could only barely see in the darkness.

Careful not to wake the others, she knelt down and grasped a fistful of the stalks to find out how the work was going, and saw that the grain had hardly been separated. *I got here in time*, she thought.

She had no idea what those men would say or how to go about the threshing. Hesitant, she went over to a stone wheel shining white in the tenuous light and sat down to wait.

The time passed slowly. The sky grew darker and the stars shone like embers. The evening air was filled with the aromas of thyme and rosemary and lavender. It was lovely! *And what's more*, she thought, *not far away, "white as the snow and scarlet as a pomegranate," is the enchanted king*!

Then she heard someone yawn. One of the men got to his feet and looked up at the stars to see what time it was. "Almost midnight," she heard him say.

Another thresher rose. "What was that?"

"It's time to get to work."

"But why ... We've been at it these three days and none of the hay is cut. It must be cursed, like our king."

Margarida approached them. At first they thought she was a ghost. One of them lit a torch and, seeing a lovely young maiden, shouted, "Look! Look over here!"

The other two got up then, and they were all astounded to see her there.

"I come to help you."

"What, you?" asked the one that had risen first, who seemed to be their boss.

"A delicate girl like you?" asked another.

"I can thresh as well as any of you. I've been helping my father for years."

They lit another torch and placed it, very carefully so as not to set fire to the grain, in a pine tree on the other side of the threshing floor. They put the other one at the trunk of the oak tree, giving them enough light to see the waiting stalks and the nine mules with their threshing wheels.

The men chuckled among themselves at Margarida's claim, but she was adamant. "I swear I can do all of the threshing."

"Maybe you can," conceded the one in charge, "but we haven't been able to do a thing. This grain seems to be bewitched."

"Leave it to me, then!"

"What do you say, boys?"

"Let her have a go."

"It's midnight," said one of them, looking at the stars.

"Hand me the reins and I'll get moving," concluded the girl. "You lot can go on back to sleep."

They hand the reins over and Margarida goes to the center of the threshing floor, neither hungry nor thirsty nor sleepy, and sets the mules in motion. "Giddy-up, mules!"

The threshers couldn't believe their eyes.

"This must be the work of the Evil One," said one of them. "Who's ever seen a woman so hardy and decisive?"

"No," replied another. "It can't be the Evil One, but the work of heaven. Because the denizens of hell never want to do a lick of work."

"Lie down and have a rest, my good fellows. I can handle it all," she cried.

Seeing that she drove the nine mules like a charm, they went back to their resting-place beneath the enormous oak.

* * *

Margarida went on threshing the livelong night, as though it were a lark. And she didn't feel the least bit tired.

The next day, little by little, all the folks from the castle made their way to the threshing floor—except for King Astoret. He was feeling so weak he couldn't leave his bed. At around ten o'clock Baltasar del Seny went out and witnessed the sight of that valiant, lovely maiden who drove the nine mules around the threshing floor without cease. It was something to behold! ... She even knew when she had to beat the tips of the stalks. But of course, she sprang from peasant laborer stock.

When he saw her face, the loyal counselor's blood ran cold in his veins. Wasn't this the same girl as in the flash of light in Jeremies' cave? He stared ... and stared ... "Yes, no; yes, yes. It just might be." Her face looked so languid as she worked, he couldn't be sure. In any case, he rushed back to the castle to inform the king.

But to his dismay, he found the king in a lamentable state, prostrate on the bed, his eyes staring up at the ceiling. He took no notice of anyone.

"My lord king, please hear me out," whispered the poor counselor. "There is a very pretty girl working on the castle threshing floor ..."

It was no use! He saw that the king wasn't listening.

So he called for the royal surgeon.

But he, too, was at a loss, though he did manage to administer a glass of water steeped in orange blossoms.

When news of the king's condition ran through the castle, everyone was frightened.

"The king is in a bad way!"

"Oh, oh, the king may die!"

Nevertheless, Baltasar refused to give up hope. He suspected—and rightly so—that it must all be an effect of the magic spell Jeremies had talked about. That spell had to be broken, and the astrologer must have taken measures to do so.

It also occurred to del Seny that the king's worsening condition could be connected with the mysterious appearance of the beautiful thresher. So he gave orders that no one impede her in her labor, and that two trusted men be present, unbeknown to anyone else, to guard her at all times. In the meantime he would ask Jeremies for instructions. To that effect he summoned one of the crossbowmen who had gone with them to the Camara Mountains and gave him a sealed message for the astrologer (a parchment scroll tied with a silk band and bearing the royal seal).

"Here Gilabert," he ordered the soldier, "take this to the astrologer. It's a question of the king's health; deliver it into his hands and come back right away."

All the while Margarida Blanca—observed at times by gawking onlookers and other times alone—kept on driving the mules and threshing the grain. That enormous pile of loose stalks was slowly growing smaller.

Gilabert returned before nightfall with Jeremies' answer on a parchment bearing the astrologer's seal. Baltasar convened the council, opened the missive and read aloud: "The maiden you speak of who is threshing the harvest is Margarida Blanca. Do not talk to her, nor say a word of this to the king. No one must know. Have faith. At midnight on the ninth night, the king's spell will be broken and he will take her as his wife. Your servant, Jeremies de Camara."

The council decided to follow the advice of the royal astrologer and ordered that the two guards watching her be withdrawn.

* * *

So the work with the mules continued. All of the inhabitants of the castle watched, some by day, others by night. And all of them returned with their hair on end and their skin covered with goose bumps. That young girl—so pretty, so shapely, with such a melodious voice and such luxurious cascading hair—neither ate, nor drank, nor rested, nor slept. And she didn't fall over dead from so much threshing!

However, in compliance with Baltasar's strict orders, no one moved a muscle to help her and no one spoke a word. The only thing the threshers did was eat like there was no tomorrow, guzzle down the strong local wine and, from time to time, ignite some resin-soaked torches to give her light. An occasional burst of laughter escaped their lips, so content they were, or a word of praise for the damsel.

And what about the mules? Well, that was another miracle. As tireless as Margarida, they didn't stop to rest, they didn't eat the hay, nor was it necessary to bring them pails of water to drink.

Thus the nine days went by, and the final night arrived. Meanwhile, King Astoret, to his courtiers' dismay, remained abed and unresponsive to anything or anyone else in the world.

* * *

And what do you think was happening on those very same days out on the king's hunting grounds, close to where the badger had turned into a witch? Well, the last night, when the harvest was all cut down and threshed, that is, when the main work was done, a small bonfire was lit high up in the mountains we've already seen and before it Safranera the witch set in to dancing a diabolical dance that made her skirts fly through the air as though they were the black wings of the Devil himself.

"Ha, ha, ha!" laughed the wicked hag, and then she stepped up close to the flames and cast in a fistful of magic powders, and a thick white smoke rose up above the tops of the pines.

When she finished her macabre dance she sat down on a flat stone beside the fire, took out a mirror and gazed at herself. And, wonder upon wonder! Her face was young and she looked very much like Margarida Blanca. *I'm not exactly the same,* she thought, *but that pea-brain of a king won't know the difference and I'll marry him and have the life of a queen, instead of living like a witch!*

And with that, she jumped up like a billy goat and kicked her heels in the air.

"Ah," she said aloud, "I'm almost late. Because of that damned astrologer's meddling conjurations, the spell will be broken when she finishes the work at midnight ... And that's when he'll see me, the one who brings him back to himself ... It was really Margarida Blanca, and I look like her. He doesn't know the real Margarida Blanca as I do. And he'll never set eyes on her, nor will anyone else in the world!"

She put out the fire, straddled her broomstick and flew above the pines to the castle. It was so dark when she got there that the only thing she could see on the threshing floor was the stone wheel where the torches were set. She came down to the ground and hid behind the large oak tree. The men were all sleeping nearby, and she went from one to the other, sprinkling a pinch of powdered opium poppy and green dragon leaves in their noses. Thus, they wouldn't be able to open their eyes for about 30 minutes. Then she watched Margarida at work, and when her back was turned, she rushed up behind her and cast some of the sleeping powder over her head.

As soon as she breathed in that poisonous dust, Margarida fell in a heap onto the straw. Oh my Lord, what a slumber! She just fainted dead away. The witch, full of energy, leaned down, lifted the sleeping beauty onto her shoulders, mounted the broomstick and flew right back to her cave in the woods.

In no time at all they were there.

"What good is this cave to me?" she said to herself as she laid the sleeping girl down at the entrance. "She can have it—and stay here forever!"

Then she let out a spine-curdling cackle that was answered by the screech owls and eagle owls and other malign and mysterious beasts in the forest.

She removed the large boulder that covered the entrance in the blink of an eye and left the unfortunate Margarida inside, lying on a miserable bed of dead weeds and straw. Then she closed off the entrance to the cave again with the boulder. She had the strength of a pair of stevedores.

"Ha! Let them come round here if they want. Nobody knows there's a cave in these parts. And Margarida will never be able to move this boulder before she dies of hunger. What's more, my friends and relatives, the witches and warlocks of these woods, will scare off anyone who comes this way."

Then, in another blink of an eye, she flew back to the threshing floor and broke the broomstick into four pieces, just in case someone found it and got ideas, after which she took up the nine reins and set the mules in motion. The men, of course, had been sleeping like logs and didn't notice a thing.

Soon, according to the stars, it was 12 o'clock. The threshing was done! Safranera cried out, "I've finished. It's over!"

The men, still groggy from the powders, opened their eyes when they heard her shouts. They got up slowly and looked toward the threshing floor. What was going on? "What is it? What's the matter?"

"Come quickly!" called the false Margarida. She was laughing up a storm.

They noticed that her voice was now deeper than before. But they paid little heed, marking it down to the dampness of the evening air.

"Light more torches!" exclaimed the witch.

In the light of more than 20 burning brands they placed in the few trees scattered around the threshing floor, far enough away that the very dry straw wouldn't catch fire, the men turned the harvest over with their pitchforks and saw that all of the grain had been freed and the stalks had been cut into short pieces and the chaff covered the grain like a fine coating of golden dust.

"The threshing is done!" they cried.

"Tomorrow we'll winnow, and then we'll be done for the year!" said their boss.

"It's a miracle," they said, looking at the witch without realizing she wasn't Margarida, as she did closely resemble the girl.

"It's like it was nothing at all." They were amazed.

"Here then. Drink, eat, rest," they offered.

"No need," replied the shameless thing. "I'm so happy I couldn't eat or drink or sleep."

They rushed off to the castle to give the news. They woke up Baltasar del Seny and the other notables and soon there was a great outburst of joy inside the palace fortress. Everyone threw on some clothes to go out and witness the visiting maiden's prodigious feat. And in a very short time the gates were opened as a rush of ladies, knights, man- and maid-servants, squires with lights streamed out—lanterns and more lanterns!—and all went straight to the threshing floor, led by the head counselor. There they hailed the false Margarida and led her to the castle, where she washed, brushed her hair and was presented to King Astoret. Still drowsy and melancholy, he looked at her unsteadily from his seat in the throne room, where they had managed to bring him.

Afterwards Margarida Blanca, as they believed, was taken to a sumptuous chamber, where she spent the night.

King Astoret's condition improved somewhat, but contrary to what del Seny had expected, he was still quite pallid and faint.

The courtiers were all distraught. "My Lord King," they said, "we thought you would be well by now, because the conditions for breaking the spell have been fulfilled."

"Yes, I do feel a bit better," he said in a weak voice.

"What do you think of Margarida Blanca?"

"Very nice," he answered, unenthused, "but her face isn't the same. It seemed so lovely and fresh in my dreams!"

"But do you wish to take her as your wife?"

"Yes ... yes, of course. I do ..."

"Ai, he will die a bachelor," thought the counselor del Seny, disconsolate.

The courtiers truly believed that if he married Margarida, as Jeremies had said, the spell would be lifted. Astoret neither opposed nor approved of his faithful followers' plans. He was mired in apathy.

Exactly two days later the great ceremony was held.

And the witch Safranera was made a queen.

***

Many days went by. And the king was still the same: as listless and lifeless as the day of the wedding. The counselors were frightened and confused. "What are we going to do? How can we bring him back to himself?" But no matter how much they tried, they could find no solution.

The fact is that Astoret wanted to return to normal; but, contrary to what he himself had believed, the company of his wife, who only vaguely resembled the maiden of his dreams, brought him neither the joy nor the peace of mind he had hoped for. Both day and night he suffered a spiritual anguish, a lack of ... he didn't know what.

The counterfeit Margarida did everything she could to make him happy. But all in vain. And then it crossed her mind that King Astoret might die of melancholy. And in her black and hairy heart of hearts, she rejoiced. *If he dies*, she thought, *it could be best. I'll wait some time, as the widowed queen, and then I'll marry my companion, the warlock Queroset de la Safra. We'll see how he comports himself as king.*

And from that point, it was really only a short step to thinking about how she could use her evil arts to rid herself of Astoret.

***

Meanwhile, what was going on with the real, and unfortunate, Margarida?

Well, the first thing she did was sleep for several days on end; for you see, back at the threshing floor she had inhaled a great lungful of those powders made of opium poppy and green dragon leaves. At last she woke up and realized she was in the dark in a rocky cave. But little by little her eyes grew accustomed to the dim light coming in through a small gap between the opening of the cave and the heavy boulder that blocked it.

She tried to move the stone. But how? It was impossible. She didn't have the strength of a pair of stevedores. She was trapped, with no way out! She burst into tears.

"And I'm so hungry!" she said. For of course the power of the hazelnut had now worn off.

But then, almost by accident, she put her hand in her pocket and realized that she still had the almond and the walnut that the mothers of the Winds had given her. Safranera, in such a rush to marry herself off to the king, had sealed the girl inside the cave without searching her clothes. Margarida took out the almond, broke its shell and quickly gulped down the fruit. It was delicious!

And what did she feel running through her body? A marvelous strength! She goes up to the boulder and gives it a push and away it goes, rolling through the woods! She runs outside of the horrid cave and is bathed in radiant sunlight; her ears are filled with the soothing sound of pine needles swaying in the breeze. It was wonderful! She was free!

She needed to make a plan to get back to Astoret's castle, though she thought it shouldn't be too hard, for just as all roads lead to Rome, all of the paths in the forest would lead to the castle.

"Ah, and I still have the walnut. What will happen if I break it open?"

No sooner said than done! She kneels down, picks up a couple of rocks and, bam ...cracks it in two. And what do you think she found inside? Not those two moist and tasty bites that all the other walnuts in the world contain. No, instead there were three precious pieces of jewelry that shone in the sun like nothing she'd ever seen before. One was a delicate mother-of-pearl comb with gold inlays, another was a necklace of pearls and rubies, and the third was a golden bracelet encrusted with gems of three different colors.

"And what good will all this stuff do me on a day like today?" thought Margarida.

She stood up, placed the jewelry in her pocket and went on her way. The long walk and the need to escape from her present dangerous situation got her to thinking, and before she reached the fortress, which she could just make out among its gardens and parks, she gave her forehead a smack. "That's it! I know what I have to do!"

She goes into a small orchard, reaches into the wet earth and spreads the reddish mud all over her arms and face and neck. Then she rubs it well in so that every inch of her skin is dark and she ties her hair into a bun at the back of her neck. Thus disguised, she looked like a different person. Not even her mother would have recognized her!

She approaches the castle and engages the folk going in and out in conversation. And soon she hears news of the king's marriage. It was a sad, sad blow! But she steeled herself and betrayed no sign of what she was feeling. On the contrary, she put on a happy face and strolled around the building and the homes of the laborers that had been built not far away and farther out along the road to Monòver, all the while crying: "Who would like to have a marvelous piece of jewelry? Who will buy a mother-of-pearl comb? Are there any takers?"

She only displayed the comb. The women crowded around and commented, "Oh, it's just too nice!"

"What a pity! Who has the money to buy a thing like that?"

"No one but the queen, Margarida Blanca!"

It didn't take long for word of the marvel to reach the castle. The queen's ladies-in-waiting went down to see it and rushed back all excited.

"Milady, this vendor has a comb that must be worth a treasure!"

"Oh, if you only saw it ..."

"Then bring it up to me!"

They bring it to her and of course, like everyone else, she loves it. She may have been a witch, but she was also a woman and, deep down inside, somewhat vain. And what if she could turn that fool of a king's head even more with the comb nicely set in a fine head of hair?

"Ask that vendor how much she wants."

They go downstairs and ask her.

"I'll give it to her cheap, for free, if only she'll let me spend one night in the king's bed chamber."

"Not a chance!" cries the witch. The thought of it enraged her. But after some consideration she changed her mind. "All right, yes. Tell her she can ... We'll give the king a sleeping potion and he'll be out like a light all night."

And so it was. The comb belonged to Safranera.

That evening Margarida went to the castle, as agreed. The servants bade her sit in a small waiting-room. The witch got a look at her through a door that was ajar and said, "I thought as much. It's her."

After his supper Astoret was in the custom of having a cup of herbal tea, and that night the witch had boiled two opium poppy buds and three green dragon leaves and slipped four teaspoons of the potion into his evening beverage.

Safranera didn't want him to get the slightest peek at the real Margarida. If he suspected it was she, the witch's plans would probably go awry. So when they went to sleep, each one in separate but adjoining rooms, she bolted the door between them.

Then, following her orders, the serving-girls ushered Margarida into Astoret's bed chamber. And as they were leaving her there, one of them said to herself, "How strange! If it wasn't for her dark skin, and that squeaky voice she has, and the pitiful expression on her face, I'd swear she could be the queen's sister."

That first night Margarida sat at the head of the king's bed and stared at him, full of deep emotion. Saddened, she recalled the riddle the fairy of the lagoon had solved for her: "As white as the snow and as scarlet as a pomegranate!" She cried out to him time and time again. "Oh, King Astoret, my heart's delight! I've gone through so much for you; and when I had almost finished threshing all the grain, a witch came out of nowhere and took on my form and married you! Oh, King Astoret!"

(After everything she'd been through and what she had heard, she was sure that a witch must have done it all.)

And so that night went by, and nothing changed. At daybreak the queen's servants came in and showed her to the street.

Margarida Blanca went out for a walk in the parks and gardens. As had happened with the hazelnut, she hadn't been hungry or thirsty since she'd eaten the almond. In the afternoon she went back to the castle to be a vendor again.

"Who will buy a pearl and ruby necklace? Ladies, who will buy?"

The queen's attendants hear her through the windows of the castle and go out to see it, and it all happens again.

"Milady, it's the vendor from yesterday. Now she has a pearl and ruby necklace. If you saw how beautiful it is …!"

"Bring it up!"

They do so and she sees it and asks the price.

"She said it's the same as the comb."

"All right."

Safranera keeps the necklace; Margarida Blanca goes upstairs again that night and again they give the potion to the king. He goes to sleep at once. Margarida enters the bedroom and spends the whole night vainly trying to wake him up and speak to him. It was useless! The next day arrived and they took her away by force, while the wicked queen, all alone in her chamber, laughed a diabolical laugh.

"He may not love me," she said in a lather, "but she'll never get her way. As sure as my name is the witch Safranera, he will never lay eyes on her."

Margarida thought and thought during the rest of the day. The way things were going, her plans would never work out. Somehow she had to get the king's attention. And what did she decide to do? She would find out which window gave onto the king's chamber.

She comes across an old woman who had a kindly face and asks: "Do you by chance know which window belongs to King Astoret's bedroom?"

"Yes. It looks out to the south, just above the garden with the most flowers."

"Thank-you, my good lady."

And she starts to cry out at the top of her voice, "Beautiful jewelry for sale! I have lovely jewelry! Who will buy a bracelet encrusted with gems? Anyone, ladies?"

"Madame," say Safranera's ladies-in-waiting, "it's the vendor again. This time she's selling a bracelet."

"Go down there and have a look at it. Maybe it's as lovely as the comb and the necklace."

And she thought that—a witch she may have been, but she was still a fool at times—wearing all three pieces together the king might pay her some attention at last. And if not, then something would have to be done with him!

The servants go down to the street and seek out Margarida. "Show us the bracelet. How much do you want?"

"The same as before—to spend a night in the king's bed chamber."

The perverse Safranera laughed heartily at that … "Let her spend the whole night! And a hundred nights more if she wishes!"

She takes the bracelet.

It was late afternoon and night was falling. The king, conferring with his trusted counselor in his room, suddenly had a warm, agreeable feeling. It was as though a sweet voice rose up from the garden in the quiet afternoon air, singing Margarida Blanca's song!

"It's the song from my dreams!" he shouts. He was beside himself. "The real song Margarida sang!"

"Your wife's song," observes Baltasar.

"My wife never sings it to me and I've never asked her to. But now I can hear the very same voice I heard on that night so long ago."

Astoret felt suddenly confused. He was excited and a thousand thoughts ran wildly through his mind. He realized that in his strange and hurried marriage everything wasn't as it should be. Not by a long shot.

Del Seny didn't know what to say, or what to think.

The song came to an end and they both stood there in silence.

After night had fallen, King Astoret went to supper. And afterwards he was given a cup of herbal tea, laced with four spoonfuls of the opium poppy and green dragon leaf potion. But since he had heard that song, he didn't trust anyone: the servants, his advisors, even himself, and least of all, his wife ... It was strange that he had never really felt love for her.

He stared at her during the whole supper, and noticed more and more how her face was different from the one in his dreams. What if she wasn't the real Margarida?

So, he pretended to taste the tea and, when the queen wasn't looking, poured it into a glass of red wine. Mixing it all together, he knew no one would notice a thing. And then, like the other nights, he yawned and said that he was tired and ready for bed. It was all a ruse, of course.

The king goes to his bedroom and gets into bed. Meanwhile the queen also said that she was going to sleep. But she wanted to wait for Astoret to fall asleep before she ordered the real Margarida be admitted to his room. Safranera herself went to look in on the king and she found him breathing deeply, sound asleep. Thus assured, she gave the order for the young woman to be admitted to her husband's chamber and went to her own.

Margarida steps inside, her heart pounding with uncertainty and hope, and closes the door behind her. She walks to the head of the bed and sits down in a chair. Then she whispers sweetly, "Oh my darling King Astoret! I went through so much for you and then, when only a half hour more and the threshing would be done, a witch came along and took my shape and married you. Ah, King Astoret."

What a marvelous surprise! The young monarch, who heard it all, feels his old strength coming back. He opens his eyes, sits up in the bed and looks at Margarida.

"You ... yes," he says. "You do have the sweet voice of the real Margarida Blanca, and all of her lovely features. But your color is strange."

"Just wait!" she says, jumping to her feet.

She walks over to the king's commode, pours water into the sink and quickly rinses her hands, arms, neck and face. Then she turns around and asks, "Do you recognize me now?"

"I do!" cries the king. "You're my real wife!"

She recounts for him the whole long story: how she dreamt of him every night, how a fairy dressed as a beggar came to her, how she told her to journey to the castle ... every last thing up to the recent events on the threshing floor, the cave and the two nights past.

The king was astounded ... and deeply in love.

"Oh, and that vile, wicked woman ... still here in the castle." He was talking, of course, about Safranera.

"What shall we do, King Astoret?" asked Margarida.

The young man stopped and thought for a while.

And then he said, "Look, we need to be careful, because if not, as she's a witch, she'll make an escape or still wreak even more evil on us. You spend the night here like the other two, and I'll pretend that I wasn't awake. Tomorrow they'll show you out just as before ... Go back to the garden where you were singing yesterday and wait for me to send for you. I'm afraid we'll still have to suffer a short time more."

And so it was. (His suffering had made Astoret a wiser man.)

In the morning the queen's ladies-in-waiting came in and saw the king sleeping soundly and Margarida sitting in the chair with her hands over her face as though in desperation. They threw her out without so much as a word. She hardly took her hands from her face for fear they'd see that her skin was no longer dark.

She went to the garden and sat on a bench in the shade of a leafy tree to wait for what came next. It didn't take long.

***

The king got up, had breakfast, went to his favorite room and called for Baltasar del Seny. As happy as he could be, he told the counselor all that had occurred, and especially that the real Margarida had visited his bed chamber three nights in a row and that at last they had been able to talk and make sense of the recent events.

"Now I feel completely free of the spell, my faithful friend!" explained the king. "It's amazing. The real Margarida has a face like the queen's, but that false woman has a wicked, diabolical expression and Margarida's is as sweet as an angel. You will see!" he concluded.

They decided to sneak into Safranera's bedroom and, before she had time to grab a wand or take up a box of sleeping powder or cast a magic spell, restrain her and deliver her to the executioner to be hanged from the castle's highest tower.

"It's very cruel, I know," confessed Astoret. "I wish there were some other way, but we can't trust her at all."

And thus it went. They informed the hangman, who made the preparations. Four archers rushed into the witch-queen's bed chamber, bound her securely and, in the batting of an eye had her at the top of the main tower. The hangman wasted no time and there she was, that infernal and deceptive being, swinging like a scarecrow in the warm and quiet air of a July morning. It was a horrible, horrible sight.

The executioner, the archers, Baltasar del Seny and three more counselors who witnessed the hanging, afterwards saw something else that left them all trembling in astonishment. As soon as she expired, the witch's face and neck and arms and hands were covered with wrinkles and she turned into a 70-year-old woman. The hangman, accustomed to the cruelest of scenes, couldn't control a shiver down his spine. Just imagine how the others felt! Baltasar del Seny almost fainted, and one of the archers went as pale as a sheet.

The inhabitants of the castle and its surroundings heard the news and everyone crowded around the fortress to see the body dangling from its highest tower.

After Safranera was throttled, the king ordered that Margarida Blanca be summoned. She was still seated in the shade in the garden and had heard the tumult of the people and had seen the end of the sorceress from the distance. She was sought out and brought at once to the throne room. Everyone marveled at her resemblance to the now-defunct queen, though no one could fail to see the purity and kindness shining out of her lovely, smiling face.

They were joined in wedlock that very night, and Astoret and Margarida Blanca were finally man and wife. They lived a long and peaceful life together among those golden mountains of Safra in the pleasant lands of Monòver.

And as for the witch, there remains one thing to be said. The day after the wedding the king ordered that her body be cut down and buried. But overnight she had vanished from the gibbet, and the only thing left was her wrinkled dress, hanging in tatters from the noose.

Notes

1 Seny: good sense, common sense.
2 The consonant "ç" is pronounced like a voiceless "s."
3 Marieta: diminutive form of Maria.

6 The Envious Moor of Alcalà
(a story from Castalla)

They say that more than 500 years ago a Moor, whose name was Al-Favet,[1] lived in the town of Alcalà de la Jovada. His two wives, Salima and Ravinaia, loved him to distraction, for he was a handsome man and gave them a comfortable life.

When he was a boy, Al-Favet fell into a drainage ditch and raised a lump on his back. And as he grew, the lump grew with him, till it turned at last into a large hump.

He lived in a quarter on the outskirts, not very far from town, where Christians also had their homes. Neither the Moors of his neighborhood nor the inhabitants of the town could repress a laugh or a giggle when he passed by, because he made an inordinate sight: so as not to fall over backwards from the weight of his hump, he had to walk with his head bent forward above the ground in front of him. But he never took offense.

"All the better," he'd say to the townsfolk. "I run forward like a hare to keep from falling back, even when I'm tired. That way I do more work than anyone here. In no time at all I go back and forth to the fields; I sow, water, hoe, pick the cherries and take them to market and never have leftover work to do."

But he wasn't the only hunchback in the neighborhood. Another Moor, around the same age, also had a hump—and a big one at that! This other one, whose name was Abd al-Maduix,[2] didn't lean over forward, for his was big and fat. But he had another defect, like an invisible hump: he was riddled with envy.

***

Oddly for that high, cool, picturesque land surrounded by pretty mountains, one year there wasn't much rain. Al-Favet had planted his fields with broad beans, peppers and corn, so things didn't go too badly for him. Still, the weather was so dry and the sun so scorching hot that the leaves of his plants, in spite of the irrigation, were always drooping and covered with dust.

DOI: 10.4324/9781003324232-6

Now Al-Favet was a hard-working sort, and he wasn't at all satisfied. So, on some nights he'd go to the fountain at Atzúvia and, pail by pail, bring back water to sprinkle over all of his plants to freshen the leaves. His lands were close to the Moorish quarter, located next to those of the other hunchback.

It was really something to see how the plants responded to his solicitous considerations. The following day their leaves would be clean and firm and very green. Naturally, watered at both root and leaf, they were a sight to behold.

Now I've already told you that Abd al-Maduix was envious: he envied Al-Favet because he was slimmer and his features were pleasing, because his hump was more attractive and also because his fields were better cared-for; and he envied Al-Favet's two wives, even though he'd never seen them, because he only had one. So he was always plotting some kind of mischief to play on his fellow hunchback.

This Abd al-Maduix was a mean piece of work: touchy as a blunderbuss, swarthy as a copper pot, oily-skinned and as dumb as a fence post. And there was something else—no matter how much he worked his land, since he didn't do it well, he never could produce a crop as good as Al-Favet's.

***

One day that summer when our story takes place, Abd al-Maduix goes out to his fields and sees that the leaves of his pepper and pumpkin plants and his corn stalks are dried and withered and dusty, while Al-Favet's looked thick and moist. He had a fit of envy that made him break out in a sweat.

You all know how these jealous people are: they turn things over in their minds; they put up big, black castles in the air; they lose their temper; they foam at the mouth and they end up doing one evil deed after another. So it came to pass that on that very night Abd al-Maduix went up to Alcalà at an ungodly hour in search of an unscrupulous apostate Christian, a fortune-teller by profession, who would just as soon cheat those of his own religion as those of the Mohammedan's. He was rumored to be a warlock, or something like that; and as we're going to see, he seems to have made a pact with the devil.

His name was Sanç i Bons[3] and his house was in a narrow street that led down from the church and which, at that time of night, was dark and deserted.

Abd al-Maduix knocks at Sanç i Bons' door—knock, knock—and soon a small window beside it opens and he hears the fortune-teller's voice: "Who calls at this ungodly hour?"

"May Allah preserve you!" whispers the hunchback Moor.

"Him or whoever," answers the shameless Sanç. The hinges squeak as the door opens and he invites the Moor to come in.

The Envious Moor of Alcalà   113

The entrance was eerily lit by an oil lamp with two wicks. Sanç i Bons ushers Abd al-Maduix into a small sitting room. On one wall three live bald owls, each one perched on a dried-out olive branch, looked down like souls in penance. On the opposite wall, hanging from small stakes, were desiccated serpents, leathery toads and a bunch of twigs that were rife with dead flies. And in the middle of the room were a small round table and two chairs covered in leather.

Abd al-Maduix was pleased to see so much paraphernalia devoted to witchcraft. The two of them had a seat.

"What can I do for you?" asked the fortune-teller.

The Moor didn't mince his words. "I want to do something bad to the hunchback Al-Favet."

"What did he do to you?"

"He betters me at everything: his crops, his wives and his hump. His fields are greener than mine; I have only a single wife; and his hump is prettier than mine."

"True," conceded Sanç i Bons sarcastically, "you've got a hump on your back as big as a brace of barrels. You probably don't even remember how to lie on the ground face-up. But doing him harm won't make you any better."

"I don't care!" exclaimed the Moor impetuously, sticking his hand in his pocket. "Here, take five coins. When you've worked your evil spell on him, I'll give you five more. And when you do something good for me, if you can, I'll give you another ten."

(As you can see, with that much money, he'd spent a whole year's savings.)

Faced with these pecuniary arguments, Sanç i Bons was willing to set to work. He took a handful of powder, put it on Abd al-Maduix's head, right in the center of his turban, and set it alight. A big blue flame leapt up and licked the ceiling, and the Moor noticed something burning.

He jumped up. "Oiii!" he cried.

"Quiet!" ordered the fortune-teller angrily. Then he stood up and opened a window onto the starry night. "Come here," he commanded.

And Abd al-Maduix obeyed.

"Listen."

It was true. Very, very far away, almost imperceptible, he caught the sound of broomsticks swishing in the evening sky. Soon, the swishing sound grew louder and a stench of sulfur filled the air. And finally, close by, he could hear a cacophony of shouts and cackling that couldn't have come from human mouths and would strike fear into the stoutest of hearts.

"Hide!" ordered Sanç i Bons, and Abd al-Maduix hurried to a corner and hid himself away behind a damask drape.

Sanç i Bons arranged himself majestically in his leather-covered armchair, facing the window, and in came six of the ugliest, most terrifying witches you can imagine. They lined up side by side, broomsticks in hand, before him.

The Envious Moor of Alcalà

"Witches of Islam," says the apostate Christian, "I have called you here to entrust you with a job."

"What job?" the six of them say together, with female curiosity.

"You have to play havoc, and havoc indeed, with Al-Favet. First, his wives Salima and Ravinaia must fall ill with painful bellyaches so they won't be able to cook for him or make his bed and he won't get a good night's sleep for a month. Frighten him at night so that he doesn't go out to sprinkle water on his crops again. And work on his hump to make it bigger and uglier than our brother Abd al-Maduix's."

"And for this, what will you give us?"

"Five goats and a ram I'll steal from Al-Favet for your Sabbath feast."

This made them so happy that they broke out in a flood of horrendous curses and blasphemed all things holy.

"We'll do it! Oh yes, we'll do it!" they all shouted together. And then they took their leave, one by one, through the window, laughing as they mounted their broomsticks. Soon they disappeared into the peaceful evening sky of Alcalà.

Abd al-Maduix came out of his hiding-place, confused and fearful. But there was a smile on his face; for deep down inside he was pleased.

"They're terrible," he said, with a quaking voice.

"The best there is," laughed Sanç i Bons. "If you wish to do harm to Al-Favet, you won't seek the aid of angels and seraphim."

***

As was their custom, the six witches flew back to the cliffs above Beniaia. The next day, in their cave, they were enjoying the cool morning air and uttering all manner of sarcastic, bitter invocations, plotting evil deeds to extract goats and rams from humans for the entertainment of their dark and hairy hearts.

Those diabolical creatures, intoxicated with the happy outcome of their interview with Sanç i Bons and the wicked task he had set them, were raising cane with their uninhibited frolics, insane laughter and their usual curses. The commotion was so unseemly and scandalous that Allah lost his patience and said, from his high throne on Mount Aitana, "Enough is enough. High time to bring order to Beniaia." And in a flash he was down in the Alcalà valley, where he took on the form of a majestic pastor and, with 30 goats in his wake, set out along the path that led from Beniaia to the high cave where the witches nested.

When he got there he herded the goats to the open space before the entrance—"Hey goat!" he cried, "over here!"—the herd placidly munching away at the rosemary and lavender plants, which were then in flower. The witches see this goatherd, not knowing who he is, and decide to give him a scare. They set off a terrible racket, some of them howling like a wolf, others screaming like an eagle and the rest hissing like a snake. The pastor soon tires and, replete with divine majesty, says, "Tremble to your bones, you wicked, cruel creatures! I come to tell you ..."

But they interrupt him with strident voices: "Quiet you miserable goatherd!"

"Be off! Be off or we'll take away your goats and clothes and leave you naked!"

"We'll make you a mute for finding our cave, so you won't be able to tell the humans where it is."

Of course, no one had ever climbed this far up the mountain to find these horrifying wraiths, so they were furious at his presumption.

But then the pastor brandished his staff and three bolts of lightning leapt out and struck the entrance of the cave. They were followed by three deafening thunderclaps, like the ones you hear in the tremendous storms that occur in those interminable mountains.

And with that they realized the threatening truth. "Allah, it's Allah!"

"Forgive us, Lord!" they cry, and they kneel down together at the entrance of the cave. It was so ugly it was pretty to see those twisted faces, their stringy, disheveled hair, those long necks and their fingers dried and bent like those of Death!

"Shut your gobs and listen!" threatened the voice of Allah. "I know what you are plotting, but I command you to do no harm to Al-Favet, for he is a true believer and his heart is as pure as a star. Instead, give him a blessing, something to make him happy, but not so much to change his way of life. And as for Abd al-Maduix, teach him a lesson, not too serious mind you, that will sting him for the rest of his life ... If you fail to do this, I shall cast you into eternal flames."

Filled with consternation, they swore a witches' oath to carry out his orders. And then the goatherd and his goats vanished into thin air.

**

Around midnight Al-Favet, who normally went to bed late in the summer months, took up his bucket and went to the garden plot to moisten the leaves, as the day had been a scorcher. He enjoyed the solitude of the fields, rich with the smell of plants and lit so mysteriously by the moon above the mountains. He could see, in the dim light, the expanse of the garden and beyond that the town, nestled above in its mountainside. What peaceful beauty! But suddenly:

"Allah and his Prophet!" Al-Favet exclaimed, dropping the bucket filled with water to the ground.

His moment of quiet contemplation was broken by a strange hissing sound coming from somewhere in the silvery landscape. It couldn't be the wind, for the air on that mild summer night was still. What was it, then?

He saw something glowing above the plain, close to Beniaia, at about the height of the belfry in Alcalà. It was strange lights; first they looked like long shining streaks and then like odd, inhuman figures, rushing down from the sky.

Amazed and curious, Al-Favet hid himself away behind a clump of Holm oaks. And the six witches, for of course it was Sanç i Bons' colleagues, soon landed, took each others' hands and began to dance a jig on the threshing floor next to the fields, where the hunchback threshed his wheat.

They produced that shrieking laughter we've already heard, and then they sang a weird song:

> *Waiting for the hunchback,*
> *What'll we do to him?*

sang one.

> *We want to roast goats,*
> *To please the gods*

responded another. And a third one continued:

> *We don't play with reeds*
> *So we don't cut our skin!*

They stopped their dancing and squatted down atop the pile of hay on the threshing floor. "How many goats will we roast?" asked a skinny, withered one. And they all stood up again and started their jig, whirling dizzily and singing

> *How many goats will we roast?*
> *How many goats will we eat?*
> *Monday, Tuesday and Wednesday,*
> *three!*
> *Thursday, Friday and Saturday,*
> *six!*
> *Eating goats we get our kicks!*

Then they sang it again and kept on whirling in their dance, so that Al-Favet, who couldn't stop looking, felt his head spinning too.

> *Monday, Tuesday and Wednesday,*
> *three!*
> *Thursday, Friday and Saturday,*
> *six!*

In spite of the fear in his heart, Al-Favet was losing his self-control. He was a talkative type, and he was getting restless. So he blurted out loudly:

And Sunday seven!

And that was his undoing! The witches rushed like furies to where he was hiding. One of them dragged him by the ear to the middle of the threshing floor, and they all set in on him for saying the word "Sunday," which, of course, is the day of the Christian Lord and which they cannot bear to hear. Pinches? The poor bloke suffered pinches, scratches, punches, shoves and more ... At last he says, "In the name of Allah and Mohammad! Please protect me!"

Then they recalled the divine goatherd and, fearful, they released him. He ran straight for the Moorish quarter. But the witches pull themselves together and go in hot pursuit. They catch him by the back and he feels a strong tug, followed by a sharp pain, but he keeps on running. Soon he notices that they aren't behind him anymore and that he's running more lightly than he ever has in his life.

He reaches the door of his house: Knock, knock!

Salima answers and he throws himself into her arms, all out of breath from the sprint.

"Lock it, lock it!"

"Who's coming?"

"The witches!"

"Are you out of your head?"

Salima looked down the pathway leading to the garden, lit by the light of the moon, and saw not a living soul. But just in case she closed and locked the door.

Al-Favet slumped down onto a thick rug in one corner and Salima and Ravinaia sat down affectionately beside him.

"What happened to you, darling?" one of them asks.

"You're all pale and shaking," observes the other.

"My back is killing me," he tells them.

Then Salima feels his back through a large rent in his clothing.

"Allah is great!" she exclaims.

Ravinaia does the same, and both of them, without a single word, prostrate themselves face down on the floor, full of reverence and wonder.

"What is it? What's the matter?"

They rise with joyful faces. "Feel your back, Al-Favet," they say. "You don't have a hump any more. Your back is as pretty and smooth as any young boy's, and you're half a foot taller than you were before."

Al-Favet examines his back with his hands, and then his eyes; and his heart is filled with gratitude to Allah, all-powerful sage of sages.

* * *

As he walked through the quarter the following morning, he met the admiration of all of those faithful Moorish laborers.

"Praise be to Allah!"

"Blessed be the name of his true Prophet!"

"You have been touched by Allah's omnipotent finger."

"You are a chosen one, Al-Favet."

"Oh Believers," said a doctor of Islamic laws, filled with pride, "witness our brother Al-Favet's back! Hasten to reveal this miracle to the Christians of Alcalà. Go forth and spread our faith!"

In short, those Moors raised a tremendous hullabaloo and the news spread like wildfire through the whole region. And when it reached Abd a-Maduix's ears, he simply went livid with rage. What bloodshot eyes, what slavering lips! Wasting no time, he went straight to Sanç i Bons' house. And when the fortune-teller saw him stomping through the street with that wild look in his eyes, he stiffened with fear and locked the door.

Abd al-Maduix pounded on the wooden doorposts. Bam, bam, bam!

"You villain! You cheated me," roared the red-faced brute.

"I didn't cheat you," reasoned Sanç i Bons from behind the door. "Al-Favet is covered with scratches and bruises. He looks like a martyr and he can hardly move his legs!"

"But he hasn't got a hump! Those witches did him a favor!"

"Calm down, Abd al-Maduix. What you need to do is go out tonight to the threshing floor and call for them. For all I know, Allah has decided to remove all true believers' humps so the Christians won't make fun of them."

That made him stop and think.

"All right, I'll go out there tonight. But now, let me in."

Sanç i Bons opened the small spy hole and looked out. "Better if I didn't. We've already talked enough,"

"Okay, I'll go," concluded Abdal-Maduix, "but I won't pay you the rest of the money if I don't see something spectacular."

"Rest assured, you will!"

Thus Sanç i Bons, whom we can see was as crafty as a fox, managed to rid himself of the Moor. And Abd al-Maduix? What do you think occurred to him next? To pay Al-Favet a visit.

He goes down to Al-Favet's quarter, knocks at his door and says when he opens it, "Brother, I esteem you as a fellow Muslim. I have heard and now I see with my own eyes the great favor Allah has done you. I beg you tell me what kind of prayer you offered to deserve it."

Now this Al-Favet was an irremediably good-natured sort and, the two of them standing right there in his small front yard, he recounted everything: the sudden appearance of the witches, how they danced a jig and then the song they sang, which had stuck in his mind:

*Monday, Tuesday and Wednesday,
three!*

Thursday, Friday and Saturday, six!

"And what did you do?" asked Abd al-Maduix.

"I said, 'And Sunday seven!'"

"Thank-you, my brother," said Abd al-Maduix. And he kissed him on both cheeks.

Without another word, he went directly to Al-Favet's fields to examine his plants and found them green and moist, recently watered at root and leaf. So he knew that the ex-hunchback wouldn't be going there that night. With that in mind, he went back home and waited for nightfall. When it was dark, making sure that none of the neighbors saw him along the way, he headed for Al-Favet's threshing floor. He could hardly see a thing, because the moon wasn't out: however, at the stroke of 12 his heart filled with joy—not because he saw the witches but because he heard them. The swishing of their broomsticks and the flapping of their devilish gowns filtered down through the starry sky into the valley. Feeling his way, he hid behind the clump of Holm oaks just before they landed on the threshing floor. And soon they had started a bonfire for light and begun their grotesque dance, while singing

Monday, Tuesday and Wednesday ...

When they get to the part where they would say, "and Saturday six!" the big nincompoop up and shouts, "and Sunday seven!"

They snatch him out to the middle of the threshing floor and all have at him. Kicks, punches, slaps: they tear his clothes, leaving him half naked; they pummel his whole body; they stick their nails in his hump ...

(Yes, he was in pain, but he didn't say a word! *Now comes the good part*, he thought.)

But soon he could stand it no longer. He broke free and ran from that inferno. And they ran right behind him. When he had almost reached the houses, he felt a heavy thump on his hump. *It's done*, he said to himself. And he falls flat out on the ground, too weak even to talk.

He does, however, manage to moan: "Aiiii!"

And then he hears them say, "Don't whine, you sissy. The hump is gone!"

Next he feels a lot of hands grabbing his arms and feet and he hears the witches shout, "Fly, fly, from the earth to the sky!," and they start to rise, and he rises with them. It was the finest thing he had felt in his life. He was flying! Yes, he was high in the impalpable, perfumed evening sky of the valley, being carried along by that coven of diabolical beings.

"Where are we going?" he asks. And then, frightful, "You won't let me fall?"

But they didn't utter a word. The only sound was the flapping of their robes and the swish of their broomsticks in the quiet air; although, from time to time, a muffled laugh could be heard.

Then a silvery sliver of moon appeared above the mountaintop out toward the sea. But he only saw it from the corner of his eye, for they were taking him westward, to the heights of Beniaia.

After a brief flight, they set him down on solid ground in the midst of a thick growth of underbrush. And where do you think they were? At the entrance to the witches' cave, of course, high up in the mountains, there where Allah had come and threatened them. The scene was spookily lit by a mixture of moonlight, the glow of a small fire and the flickering of torches from deep inside the grotto.

Abd al-Maduix's head was still spinning from the fantastic, dizzying flight, so they had to set him down on a flat rock beside the mouth of the cave. Witches, witches everywhere: horribly ugly, cackling madly, with hooked noses and toothless grins. They circled around him, fawning, chattering and cursing up a storm. Nevertheless, the Moor's heart was filled with promising hopes.

At last, he dared to speak. "Where am I?"

The question was met with a cacophony of deafening cries from that swarming, evil agglomeration.

"Fool!"

"Numbskull!"

"Where do you think you are, you feckless knucklehead? Biterna, this is Biterna."[4]

Abd al-Maduix came back to himself. He felt his back ... and it was flat. He didn't have a hump! "OK, it's done. What else have you got in store for me?"

The one who seemed to be their leader, a tall, tall witch (who looked like she was standing on stilts), leaned over and looked into his face: "Don't be a 'fraidy cat! You've no need to fear. You've been highly recommended by our brother Sanç i Bons."

And then she gives him the big news: "We're going to soak you in pickle brine!"

The Moor's hair stood on end. "Is that really necessary?"

"I'll say it is ... If not, the hump will grow back."

"In pickle brine!" He was horrified. "Like any old cucumber!"

But how could he say no?

"Take off his clothes!"

Several of them carry him into the cave and start to strip him down and before he knows it he's as naked as the day he was born.

"Aa-choo!" he sneezed, the unfortunate wight.

In a hidden corner at the far end of the cave there was a row of vats, and they stick him feet first into the one in the middle. Luckily, the water was lukewarm; no, it was warmer. It was nice! It nearly reached his neck. Then the witches started coming in with handfuls of herbs that they placed in the water, so close to his body it scratched his soaking skin.

"Thyme!"

"Savory!"

"Rosemary!"

"Pennyroyal, to bring down his blood!"

And at last the leader, who was directing the operation, yells out: "Salt!" Another one brings in a couple of pounds of salt in a sack and pours the whole thing in. In no time at all the water was saltier than the sea. Finally, they bring the lid and place it down over his head. Lucky for him, it had a hole to breathe through in the middle. But the Moor thought he was dying.

"I'm going to drown!" he shouted from inside,

"Silly us, we forgot the fennel!" says the leader.

They take off the lid and put the fennel on top of his head. "We have to soften you up. If not, it won't work."

Abd al-Maduix didn't speak another word. Mouth firmly closed, he awaited the second miracle.

For most of the night he heard their devilish goings-on from inside the vat: singing, dancing, eating roasted meat and probably drinking large amounts of wine. In the morning, there was a frightful silence. The water in the vat had gone cold, and Abd al-Maduix let loose such a chain of sneezes that I don't know how the contraption didn't burst. And still worse, since the witches had weighed down the lid and the cooking pot was short, he had to stand there with his legs bent and one arm in a highly uncomfortable position. So uncomfortable it had gone to sleep. "Anything for the de-humping," he thought, to console himself.

Then suddenly he heard a sound and the lid came off. The head witch reached in and felt him here and there and announced, with the confidence of an expert in the procedure, "He's softened now. Take him out!"

They extract him from the vat, dry him off, dress him and put his turban on his head. Then the leader, in person, gives his right arm a vigorous yank.

"All done. Take him to his house."

"Thanks be to Allah!" says the envious idiot.

The witches meet this with a chorus of hideous guffaws.

They take him to the entrance of the cave. Over the sea the sky was beginning to glow, but the valley was still dark and mysterious-looking. They take hold of him, lift him up and begin their mad, frightening flight above the plains and ravines, till they reach the edge of town and leave him at the door of his house. And then they disappear into the sky.

Abd al-Maduix, beside himself with joy at the thought that he no longer had his hump, knocks at the door and calls out for his only wife, Jasmir. She was slow to answer, as she was still sleeping. The house was half-dark, and he walks in.

"Abd al-Maduix, my husband," she exclaims, "I was worried. You've been out so late. What happened?"

He was bursting with joy. "Light the lamp and see something marvelous ... But oh, how tired I am. I can hardly move my legs."

Jasmir lights the lamp and Abd al-Maduix takes off his shirt. "Look! My hump, it's gone!"

But to his great surprise, her eyes were as wide as a frying-pan, and she didn't utter a word.

"Aren't you happy, you fiend of a woman?" he curses. "I'm a man like all the others! Now you have a husband you can be proud of!"

"No, no!" cries Jasmir, stepping back with a frightened look on her face.

"What do you mean, no?"

"Who did this to you?" she exclaims.

"The witches ... at the behest of Sanç i Bons!"

She covers her pretty face with her hands and bursts out in tears.

"What is it, Jasmir? What mystery is this?"

"Abd al-Maduix, you're half a foot shorter than before," she tells him sadly, "because you're so bow-legged now that a hog could walk right between your knees without touching either one."

Then Abd al-Maduix looked down at his legs and he felt a black rage running through him from his head to his feet. Next he raised his hands to his head. One of them couldn't touch it and the other circled it twice. One of his arms was longer than the other!

"Brrrr!" he roared like a bull.

The day had begun and the streets were filled with people on their way to work. Abd al-Maduix felt his blood rising like a fog that blotted out his senses and he found himself half-naked in the middle of the road. Only his pantaloons covered him from the waist down. He shrieked like a madman, piercing the peaceful glory of the morning.

He takes off down the road, heading for Alcalà de la Jovada! Mad as a rabid dog, the Moor, whom we know was touchier that a cannon filled with nails, comes to the fortune-teller's house.

And it took him quite some time, for with his legs bent out of shape he couldn't run half as fast as when they were straight.

Bam, bam! He pounds on the door like a drum.

"Come out, you two-faced thief!" he shouted. "Come out and look at my arms and legs! I look like a cripple because of you!"

Sanç i Bons steeled his heart and opened the door and stepped outside. He was dumbstruck at what he saw. In the wink of an eye he rushed back in and slammed the door behind him. You could hear the sound of a lock being turned and two or three bolts sliding into place.

**

The years went by, and the heart of Abd al-Maduix, the envious Moor, grew softer through his misfortune, just as the diabolical pickle brine had softened his body. In time he was resigned to his deformity, realizing that it was a just punishment for his inordinate envy. And, by the will of Allah, he and Al-Favet became close friends and lived in peace; and thus they both grew old and were living examples of divine justice, which always allots to each and every one what they deserve.

Notes

1 Favet: diminutive of *fava*, bean. Also slang for fortunate, blessed or naïve.
2 Maduix: play on *maduixa*, strawberry. The consonant "x" is pronounced like "sh."
3 Sanç i Bons: While not an uncommon surname, *sanç* is also a homonym of *sants*, saints or saintly. Bons, plural of *bo*, good.
4 According to a wide-spread belief in Catalan territories during the Middle Ages, a place where witches convene to renounce God and worship Satan.

7 The Saddle-Maker of Cocentaina
(a story from Muro)

In that noble town at the foot of Mount Mariola there lived, more than a century ago, a good man who was called "the saddle-maker" because he made pack saddles, panniers, harnesses and all types of gear for mules and other beasts of burden. He was renowned throughout the Cocentaina plain, the Travadell, Perputxent and Seta valleys, and even as far away as the Penàguila Mountains, as one of the finest saddle-makers there was.

And though he was upright and honest, a hard worker and a desirable catch—he had a sturdy frame, was slender and tall, with a handsome face—he had never taken a wife; for he was set on finding a woman from somewhere else. The local girls, "home-baked" as they were called, didn't please him in the slightest, even though they were said to be the loveliest women in the entire Kingdom of Valencia. He was one of those fellows who believe that the saint from another place produces better miracles.

***

One year there was a lively festival to celebrate the saint day of Saint Hippolyte.[1] And aside from the processions of "Moors and Christians,"[2] the mayor decreed that there be dances and publicly invited all of the unmarried youths in the region to attend. So that year many unfamiliar faces were seen in Cocentaina: from Alquerieta, Alcúdia, Muro, Turballos, Beniarrés, Benilloba ...

Ciril—that was the saddle-maker's name—cut a fine figure in the town square, because he was an excellent dancer. The drum made hearts beat with its rhythmic "bam, ba-ba-bam" that echoed against the grandiose, high walls of the castle and frightened the many seagulls and ravens that perched there. The dancers in couples began the dance! And Ciril, leaping and twirling to left and right, was pleased to notice among the crowd of curious onlookers, at around mid-afternoon, a young lady who couldn't take her eyes off of him. She was thin and tall—very tall—and odd, but also pretty. "What does this stranger want," he thought, "a dance with me?" And no sooner said than done, he walks over and very courteously invites

DOI: 10.4324/9781003324232-7

her to dance, to which she replies as nice and friendly as could be; "Why yes, I'd be delighted to dance with you."

They move into the circle and begin to perform a series of graceful, complicated steps, which they carry off to perfection. Ciril himself was amazed. With this damsel at his side, his two feet seemed to have wings.

What a flurry of gossipy whispers rose up among the women of Cocentaina!

"Just look at that Ciril. There he is, with a girl from another town, as if there were no good catches here!"

"And look at those leaps and bounds! He spins like a top!"

"And what about her? She looks like a fishing pole."

"Well, she's not all that bad: skinny, yes, she's skinny, but not bad-looking."

While they danced, Ciril asked his partner, "And what might your name be?"

"Vicenteta, and yours?"

"Ciril, the saddle-maker."

When the dance was over—it was the last day of the festival—Vicenteta said good-bye and disappeared into the crowd. And the truth is, her departure was somewhat mysterious.

But Ciril kept on happily dancing, as though the music were still playing in his head. He went back home to his house on a small street close to the castle, with his heart full of poetry. He noticed things he'd never paid attention to before, like the gentle breeze that caused the tufts to sway on the branches of the acacias at that time of day and pushed against the cornstalks growing in the fields along the banks of the Alcoi River.

* * *

For the following year he heard nothing of Vicenteta, though he missed no opportunity to question anyone from outlying villages or the most distant farms. It was all his fault of course—the fool!—for not having asked her about herself while they danced. But everything had been so sudden and enchanting!

Now this Ciril was generally a high-spirited, happy-go-lucky fellow, but the lack of any news of her was bringing him down. And so he had a very dull year and devoted himself in heart and soul to his work in an effort to lighten his mood. He thought to himself: *I'm 30 years old—not a spring chicken anymore.*

But the festival of Saint Hippolyte came round again—with its parties and dances—and the mayor, an inveterate party-goer, had decreed four days this time. One more day than the year before!

He didn't know quite why, but Ciril felt a new burst of hope in his heart. What if Vicenteta showed up? Anything could happen. And so it went: the first day came, and nothing; the second day, nothing, and the third. But on the fourth day he saw her (all smiles and laughs and nicely turned-out for the dance) at the flageolet-player's side.

"Hello, Vicenteta."

"Hello, Ciril," she said, just as natural as you could imagine.

But what a look she gave him!

They danced together the whole afternoon. At twilight, when the dance was almost over, Ciril says to himself: *I'll ask her where she's from; she won't get away this time.*

But what bad luck: a pair of silly chatterers comes up and walks between them at that very instant.

"Vicenteta!" he cries.

And he hears coming from the crowd of dancers, "Ciril!"

But they can't see each other. He hurried here and there, but it was useless. She was gone.

"Vicenteta, Vicenteta!" He frantically searched the square, to the amusement of all of the townsfolk in the crowd.

Suddenly the flageolet and drum fell silent, and the dance had come to an end.

He walked home, not really seeing where he went, blinded by the heavy blow to his heart.

Useless idiot, fool! he said to himself, pulling at his hair.

And that was the end of that.

***

Days went by, then weeks; the summer ended; autumn came and after that the snows of winter. Then another joyous Cocentaina spring came round, filling the olive trees with silver flowers, the almond trees with green leaves, the fields and meadows with colorful poppies, all, of course, at the foot of the tall crest of Mount Mariola.

And in Ciril's smoldering heart, now contemplating 40, a tenuous flame began to grow as the month of August and the festival of Saint Hippolyte approached. Would he see Vicenteta again? Would that thin, friendly being show up once more? If not, he'd have no choice but to marry someone from town; and he, well, he was enamored of that outsider. "She's the one that would be right for me," he told himself, "because she's good-looking, polite, a little bit skinny but full of life, and she looks at me with loving eyes. Her age should also be a good fit, she must be around 30 years old … Yes, yes, a youngster like myself."

And he laughed at the thought.

That year, their third mysterious meeting, was the big one. As soon as the "tram-tra-bam" began, there she was in the square, dressed to the teeth, leaning elegantly against a doorpost just behind the flageolet-player.

"Vicenteta!"

"Ciril!"

He strides up to her and takes her hand, "Will you marry me, Vicenteta?"

She won't get away this time.

"Ciril," she answers, "I have neither father nor mother, and I have no dowry ..."

"Who cares?" says Ciril enthusiastically. "Neither do I. But I have my own house, my profession and enough money for your dowry."

That evening, after the dance, they went straight to the priest and he told them what they needed to do. She left that very night—she said she was from Agres—and three days later she brought back all of the papers she needed for the wedding. She was accompanied by two odd old women that she said were her aunts. In a week's time all was ready, and the marriage of Ciril and Vicenteta was the talk of all the town and surroundings.

***

So Ciril is now a married man! A month goes by, then two, then three; and their newlywed time was the oddest thing in the world. As soon as they were married, Vicenteta's behavior began to change. She was no longer that laughing and open girl of the festival dances. On the contrary, she began to be moody and uncommunicative. Above all, she acted as though she were tremendously bored, yawing from morning to night, having fits of nervous laughter ...

This is because we don't have children, Ciril thought after several months; for the festival of Saint Hippolyte came round again, and no sign of a baby.

For one thing and another, the saddle-maker was worried. "My wife looks down in the dumps," he sometimes muttered between clenched teeth when he saw her so listless and languid, so disinterested in everything.

"Give me some help," he told her one hot September afternoon, flies buzzing heavily and the air so close that even the sun seemed to have fallen into a doze.

"Help you with what?" she asked, her slack-jawed mouth gaping open.

"You could help me make panniers, stitch together saddles or harnesses. Look ... if you start to wax leather, or thread needles, or sew hides, the time would go by in a flash."

"Oh, I just don't feel up to it," she moaned. "Ciril, I grew up on a farm on Mount Mariola. I'm no saddle-maker. The only thing I like to do is take care of hens and barnyard animals, collect eggs and most of all go out in the fields and look for grass and herbs for rabbits."

"Well woman, why didn't you say so before?"

At last he knew what was wrong with his skinny wife!

Wasting no time, he bought her some rabbit hutches, a half dozen hens and a rooster. There was a little open space behind the house where he set it all up.

For a time things seemed to go better. But then another problem cropped up. Each and every afternoon the poor saddle-maker was left alone because Vicenteta was dead serious about going out to pick grass and herbs for the rabbits. After lunch she would wash all the dishes, take a short nap in her room, pick up a basket and a hoe and make tracks for the open fields!

Sometimes she went out to the lovely farmlands along the banks of the Alcoi River just beyond town, others she'd go to the olive groves on the slopes of Mount Mariola close to Agres, or she would walk through the gullies beneath the other mountains, behind the Saint Cristòfol Hermitage ... She never wished to go with any neighbors because she said they chatted too much and distracted her so that she couldn't find the good herbs.

And so the next two years went by.

***

Freezing December came again and brought that day we know is so short, which is even shorter in the town of Cocentaina where the sun hides itself early behind the high peak of Mount Mariola. It was as cold as the North Pole because a strong northern wind had come in, and the mountaintops were covered with snow.

"Where are you off to in this weather?" Ciril asked, hoping to change her mind.

"Where do you think?" she answered. "The poor little rabbits haven't got a bite to eat. There's so little grass growing in this freezing cold ..."

So Ciril set to work on his saddles. And Vicenteta walked out of town along the path that goes behind the St. Cristòfol Hermitage and went to the Penya Banyada, beneath the slopes heading up to Mount Montcabrer.

The saddle-maker was absorbed in a rush job for a farmer from Benimarfull and lost track of the time; when he glanced through the window of his workshop he saw that night had fallen.

"And that woman still hasn't come back," he muttered.

A half an hour later, feeling nervous, he stepped outside the door. There were clouds in the sky and the night was dark; the wind howled over eaves and through the streets. At that very moment, through the rushing of the wind, he made out the bells in the belfry striking eight o'clock. The slow ringing seemed to drift away into the fields and the ravines on the wings of the storm. As he stood there, Ciril noticed something stinging against his cheeks. Frozen snow was falling from the storm clouds towering above the invisible summit of Montcabrer.

"Mary mother of God!" he exclaimed. "It's sleeting and that woman is out in it all alone. If I just knew where she went I'd go out to find her ... But who knows where she could've gone? And no supper on the fire ... What a mess!"

But just then he heard the sound of footsteps on the road and he could see the form of a shadow coming toward him.

"Is it you?"

"It's me."

The saddle-maker's spirits rose. "I thought something had happened to you."

"No, no," she assured him calmly, "it's just that there's not a single blade of grass that hasn't been blanched by the frost, so I had to go all the way to the open meadows close to the Frare rock face to find something worth the trouble."

They went inside, where Ciril had his workshop off the entrance. He looked at her in the light of the two oil lamps there and a chill went down his spine. Oh Lord, her face! She was skinnier than ever, almost flesh and bone, her eyes looked wild—she wouldn't look at him—and her cheeks had a sinister dark hue that contrasted with the yellowish tone of the rest of her skin. It was his wife, yes, but how different she looked! And to top it all off, Ciril noticed a strange smell in the air—like sulfur. Yes, it was sulfur!

But he didn't say a word. He sat down on his bench and went back to work until she called him to supper. And that was another odd thing that made him shiver. She had hardly been in the kitchen for five minutes when everything was ready on the table. How was that possible?

* * *

From that day on, he noticed more strange occurrences. Her mysterious outings and late arrivals became more frequent for the rest of the winter. And she always came back at night. And it reached Ciril's ears that a woodcutter had seen her kneeling on a high hill between two clearings in the Penya Banyada Ravine. No one could figure out what she was doing there.

When spring arrived, Ciril noticed three more worrisome things about Vicenteta. First: she was growing thinner and thinner—but she was still strong! Second: her voice was getting hoarse, like a mule-driver's. Third: (and this was strangest of all) she had grown taller! It was truly frightening. He could see it happening from one day to the next. By the month of May her head touched the kitchen ceiling; and only a year before she missed it by half a foot. This growth had begun after that mysterious evening in December.

She had never had a pretty face, as we know, but she wasn't unattractive either. Now though, she was downright ugly: her nose was too long; her chin was too sharp; her eyes bulged out.

* * *

Around mid-September of that same year, on a night when the moon was full, Vicenteta said something strange to Ciril after supper. "Look here Ciril, a cousin of mine from Orxa sent me these herbs to take after supper so the food won't upset our stomachs during the night."

"OK; it might do us some good," Ciril admitted. At times, perhaps from sitting too long in the chair, his stomach bothered him.

So Vicenteta brewed two cups of the infusion. Ciril drank one—it was good!—and she pretended to drink hers; but when he wasn't looking she poured it down the drain.

As soon as Ciril's head hit the pillow that night he fell into a deep slumber. It was a Saturday. He slept so soundly that the following night he asked for another cup, but Vicenteta told him, "My cousin said not to take too much. It would be better to use it only once a week, on Saturdays."

Ciril didn't argue. "OK."

The next Saturday night the same thing happened. But this time Ciril wanted to keep an eye on his wife. He wasn't a total idiot, and after so many unsettling things had occurred he didn't completely trust her. He took his time, stirring the brew and sipping it to see if it was too hot. Meanwhile, he saw that Vicenteta didn't drink hers. So when she went into the kitchen for a moment, he rapidly tossed his drink out through the window.

When she came back in he said, "Ah Vicenteta, I can't keep my eyes open!"

And he was as wide awake as an owl!

He glimpsed a glint of satisfaction in his wife's bulging, bluish eyes. It was only a second, almost invisible, but that was enough for him. (This saddle-maker was turning into a very clever fellow!)

So after she did the washing up and cleaned the kitchen and he put his workshop in order they went to bed. Ciril pretended to be sleeping like a log. He even snored a little, but he was alert and listening with all his might.

A half hour went by, and nothing. Then an hour—and nothing. He was too curious to sleep, and that was the last thing he wanted to do.

There he was, on tenterhooks. And then, around 12, he felt his wife move quietly beside him in the darkness. She slowly got up and went to the kitchen, which was just next to their bedroom. A faint glow came through the partly-opened door; Vicenteta had lighted a lamp.

Ciril got up too, careful not to make a sound. He tiptoed in his drawers to the door and looked through the crack. What he saw there took his breath away. His wife, standing before the hearth, had taken off her camisole and was as naked as the day she was born. From a small bottle in one hand she poured an unguent into the other and spread it very carefully over her whole skinny body. When that was done, she straddled a broomstick, knelt down in front of the fireplace and said in a low but forceful voice: "I do not believe in God, nor in the Virgin Mary!"

Then she prayed a blasphemous prayer, addressed no doubt to the devil; but her teeth were clenched and Ciril couldn't make it out. After that she set alight a handful of twigs and threw some powders onto the flames. A thinnish smoke rose up, and she rose with it and vanished right up the chimney.

As you can well imagine, Ciril stood there trembling like a leaf. But he was no coward, in spite of his mild-mannered appearance. He decided to anoint himself with the unguent too—the bottle was on the mantel piece and beside it, the box with the powders—and follow his wife to find out what was going on. But then he reconsidered. He took up the unguent and went into his workshop, where he used a skiving knife to spread it over a saddle he had just finished making. He sat down to see what would happen. But five minutes passed and nothing changed.

"Oh," he exclaimed, "the powders!"

He took a pinch of powder from the box on the mantel piece and put it on the ground beside the saddle and set it afire with a length of hemp he lighted in the lamp. In no time at all the saddle began to buck up and down, hitting against the ceiling, like the very Devil. **Boom, boom, boom!** Ciril clapped his hands over his ears and knelt down behind the chair in case the thing knocked him cold with a single blow. In the end, as the saddle had no way of getting out of the workshop, it battered itself to bits.

Ciril gathered them all up and burnt them in the fireplace so that Vicenteta wouldn't suspect anything when she returned. Then he went back to bed and didn't fall asleep till early in the morning.

When he woke up the following day, his wife was lying by his side, as though she had been there the whole night through.

* * *

That Sunday, and for the rest of the week, Vicenteta was light-hearted; she smiled most of the day and often sang something in that strange, hoarse voice she had acquired. She had clearly gotten over the old boredom she had felt for years—or it could be that some dark and shadowy power was working a good effect on her.

Well, thought Ciril, *at least she doesn't seem to be so eager to look for herbs for the rabbits! We'll see where this leads.*

She was taking better care of him now; she cooked him nice meals and even began to give him some help at his work. But it was all done to butter him up.

That pleasant week went by and Saturday rolled around—which would be the proof of the pudding. She made him the infusion that we know about, and again Ciril didn't drink it. They go to bed and, in the darkness, Ciril keeps his eyes wide open like plates. It's almost 12 and she creeps quietly out of the bed, and very soon after, Ciril is spying through the partially opened door. She again takes off her clothes before the hearth and covers her body with the unguent. But exactly then—and this took guts!—Ciril makes up his mind, opens the door and approaches her.

"Oh! You nearly scared me to death!" she says, seeming to be upset.

"I'm going along with you," says Ciril, as calm and natural as could be.

"Good," she replies with a smile, "you won't be sorry. It's all great fun."

She finished oiling her body and then she oiled his, after he had taken off his clothes. (What a sight they made, standing there buck naked. A couple of skinned foxes couldn't have looked more ridiculous.)

"Have you got another broom?"

"Here you are."

They both straddle their broomsticks, kneel before the fireplace and pronounce the blasphemy: "I do not believe in God, nor in the Virgin Mary."

(This made Ciril's hair stand on end, as he was a faithful believer. However, he trusted that God would make allowances since he was doing it all with good intentions: to discover some devilish plot.)

Holding hands like a couple of inordinately ugly sweethearts, they rose up through the chimney, then higher and higher in the air. It was a fantastic journey. The moon illuminated everything; the mountains seemed to grow larger as they ascended. Ciril couldn't stop sneezing.

"I'm going to catch my death of cold."

"Oh, be quiet," she urged. "What are you muttering on about?"

"Where are we going?"

"Out to the Alcoi Canal."

Then Ciril heard some cries and laughter and saw a number of outlandish beings flying not far away through the clear, starry night.

"Who are they?" he asked Vicenteta.

"More witches and warlocks, like us."

"Oh my. Oh my."

Ciril didn't much like the idea of being called a warlock, but he desperately wanted to follow his wife and get to the bottom of this whole imbroglio.

They flew on over the few lights Alcoi would have had back then, many hundreds of feet below them, and then crossed above the Ravine of the Battle and came to that high plain known as the Malany Fields, not far from the beginning of the Castalla Valley. They set down in the middle of the plain, which had recently been harvested, and Vicenteta says; "You see that lonely farmhouse?" It was a large building nearby, at the foot of the Cantal de Corbó.

"Yes," said Ciril, "just by that clearing in the woods."

And at that moment he was alarmed to see the field become crowded with stark naked witches and warlocks, all as dried-up and skinny as his wife, or even more so. They began to scream like crows and, Ciril and Vicenteta in their midst, rushed toward the farmhouse.

When they came to the front of the building, Ciril was astonished to see them go in through the keyhole, one after another.

"Get a good grip on my feet," Vicenteta ordered.

He did so, and immediately felt his body getting thinner and thinner, until it was as small around as a yo-yo string. And then they went in through the keyhole after all the rest of those diabolical beings. Once inside, they went right back to their natural form.

That place was a big wine cellar; its walls were lined with seemingly endless rows of barrels and vats. Ciril looked around—the warlocks had lighted a few torches that gave off a weak glow—and reckoned there must have been 30 or more in the coven. They were raising a terrible ruckus. There was an open tiled floor in the middle of the cellar where they began to construct a makeshift table big enough for all. Some of them dragged buckets for collecting must and placed them so as to form a large square. They lay long boards from the wine press on these; someone produced some big table cloths and they started to set the table. In one corner, some others produced a gigantic paella pan—who knows where that came from. It was four times bigger than a winnowing sieve. Others started the fire and the smoke floated out through the large, barred windows they had opened high in the walls. Others filled bottles and wineskins with wine from the casks. Afterwards, when the table was set and the paella was cooked, giving off a succulent smell of lamb and chicken, all 30 of them clasped hands and danced a jig around the table at a dizzying speed while they sang horrible songs full of the most devilish blasphemies. The whole crew seemed to be enjoying themselves immensely. Ciril's wife was laughing louder than anyone else and looked exceedingly happy.

What have I gotten myself into? thought the saddle-maker, feeling sorry for himself. "No more marrying outsiders for me!" But of course, he kept these sentiments mum.

"Time for supper!"

The dancing stopped. Then a very skinny, very naked, stooped-over fellow with a long, white beard and the face of an ancient peasant, who seemed to be presiding, said: "Everyone to the table!"

With a great deal of noise and confusion they all took seats. Ciril was beside his wife and on the other side he had a witch who looked him avidly up and down. She must have been more than a hundred, but she seemed to be tough and vigorous.

"What do you think, stranger?" she asked.

"Oh, it's a fine party, a swell party!" he said to calm his nerves. "I'll come back every Saturday!"

But his stomach turned over to see that grotesque congregation of wrinkled, naked bodies. He could never have imagined such a detestable and shameful picture. (He kept up his courage though! He had to find a way to rid himself of that witch of a wife and her unholy get-togethers.)

All of a sudden the old witch at his side cries out, "Curses!"

"By the Devil's horns!" shouted a warlock, "this paella has no salt! Where's Jirònia?"

Jirònia was the witch in charge of the salt, but she was nowhere to be seen.

"She didn't show up!"

Then ensued an argument to beat the band. Some of them took her side and others roundly cursed her. And their tempers were inflamed by more and more wine. Ciril's head was spinning just watching it all.

Those crazed hotheads grabbed up bottles and slurped from wineskins, and the delicious liquid streamed from the corners of their mouths over cheeks and ribs.

"To Hell with Jirònia!" some of them exclaimed.

"Long live Jirònia!" said others.

"We'll eat it without salt! Salt is Christian!" shouted the ones farthest away.

"This paella is no good!" complained a few more.

But the fact is Ciril, horrified as he was, was also as hungry as though he hadn't eaten for days. It seems that flying naked through the cold night air had stimulated his appetite. "What a shame," he thought, "I really do love a good plate of rice." He dared to sneak a taste but, to tell the truth, without salt it was inedible.

As the raucous confusion grew, there was a hiss at the keyhole and a witch with hair down to her feet appeared.

"Jirònia!" they all cried.

"Thank the Lord," said that empty-headed Ciril. He was so happy the salt had arrived.

"Aiiii!"

Boom! There was a terrible peal of thunder and a great sulfurous flame lit up the whole cellar, singeing Ciril's hair.

What a commotion! Darkness—the torches went out—shouting, turmoil, but all in a flash. The witches and warlocks vanished, including his wife, hissing like the wind, in no time flat. And then there was only silence.

A beam of moonlight came in through one of the windows, and in the dimness Ciril could see that he was all alone, still seated at the table. The tablecloths, the paella, the spoons and napkins, everything had disappeared. There was nothing left on the boards but a few burnt-out embers.

When he recovered from the shock and surprise of everything that had happened, Ciril walked in the moonlight to the door. It was locked, and he didn't know the magic words to make himself as small as a needle to get out through the keyhole. He ran his hand along the walls to find any openings, or a window without bars; but it was closed tight. In the end he got behind some casks, still naked, as we know, and shivering with cold. He hunkered down beneath some dirty baskets for dried must to cover himself and, exhausted from so much fear and excitement, finally fell asleep.

The joyful sunlight pouring through the windows brought him out of his slumber. But what woke him up completely was the sound of men's voices outside the door. His whole body stiffened with fright. He heard someone put a key into the lock. From where he was he couldn't see who came in, but he could make out everything they said.

"Not again! Just like the other day," said the voice of an old man.

"What mischief has been going on here?" exclaimed someone who sounded younger.

"It's too bad we can't catch the thieves, or the devils or the ghosts that are drinking grandfather's wine," complained another voice.

So there were at least three. Ciril knew he was in trouble now.

"Look around to see if you can find how they get in," said the first voice.

The saddle-maker heard them remove the boards of the wine-press, drag the buckets back to their places and reorganize all the rest that the witches' coven had left topsy-turvy. And soon, searching the whole place carefully, one of the men caught sight of Ciril's naked back.

"There's a cat in the bag over here!" he shouted.

The other two came round and with a couple of heaves they pulled off the baskets that were covering the poor saddle-maker.

"This looks like the Devil's work!" said the old man's voice.

They were the owners of the cellar: three farmers from the Riurau farmstead, the father and his two sons. The father, advanced in age, was tall and slender and handsome. The two young sons were dark and sturdy; they looked like they could tackle a bull.

Ciril stood up, trying to cover himself with a sack from the floor. The sons pulled him out on the spot and were going to give him a beating.

"Forgive me!" pleaded the poor baboon. "I'm not a bad man; I'm the saddle-maker of Cocentaina."

The youths looked to their father, and he looked carefully at Ciril and at last said, "Yes, it's true. I know this man. But how is it that someone like you is standing here without any clothes?"

"It's my wife's fault. She's the reason I'm here like this." His voice was somewhat calmer now, seeing that he was safe. "If you will permit me, I'll be happy to explain it all."

"We'll get you some clothes. Toni, go to the farmhouse and see what you can find."

One of the boys ran back to the house—it wasn't very close—and brought back some used clothes to dress the miserable fellow decently and then they took him to the farmhouse and gave him a good breakfast and a glass of fortified wine to buck up his spirits.

Relieved and tranquil at last, Ciril recounted the horrible and incredible adventure he had had, beginning with his wedding.

"So," said the old man, "everything happened because you followed your wife to uncover the mystery."

"And because I spoke the Lord's name," concluded poor Ciril. "Because I believe that if I hadn't said, 'Thank the Lord,' I'd still be mixed up with that group of demons."

* * *

Ciril took his leave of the Riurau family and started back to Cocentaina on foot. He was apprehensive and in no hurry to get there. He made sure not to arrive until night had fallen. He found the door of his house locked, just as they had left it. He had no key, so he had to go round the back and, with great effort, climb the wall of the back yard and enter the house from there.

He was completely worn out and went straight to bed, where he slept soundly for ten or twelve hours.

In the late afternoon of the following day, he went to the priest's house and told him everything. The priest was amazed and vigorously crossed himself.

"Listen Ciril, you were lucky to get away! Vicenteta was an evil spirit who had undoubtedly come to get you and take you to hell."

"I'm sure she was, Father!" agreed Ciril. He shivered again from head to foot to think how close he had been to perdition.

"Ciril," continued the priest, "you didn't know that Vicenteta never came to Mass?"

"No Father, I didn't."

"She pretended to come but I know she never again set foot in the church after the wedding."

He fell quiet then, pondering how strange the ways of God are in this life: if Ciril hadn't been so hungry to eat rice on that terrible night, in spite of how frightening those witches and warlocks were, and if he hadn't said "Thank the Lord," he would still be under the diabolical Vicenteta's power.

"What will happen now, Father?"

"Oh, you'll never see her again. But in any case, I'll make sure of that."

The next day the priest, the vicars, the sexton, all of the altar-boys and a host of people from town, including the mayor, went to the saddle-maker's house. The priest sprinkled lots and lots of holy water over everything, from the front door to the attic. And there was another mysterious thing: they didn't find a single thread of the dowry Ciril had bought for Vicenteta, and the hens and the rooster she always cared for, as well as the rabbits and their hutches, had disappeared. It was all gone. The saddle-maker's house was just the same as before he had married.

The prayers and blessings and exorcisms required by canon law were made and the crowd retired, everyone congratulating Ciril on having safely escaped that horrible fate.

And the next year, given that his marriage to a witch was annulled by the Authorities of the Church, and fearful of falling once again under the evil spell of a mysterious being disguised as a woman from another town, Ciril married a second cousin who lived a few houses away from his. At last he admitted that the old saying was true:

> *Don't ever leave your home*
> *to find a woman for your own.*

And they were very, very happy and had lots and lots of children; and they'd still be alive today if they hadn't died.

Notes
1 On August 13.
2 *Moros i Cristians*: various festivities celebrated mostly in the southern areas of the *País Valencià* to commemorate the battles between Muslims (Moors) and Christians during the period of the *Reconquesta*.

8 The Gambling Man of Petrer
(a story from Castalla)

These events took place in the olden times when elegantly dressed demons would visit farmlands and villages if anyone summoned them.

It was the picturesque town of Petrer, set gracefully on a high hill between the great Cavall and Cilla Mountains and having in view at its very feet, you might say, the delightful expanse of the Elda Valley. And farther away to the south is the noble city of Monòver, with its many cultivated fields, its dusty hills, its broad esplanades and the lovely, pine-covered peak of Mount Safra.

In a house as large and imposing as a convent, located in Petrer's High Street, there lived all by himself a confirmed bachelor whose name was Pere Mestre. He was an only child, around 40 years of age, and so had inherited the house and a considerable fortune from his parents.

He and a group of his friends were partial to the high life, and they often went out carousing, serenading pretty girls and delighting in delicious dinners—sometimes in Squire Pere's splendid dining room. And always, for one reason or another, they got back home in the early hours of the morning, be it summer or winter. Now Squire Pere had one more vice, which was gambling. And like every gambler there has ever been in the world, he always ended up losing in the long run. For that reason he often found himself in dire straits.

After he turned 40 though, the vice of gambling became too strong for him to resist. He left off serenading because his voice was getting hoarse; he left off the big dinners because the overeating was ruining his digestion … So gambling was left! First, he gambled away all the money from his harvests; then he sold a plot of farmland to get more money to bet with, and later an entire farm; and in the end he lost his whole inheritance. From one gambling den to another, from one disastrous bet to the next, he finally ended up with nothing left but the house on the High Street.

He had had an aged servant—her name was Francisqueta—who was very, very loyal … She had cared for him from birth and she catered to his every need and whim. During the latter years she had even stayed on without any pay. (She was willing to forgive her fine little gentleman anything). But Francisqueta passed away when he fell into poverty. And little by little,

DOI: 10.4324/9781003324232-8

the whole town came to know that he had neither land nor money; and no one wanted to work for him anymore.

That same year they had a very wet October for those arid lands. One night Squire Pere Mestre was preparing himself a miserable meal alone at home when he began to feel the proverbial itch. "Ah, if only I could gamble again," he said to himself. "If only I could gamble, now that I've thought and thought and come up with a fool-proof way to win at *golf* and at *monte*[1]... I'm sure I could win back everything I've lost. I'd be a millionaire! And I'd buy back that wonderful plantation, Molí de les Reixes. How it echoes with the songs of nightingales, orioles and blackbirds up in the harsh mountains, and the murmuring sounds of the stream sliding down the mountain slopes to fall at last in leaping cascades. Yes, yes!" He was growing exited at the thought. "And I'd also get my hands again on that blessed house in the Falsa Valley, with its pond surrounded by enormous pines where the turtle-doves nest, and the Clot de Catí farmstead, the flower of the highlands, with its lofts brimming with heaps of apples and all the sweet perfumes of Paradise! ... But I haven't got a penny to my name!" he bellowed. "Curses! I haven't got a penny and I'll never gamble again. I'll just rot away in this big, empty house and one day they'll find me in my bed, dead from poverty and hunger."

He had his meager supper: a bite or two of cod, soaked in olive oil, a hunk of barley bread and a few swallows of water. After eating, he remained seated, staring off blindly into space with his mind absorbed in a painful and anxious fog.

Outside, there was thunder and rain and hail, and a frightful wind was blowing.

"Well, time for bed," he said at last. He brought his once lithe and now bony frame of a knight of chivalry to his feet and exited the ornate, dusty dining room. On his way to his bedroom with an oil lamp in his hand, he glanced at a tarnished old mirror hanging in the hallway and he noticed that his aquiline nose seemed to be glued onto the face of a corpse, his cheeks stuck out like doorknobs and his fine, blond beard and elegant moustache were gray and unkempt, like an exile's.

He halted, trembling all over to see himself so diminished. "Ah, what a fall is here!" he murmured bitterly. "I have to get rich again, no matter how!"

Then a horrible thought entered his laborious brain.

"If I could be wealthy again," he swore in a loud voice, "I'd gladly give my soul to the Devil."

Up in the sky there was a tremendous clap of thunder and a lightning bolt split the clouds like bat's wings on high from the black peaks of the Camara Mountains to the summit of Mount Cavall. And that noise shook the ancestral house of the Mestres down to its very foundations.

At that moment Squire Pere ceased hearing the storm, for he was motionless, not with fear but with wonder. Yes, he was truly courageous; and what's more, he felt desperate. So there he was, dumbstruck, because at the end of the hallway, in the dim light of the oil lamp in his hand, he just made out a tall, well-dressed gentleman with an air of refinement. That figure gave a subtle, aristocratic bow as he spoke these words: "You called me, Squire Pere?"

"Yes, I did. I called you," Pere calmly responded, while thinking, "So this is the Devil." He was happy to see him. "Do come in," he said politely.

He led the mysterious visitor to his nearby writing desk, and they sat down in two very artistic and comfortable armchairs beside that ornate piece of furniture.

"Although I gather you already know, I am a demon," said the visitor, "and my name is Capralenc el Fi."[2]

Squire Pere replied, truthfully, that he was delighted to see him.

"I heard you mention that you desire to be wealthy," delicately observed that agent of hell.

"Yes indeed; you're not mistaken. I wish to be rich again. And that's why I requested your assistance," remarked Squire Pere, just as cool and collected as though he were discussing a business venture with a peer of his social class.

The demon smiled. "Oh, you will be. I'm just the man for your case. I live in the Castalla Mountains and have in my charge the bodies and souls of all of the important men who own the great plantations and farmsteads in Catí, les Fermoses, Puça, Planisses, Caprala, l'Arguenya and other places I won't bother to name. In these days a rich landowning class, like a small royal court, is scattered all through the hills and dales and ravines of the Castalla Mountains. They gamble, they drink, they play and they suffer. There are love affairs and virtues and loyalties and betrayals. And I'm a part and parcel of them all. And so, when my Master heard how you were drowning in sorrow, he sent me to come to your aid."

"In that case, aristocratic demon of the hills," asked Squire Pere tactfully, "how can I regain my fortune? Mark my word, I'm willing to do whatever it takes!"

"Well then, my distinguished fellow," explained Capralenc, "in order to avoid raising suspicions in Petrer, you should go back to gambling." And, at a gesture from Pere, "Yes, go back to gambling, for I've brought you money ... and from this day on, you'll always win."

Squire Pere wasn't convinced.

"I know what you're thinking," added Capralenc. "You're feeling ... as you humans say in this world, remorse, and what we call a fainting heart. Yes, it might bother your conscience to profit from ruining your friends." Here the demon chuckled and his eyes flashed like lightning. Then he said venomously, "You might as well know that you've lost so much because they've cheated you more than four times ..."

Pere lowered his head. Capralenc el Fi produced a sack of gold coins from beneath the fashionable cape of the day he was wearing and set it down on the writing desk. The Mestre family heir made not the slightest move to pick it up. He had his gentleman's pride.

"So how does all of this work?"

Capralenc smiled and brushed back several locks of hair from his forehead, revealing the tips of his horns. They were, indeed, slender and elegant, quite suitable for a devil who dealt with wealthy heirs, mayors and the like. He placed his hand over his heart, but it was to take out a parchment scroll from beneath his cape.

"Here, Squire Pere. Read this."

"So you've drawn this up on the spot?" asked Pere.

"No ... We already have them pre-prepared ... two or three models. I only needed to fill in the blanks with your honorable name."

Squire Pere read through the document; it had all of the customary clauses: he accepted the sack of gold coins that would make him rich in exchange for a promise to give his soul to the Devil after a period of ten years.

"Is ten years good for you?"

"Yes."

"You'll have time to be happy. You can marry a rich heiress; you can have children and begin a dynasty. What's more, I won't come round to collect your soul till the 11th year, and we may take a few months to get here if there's a good harvest (of souls, of course) that year. We usually take on the newly-acquired ones only as needed."

"All right," agreed Squire Pere, "but I want to add on one small condition. I shall gladly give up my soul in ten years from today, or any time after that date; but you can only come to collect it when there are no locust beans on the carob trees."

The demon smiled, "And why this request?"

"You see," explained Squire Pere, "I've always loved to harvest locust beans, and it would be such a shame to have to leave when there were still some growing on the trees. I'm sure you understand a landowner's whim."

"No problem," conceded the demon. And he affixed Pere's stipulation to the curious parchment.

Then the squire signed the contract, followed by Capralenc el Fi. And, with a burst of sulfurous flames, as short and discreet and as his horns, the demon disappeared. Pere was left staring at the empty armchair. He sat there thinking for several minutes and, at last, gave a hearty belly laugh. The sack of gold lay on the writing desk. He opened it and counted the coins: there were 30—just as with Judas.

**

He figured it must be around midnight. *The monte game run by Squire Antoni from Pla de Dalt must be in full swing now*, he thought. And he still had the energy to put on a pair of high-topped boots, some leggings made of heavy cloth, a thick waistcoat and a waterproof cape with a felt lining. He also put on a hunting cap with wide wings to protect his head. Then he went downstairs, opened the large doors of the main entrance to the house and stepped out into the pouring rain amid frequent flashes of lightning.

"Thunder, thunder!" he growled contentedly, pressing his hand over the sack of coins in his pocket. "Bring on the rain! Drench the mountain slope and valley; swell the stream that turns the wheels of the Reixes mill; ready me well the terraces and fields and farmsteads I'm going to buy ..."

He walked with care up a cobbled street to a small square where the wind and rain were even stronger and halted in front of a nondescript door in a shadowy corner. He listened attentively. Yes, there was a muffled confusion of voices inside. He rapped on the wood with the edge of a coin and the voices suddenly stopped. Then someone spoke from the other side of the door, "Who's there?"

"Squire Pere."

A bolt slid back, a key turned in a lock, a chain was released, and the door opened just enough to allow him to pass through. A servant with an oil lamp gave a respectful bow and led him in to where the game was being played. There were five men at a large table: three local landholders, a businessman and Squire Antoni from Pla de Dalt, the master of the house. Squire Pere greeted them all.

They stood up and welcomed him effusively, *too effusively*, thought Squire Pere. Who could he trust?

"It's been a long time since we had the honor!" said the youngest one there, a young blond baronet.

And then they all made similar comments.

These lazy rascals think I have no money, Squire Pere said to himself, *and they won't want to give me credit to play now that I'm broke. What hypocrites!*

"Did you wish to play?" asked Squire Antoni smoothly, while offering him a comfortable chair.

Pere handed his cape to the servant and sat down. "That's why I'm here," he said, "but the pot looks kind of slim. Maybe I brought too much money."

And with that he took out the sack and plopped it on the table. He untied its strings and the gold coins inside shone in the lamplight as though they were fresh from the mint.

"Mother of God!" exclaimed the Hortís family heir, an old graybeard.

"That's good money," said the baronet, "a gentleman's money."

They were surprised. But soon the game began.

"Squire Antoni is the bank," said the baronet.

"As usual," replied Squire Pere with a smile.

"The game tonight is *monte*."

"That's fine with me."

The first four cards were dealt.

"The Jack!" said Squire Pere, pushing two coins bright as suns to the middle of the table.

And a Jack turned up, with a smile behind its beard. He recalled a ditty from his childhood:

Jack on the spot,
turn up the pot,
don't leave a drop.

The next card was a seven. As he pushed in two more coins, Squire Pere remembered a nursery rhyme:

Seven, seven
sevens will show
and then to prison
you'll have to go
and from your cell
you won't see me
closed in well
with lock and key.

And the seven of cups[3] turned up, sparkling like a piece of expensive jewelry.

He won two games in a row. And his bets were higher than the others so he raked in piles of money.

"The King!" he cried, and set down 20 coins beside the card. The baronet did too. He knew a lucky streak when he saw one.

"Don't turn on me; he'll clean me out," said Squire Antoni, hiding his discomfort behind a forced smile.

Another king turned up,

dressed in red
with tattered stockings
and hatless head

as the village children like to sing.

Then Squire Pere bet again. "The Jack of swords."

And it didn't take long for another Jack to come out of that accursed pack of cards

bouncing up
and bouncing down
from so high up
to so far down

as the old song said.

Pere Mestre won so much dough that night they had to give him another sack to be able to carry it all.

The others were astounded. It seemed like the work of the Devil.

By three a.m. Squire Pere had 200 gold coins. Then Squire Antoni dealt out the four cards again, and everyone was silent. They were all done in and couldn't' move a muscle.

"Aren't you going to bet?" asked Squire Pere.

"How can we bet?" responded the baronet. "I've got no more money. But tomorrow you'll have to let us get our revenge."

"Not tomorrow, by God," chimed in Hortís. "Let's play again on Saturday."

They all agreed and the game was over.

The same thing happened that Saturday. The landowners and gentlemen had sold paintings, furniture, farm fields ... the businessman had borrowed money on credit and that night they met, as agreed, at the home of Squire Antoni from Pla de Dalt. There were also a few more players there, sticklers and irritable types. But there was nothing to be done. Pere cleaned them all out mercilessly.

"What devilish luck!" said the businessman. "If this keeps up, in a month you'll ruin us all."

"You can say that again!" growled Squire Pere between his teeth.

But why go on? In less than six months he was once more a wealthy man. He purchased all of his family's old properties, no matter the price. Land, houses, whatever he wanted, everything. So of course, some people took advantage of him; but what did he care? He just kept on winning and winning. And not all of the money was from Petrer. Because when there was nothing left there, he went to Monòver and to Novelda. He fleeced them all wherever he went, be it *golf*, or *monte*, or even *set i mig*.[4] His luck was shameless and infallible. In some shady dives they conspired to cheat him. But the more they tried, the more and faster they lost.

When a year had gone by he gave up gambling. The gossip was getting out of hand; and anyway, what did he want with so much money? He finally had enough. It was time to find a wife. And he did, in Novelda. She was 27 years old, tall and fit, as fair as gold and with blue eyes like in a fairy tale. They soon got married and she became the brilliant mistress of the house on the High Street. She bore him three handsome sons and a delightful daughter. And meanwhile, the ten years of earthly joy the demon had stipulated in his contract flew by.

* * *

Squire Pere had been happy indeed—fulfilling the sweet obligations of married life, bringing up his children and overseeing the harvests on his many and extensive farmlands. But sometimes, in the night, a gnawing like termites ate away at the back of his mind. His contract with Capralenc el Fi was all in order, as we know, but any confrontation with a demon, no matter how courteous the manners, is always a narrow thing. Now though, on the other hand, he was no longer that carefree, fun-loving, high-living bachelor who spent all his time and money drinking and gambling. No, now he was a serious heir and landholder, his character made mild by the sweet company of a pretty wife and the love of the cute little children the lord had given them ... So he would have to keep his nerve and make sure the contract held good; if not, all would be lost.

"I know I can do it. And anyway, I'm right ... my wit is on my side," he said to himself, reawakening the strength and resolve that had been dormant so long in his heart.

And the 11th year rolled round—the year when Capralenc el Fi would come back to collect his soul and carry it to the fearsome and unquenchable confines of hell.

That year there was a magnificent crop of locust beans. And one August night the demon left his aristocratic plantations in the Castalla Mountains and went down to the Petrer Valley. He went straight to the orchards on the slopes of Mount Cilla and halted beneath a fine, big carob tree. In the early morning light the locust beans looked to Capralenc el Fi like strange, fat, shiny pods. They were already ripe; at a touch they fell to the ground. There were piles of them under all the trees!

Capralenc whispered to himself, "In 15 days there won't be a single one left on the branches. Then I can take that rascal Pere's soul." Then he spoke a little louder: "You've had your way in this world, my good sir. Now, your time is almost up."

But he reconsidered. "On second thought, I'll give him one more month, just to be sure there are no more beans in the trees to spoil the deal."

In late October, having a peaceful after-dinner chat with his family, Squire Pere noticed the elegant figure of Capralenc el Fi at the door. His heart gave a thump! *So here he is*, he said to himself. But no one else could see him, for neither Pere's wife nor his children made the slightest move. However, just to be sure, Pere said, "Maria, does the curtain there to the left of the door look dusty to you?"

(Capralenc el Fi was standing right next to that curtain.)

They all looked that way.

"No, Pere," answered his wife, "I think it's just a shadow from the lamplight."

The maid, who'd just come in, also looked; and no one said a thing about Capralenc. If they had seen him, what a commotion there would have been!

The demon gave a laugh. "Nobody can see me but you, my good heir Squire Pere. And they can't hear me, either. If you stand up and say that you're stepping out to Squire Antoni's house, your wife won't be surprised or worried."

Squire Pere got to his feet, trembling all over. "I've just remembered," he said as naturally as he could, "I promised to go see my friend Antoni from Pla de Dalt this evening."

"Well, don't come back too late, dear," said his wife affectionately.

"Give us a good-night kiss," said the children. And Squire Pere gave a kiss to each one.

"Please do kiss your wife," said Capralenc sarcastically, "and finish the job. It's a pity, but you won't be seeing them ever again."

Squire Pere's expression was blank.

"Put on your cape," said his wife. "It's cool out tonight."

The maid brought it to him and Squire Pere left the house with his hat and cape to follow the demon.

In those long-gone days the streets were dark if there was no moon. But that night there was. And, on some house fronts the candles in the small compartments for the images of saints were lighted.

The streets were empty.

"So give me your soul!" demanded the demon. "There's no need to tire yourself out by walking any farther. This isn't a bad place for them to find your body. People will think you had a colic from eating too much supper."

"Hold on there, Capralenc ... a deal is a deal," responded Squire Pere with a calmness that surprised the demon.

"What deal? The deadline in the contract ended months ago!" argued that hellish character.

"Now just slow down, my friend," said Squire Pere politely. "You people have a reputation for being serious and correct, and always keeping your promises, be they good or bad."

"OK, OK," muttered Capralenc. "But I'm in a hurry."

"Yes, but the locust beans ... We have to check the carob trees."

The demon gave a laugh. "There aren't any left. I came down from the mountains three or four times and saw how the farmers were collecting them. There aren't any lying on the ground or hanging from the branches."

"That's the thing," said Squire Pere, "the two of us have to examine the trees very closely together to be sure."

Capralenc relented at last. "All right! Let's go to the orchards. The fact is you're right. But I'm in a hurry tonight because a certain ... amorous issue has come up at the Litero farm ..."

They went on down the street and took the road to Elda. In all of the fields on their left carob trees loomed as large as churches, their shadowy boughs in the moonlight full of sleeping birds.

The gentleman and the devil made a halt beneath the first one they came to, since all the trees would be the same.

"The moon's almost full," said the demon, "see if you can find any locust beans anywhere in this tree."

"As you desire, demon Capralenc. But you're mistaken when you say you've seen all the locust beans gathered in the harvest. Come up closer and have a look."

With a saintly smile on his face, Squire Pere pointed to the tender new beans that had sprouted on all of the branches, both high and low. There were even a few bunches growing out of the sturdy trunk.

The demon was disconcerted. "What's that?"

"This invalidates the contract, Capralenc," Squire Pere said firmly, "because the carob tree never stops producing its beans. When the ripe ones fall, the green ones sprout!"

"R-r-r-r." Capralenc began to shudder and shake and all of a sudden his guise as an infernal gentleman fell away and his real beastly appearance showed through. He writhed, he tore his stylish suit to shreds, he cast his hat into an irrigation ditch and he jumped furiously up and down, scratching his body on the branches of that unknown, heavenly carob tree that had cheated him out of a soul.

"You ... you gambling man!" he roared in the quiet, transparent night of Petrer. "You're a gambler and you cheated me in the game of the contract."

For you see, that demon lived up in the mountains, where there are no carob trees, and he knew nothing at all about how they grow their fruit. Lying farther inland, Petrer is the last town where those trees can live.

"It's your own fault if you don't like the deal," said Squire Pere, staring at that scoundrel and standing stiff as a board. For he couldn't be sure if the demon would do something horrible to him, like throw burning sulfur in his face. What should he do? Turn tail and run, leaving his backside unprotected? Or stay there and wait for this fit of pique to calm down and see how it ended? And then an idea struck him; he'd commend himself to the patron saint of the village, the glorious St. Boniface. "Our father, St. Boniface ..." he said aloud.

And Capralenc was silent, quaking from head to foot.

"You win, Squire Pere. You've beaten me. I'm off!"

A yawning chasm opened up in the ground and Capralenc el Fi disappeared forever in a great ball of flames.

Squire Pere slowly strolled back home. Before he turned in, he looked at himself in the mirror in the hallway. For a long time now his nose hadn't been thin and pointed; his cheeks hadn't been boney; nor his beard peppered with gray.

The whole house was quiet. One and all—his wife, his children and the maid—were sleeping safe and sound.

Notes

1 Two popular card games of the wealthy classes in Valencia. In *golf* a total of five cards is dealt to each player. When the first two have been dealt, the players may bet or not, and the betting continues after each of the remaining three cards is dealt. At the end of the hand, the value of the three highest cards of the same suit is counted, and the player with the most points wins. In *monte*, four cards are dealt out face up in the shape of a square on the table. The players may place bets on any of these cards. The remaining cards are then turned up one by one, and when a card appears with the same value as one of the four on the table, the players win or lose, depending on whether they bet for or against it.

148 The Gambling Man of Petrer

2 *Capralenc*: play on *cabra*, goat, thus suggesting goat-like or goat-man + *el Fi*, the slim or delicate one.
3 The suits of Spanish Catalan playing cards differ from those of the English deck. They are cups (*copes*, usually depicted as a golden goblet), swords (*espases*), coins (*monedes*) and clubs (*bastons*, usually depicted as a long wooden club).
4 Seven and a half: a card game similar to Twenty-one. It is played with a deck containing number cards 1–7 and the face cards. The former have their numerical value and the latter a value of ½. The winner is the player who gets closest to 7½ without surpassing it.

9 Peret

(a story from Castalla)

Many years ago there was a very clever man in Castalla whose name was Peret. When he got married to a fine-looking woman from town named Carmeta, he owned nothing more than the clothes on his back. But because he was an enterprising sort and a hard worker, he soon began to rise in the world. It wasn't long before he could buy a yoke of land in the Marjal, a newly-planted vineyard in Altet de Todora and an olive grove in Torrià.

But his fortunes really started to change after he became close friends with a man by the name of Jeroni, who was very rich indeed.

Now this Jeroni was married to Carmeta's first cousin, Maria. That relation, of course, led to their husbands' friendship and eventually to the notorious story I'm going to relate.

***

Every time he met with Jeroni, Peret managed to turn it into some kind of competition. If they went out to the mountains, it was which one could cut and load the most firewood in the shortest time. Peret was a quick-witted devil and knew how to choose a field with rosemary and rockrose, which are softer to the touch, and maneuver Jeroni into a place full of thorny furze, wild rose and broom. So of course Peret cut away as he pleased and bound up any number of sheathes, while Jeroni's skin got scratched and his clothes got torn. Peret won the bet and pocketed Jeroni's money without a second thought.

Sometimes he'd say, "Come on then, let's have a race."

"Don't make me laugh, Peret," answered the sturdy Jeroni, "my legs are longer than yours."

But Peret managed it so that Jeroni had to run along a path that was strewn with large rocks, while he, claiming that his way went uphill and furiously hunching his shoulders, took a path where he could open his stride like a hare.

And so, Jeroni was always handing out the pesetas and Peret was always raking them in and stuffing them into his pockets.

***

DOI: 10.4324/9781003324232-9

The day finally came when Maria found out about the dirty tricks her cousin's husband was playing on them and she went to see Carmeta to clear things up.

"All of that's between the men," said Carmeta, who was just as clever as Peret. "I'm not going to get involved."

Maria could see that her cousin was just as eager as Peret to cheat Jeroni out of his money and decided it would be a waste of time to try to change their minds. Instead, she'd work on discouraging her own benighted husband from taking the bait.

So she reasoned with him about the dangers of betting and competitions and even reproached him for buying things that Peret offered him. But Jeroni was so fond of his friend that he couldn't be convinced. Maria would manage to plant some second thoughts; but when he was around Peret, those were all dispersed. Peret was so much fun to be with—he told such entertaining stories and anecdotes (he knew hundreds), he hummed the delicate melodies of the dances at Tibi—Jeroni just couldn't resist.

Then when he went back home he'd hear Maria's warnings: "He's fooling you. He's pulling your leg. He's stealing your money."

And his spirits would fall again. The next day, though, he'd meet Peret in the street and all that was forgotten. Peret gave him four friendly pats on the back and invited him to have lunch at Pinar del Clot or Basseta dels Confiters, and the bad feelings vanished in a flash and his heart was as open and warm as a morning in May.

* * *

Peret was fond of Jeroni, but he liked his money even more; and the truth is he was happy to take it, the more the better.

One day, when he went out to see how the hay was drying, Peret found two very handsome rabbits in a hutch. They looked exactly the same. They were almost white, with a star-shaped patch of grey above their eyes and all four paws of that same color.

He took one back to his wife and said, "You see this rabbit?"

"Oh yes, it's a nice one."

"Well, there's another one that looks just like it. And I'll tell you what, Carmeta. With these two bunnies I'm going to get 500 pounds out of Jeroni!"

Carmeta laughed. "You devil, you!" She admired how inventive he could be. "But 500 pounds ... it seems like too much."

"Look, I'm going to make him think the rabbit understands what we say and will do what we tell it to. Tomorrow Jeroni and I will go out to the fields in Altet de Todora and I'll take one of the bunnies along. He'll come here to meet me, and when we leave you'll ask me, 'What would you like for lunch, Peret?' And I'll say, 'We'll decide that later on, depending on how hungry we feel. Jeroni can eat here, and we'll send word back with the rabbit.'"

Carmeta saw one flaw in the plan: "But how am I to know what you and Jeroni decide on for lunch?"

"Oh, that'll be easy. At around ten you go out to the fields while we're working, but don't let us see you. Hide behind a slope. Just take the old road to the tile factory that can't be seen from where we'll be. When I'm sure you're there I'll start the conversation. But you have to be there at ten o'clock sharp! After that I'll let the rabbit go, and when we come back, you'll show him the other one. He won't know the difference."

* * *

So it was agreed and so it was done.

Peret called his friend over to show him the rabbit. "I bought it from a fortune-teller in Biar. It cost me 500 pounds. And it has special powers: it understands what we say and can carry messages and do other things."

Jeroni was hooked. "That can't be true."

"I'll show you tomorrow."

The next day he put the rabbit into a haversack with its back legs firmly tied together. And when they got to the fields in Altet de Todora—each one had a vineyard there—they contentedly started to dig up the earth around the trunks of the vines so the grapes wouldn't touch the ground when they grew fat and heavy.

Soon they heard the church bells in the distant village striking ten, and Peret, knowing that Carmeta would be hidden behind a slope somewhere, said in a loud voice, "Who in the world invented this thing of digging? He must have been out of his mind. I'm already feeling famished."

"Say, Peret, now that you mention it, shouldn't we think about what we'll tell Carmeta we want her to cook for lunch?"

"We can do that in a jiffy. What would you like to have?"

"A chicken pilaf," replied the poor dupe.

"Oh yes, that's good!" praised Peret. And to make sure Carmeta heard it correctly he repeated loudly, "Chicken pilaf! There's nothing like it in the whole wide world ... Come on, then, let's give the rabbit the message."

They set down their hoes and went to the spot where they had left their blankets and the haversack and took out the animal.

"Oh, he's a pretty one," said Peret, stroking its fur, "and smart as a whip."

He carefully untied its back legs and whispered into its ear. "Bunny rabbit, go tell my wife to cook a chicken pilaf. Can you do that?"

The rabbit squirmed in his grasp to get away.

"See how he's nodding his head, Jeroni? He's saying he can."

Carmeta, hiding at the bottom of a nearby embankment, heard the whole conversation between her rascal of a husband and the poor fool Jeroni and had to stifle her laughter. I don't know how she managed, but if she hadn't the plan would've gone to pot.

At last, they let the rabbit go in the middle of the vineyard and it scurried away as though it had ten dogs on its tail. It was never seen again, but Jeroni was firmly convinced that it was on its way to Castalla to give Carmeta their message about lunch.

***

Carmeta went home undetected by Jeroni. Once there, she slaughtered the chicken and cooked a rice dish that could revive the dead. Around midday she heard the two friends coming back.

"Where's that rabbit?" Jeroni asked first thing. "Did he come and give you the message?"

"You better believe he did," said the clever vixen. "The rice is all done, and it's going to be delicious!"

"And what about the rabbit?" insisted Jeroni.

"I've got it here, in the pantry," she told him. And she went to fetch the twin rabbit that had stayed at home.

"How did it give you the message?" asked Jeroni, looking amazed.

"Oh, it did it, all right! Of course, it doesn't talk. That would be the work of the Evil One! But it doesn't need to. I heard a scratching at the door and opened it and there it was. It hopped right into the house and straight to the pantry. I opened it and he stuck his nose into the sack of rice. I said to myself, 'I know what they want!' But the rabbit kept hopping about and went through the whole house and out to the chicken coop ... and I was right behind. When I got there it was trying to bite a chicken ... 'They want a chicken pilaf,' I said to myself. Oh, what an animal! It was easy; so he must give all the messages that way."

Jeroni was gobsmacked, staring from one to the other, speechless with the powerful impression it made. And Peret, to be even more convincing, also looked around with assorted expressions of surprise on his face.

They had a lunch fit for a king, followed by several glasses of good local wine. Jeroni, enthused with it all, finally asked if he could purchase the white rabbit. Peret said he'd sell it for 500 pounds, which was what he had paid; and Jeroni rushed out to get the money right away, just in case Peret should change his mind.

***

He took the rabbit home and showed it to Maria, all puffed up with pride and joy. He told her about the messages, the chicken pilaf and all the rest they had enticed him into believing. But she was only displeased—very, very displeased.

"You're as mad as a loon, Jeroni. What are we going to do with you? Peret and my shameless cousin have fooled you again!"

"Oh be quiet, Maria," answered Jeroni self-righteously. "You women never know when to keep your mouths shut. How do you know what that rabbit is worth? Have you ever in your life seen a rabbit that can carry messages like a servant? And what a difference between giving room and board to the one and nothing more than a few bunches of weeds to the other!"

"But ..." she was exasperated, "how can you be such a dope? You really believe all that poppycock?"

"Poppycock? ... Now look... don't get me riled up, or things will get hot around here! I've just seen the proof with my own eyes. Here it is, with nothing sneaky at all!"

Maria's face was a mixture of indignation and pity for her husband's gullibility. Jeroni only told her once again the story of the chicken pilaf.

"They had to be playing you some kind of trick, Jeroni."

"Then how do you explain it?" he argued. "That bunny rabbit was half an hour's walk from town and it found Peret's house. Doesn't that prove it's smart? If it had been any other run-of-the-mill rabbit, it would've scampered off and disappeared as soon as we let it go in the middle of the field and we would never have seen it again."

Maria, too, was beginning to have her doubts.

Jeroni insisted, "What do you say to that?"

"Well, nothing, but ..."

"Look here, Maria. If I had listened to you, I would've given Peret the cold shoulder; and I always have him eating out of the palm of my hand. You should've seen Carmeta's face. She didn't want to sell that rabbit for all the money in the world."

So there things stayed, at least for the time being.

***

The next morning Jeroni went out by himself to an olive grove he had close to the mountains on the road to Saix, an hour from the village. He took along the bunny rabbit he had bought and, around ten a.m. he went through the ritual we've already seen and sent it to tell Maria to make a nice gaspatxo[1] for lunch. Of course the rabbit, just like its twin the day before, was up in the hills in three big hops and was a gone bunny forever.

"Did you make the gaspatxo?" Jeroni asked as soon as he walked through door. "I'm as hungry as a horse and dying to get my teeth into that hash!"

"What gaspatxo? What in the world are you talking about?" answered his wife, as hot as a pepper corn.

"Didn't the rabbit come?"

"The rabbit?"

"Yes, sure, the rabbit," repeated Jeroni. "Who else? I took it out this morning and I sent it to tell you I wanted gaspatxo for lunch."

"Taken for a fool again!" said his wife, livid with desperation.

And then all hell broke loose: Maria shouting that her husband was a hare-brained idiot and she herself crazy for believing that outlandish story; Jeroni searching high and low for a large knife they had, to go to Peret's house and give him his just desserts.

***

Jeroni and Peret lived in the same street, seven or eight houses from each other. And so, when Jeroni rushed out armed with the knife to kill his friend, it just so happened that Carmeta had opened the door at the same time and saw him coming her way like a bat out of hell. She jumped back in and closed and bolted the door. Then she ran to warn her husband that something unpleasant was in the works.

"Here comes Jeroni! And this time he's going to kill you, Peret! What'll we do?" the wicked woman wailed.

"No need to worry or to be afraid, Carmeta. There's a remedy for everything in this world. Run upstairs as fast as you can and bring me the lamb's bladder filled with blood from the bull we slaughtered yesterday."

She fetched it in a jiffy.

"Now, put it beneath your blouse next to your chest. You know what we have to do."

"Yes, yes, Peret," said Carmeta, placing the bladder between her breasts. But she had her doubts, even though she always trusted in her husband's wit and ingenuity.

Bam, bam! There were two stout knocks on the door, strong enough to break it down. And of course, it was Jeroni.

"Hurry up and open it! What a beast!"

With the lamb's bladder well hidden beneath her blouse, Carmeta nervously opened the door. Jeroni shot in like a bolt of lightning.

"Where's that husband of yours?" he brayed, brandishing the shining knifeblade through the air.

Carmeta began to scream and squirm. "Oh, for the love of God!" She was really scared, but she blocked his way.

"Where are you, Peret, you coward? Come out and take what's coming to you!"

Peret, who had hidden in the kitchen, came out meekly.

Carmeta was a strong and hardy woman; she tried to hold Jeroni back.

"Jeroni! Jeroni!" cried Peret, "please forgive the misunderstanding and let me explain ..."

"No explanations!" shouted Jeroni, moving toward him, while Carmeta was pulling him back.

"Just let me speak and you can kill me afterwards, if you want, Jeroni," said Peret in a humble, resigned tone of voice. "It's a right that all condemned men are given."

Jeroni hesitated. Carmeta grabbed the knife from his hand and ran out of the room. Peret embraced his friend.

"You and I are men and we've always acted that way; but these women always ruin things for us ... Your wife, making you feel bitter, and mine, making me do bad things to get your money ..."

"Well ..." said Jeroni doubtfully.

"I can prove it to you whenever you want ... right now! These two cousins we've married are a pain in the neck. Maria poisoning your mind against me, and Carmeta making up that tale about the rabbit. I'm sick and tired of my wife. And just to show you it's true, I'm going to kill her right here, before your eyes. Your friendship is more important to me than anything else in the world! Carmeta!" he shouted, and he took a knife out of his pocket.

She had been waiting by the kitchen door and came right out. Before Jeroni could stop him, Peret stabbed his wife in the middle of her chest.

"Aiii, I'm dead!" she moaned, and fell to the floor in a heap.

Jeroni was flabbergasted. He took a step back and gave out a terrible scream.

"Mother of God! What have you done, Peret? Look at all that blood coming from the wound!"

The lamb's bladder emptied and the blood was streaming out horribly all over the floor ...

***

This scene had a tremendous effect on Jeroni. His whole body went limp and he was wracked with remorse to think he was the indirect cause of that horrible crime.

"You didn't have to do this evil deed, Peret!"

"Didn't you want to murder me?"

"Yes ... but now ... I've changed my mind. It was only money ... and you and I ..."

Peret remained silent.

"We have to do something to save her life!" Jeroni suddenly exclaimed.

"She's lost a lot of blood," observed Peret. "But the truth is, I can find a solution for anything."

"How?" asked Jeroni hopefully.

"I have something ... but it would be better not to tell you. You'll never believe me again."

"Yes, yes, Peret! Believe me, I'll believe! You've always been so smart. Do something! Save her, for the love of God!"

Carmeta was playing dead like the only thing she'd ever done in her life was die. Lift an arm? Bam, straight to the floor! Lift a leg? Flop, straight to the floor!

Peret went to the kitchen and brought back a small bellows, like the ones used to blow on a fire, but highly decorated and shiny.

"You see this bellows?"

Jeroni nodded his head.

"You'll soon find out the kind of power it has."

He placed the nozzle close to his wife's nose and gently blew air into it. After about 30 seconds Carmeta began to stir. She took three or four deep breaths, raised her arms, stretched and shook her legs, opened her eyes and asked in a very weak voice: "Where am I? What happened?"

"It was nothing," said Peret in a serious tone, as though it weren't anything important. "You're all right now. Go inside and dust yourself off and comb your hair, and then get a rag and clean this up so we can have lunch."

Carmeta got to her feet as if nothing at all had happened. Jeroni, dumbfounded, hugged Peret. "This was miraculous, Peret. Can you forgive me?"

"You're forgiven!"

"But ... now you'll have to sell me that bellows ... because you can never tell how these women might act. Sometimes you might get a bad thought in your mind, or a sudden fit of anger and you knock them out; why if you haven't got the bellows, who knows? Let me have them; you just name the price."

"No, no. None of that, Jeroni, please. I don't want to have any more deals with you or with your wife. We'll just be friends, and no more deals."

But Jeroni was so hard-headed that in the end Peret couldn't say no and sold him the bellows for 500 pounds. In the dark of night, Jeroni snuck the bellows into their house while Maria was cooking supper, so she wouldn't know a thing about them.

***

The day after the deal with the bellows, Jeroni's wife was checking the money they kept hidden away in the chest of drawers and found, to her surprise, that 500 pounds were missing—the amount Jeroni had taken out. She was sure they had pulled the wool over his eyes yet again.

So there was another set-to when he came back from the field at midday.

"This was another con!" she shouted. "And they've already cheated you a hundred times!"

"Just quiet down," said Jeroni calmly, "you drive me to do things I don't want to do."

But his wife kept it up, and then some.

"That's enough!" he blurted out. "I'll show you who's boss!"

He took up the knife from the table and stabbed her in the heart.

Poor Maria collapsed to the floor without a sound, and she gave up the ghost on the spot.

Jeroni saw her dead body and smiled. "That should teach her a thing or two. Now I'll revive her and she'll never talk back to me for the rest of her life!"

He got the bellows and started to blow air into her lifeless nose, just as Peret had done with Carmeta. He pumped and pumped, for at least 15 minutes. And Maria? She didn't move a muscle.

When he finally realized that his wife wouldn't come back to life, he went mad with desperation and he swore to God that now he would murder Peret—no ifs, ands or buts.

But first he had to cover up his crime. He did so by throwing Maria's body into a very deep well that gave onto an underground river. No one knew where it led. He'd say that his wife had gone out and hadn't come back; and no matter how much they tried, no one would ever find her. What's more, they were known to be a couple that always got on well together.

It was clear that Jeroni was useless for everything but crime. And as usually happens, he had a special talent for evil deeds.

***

Jeroni ran straight to Peret's house. But he wasn't carrying a knife this time, because he didn't want to see any more blood. Instead, he had a very big sack made of thick burlap and a good hempen rope.

When he got there he asked Peret to go out and help him carry back a sack full of melons. Two would be able to tote it better than one. Knowing nothing of what had occurred, Peret agreed to go. But when they were well out in the countryside, Jeroni took him by surprise and, being the stronger of the two, hastily tied him up with the rope and stuffed him into the sack.

"What are you going to do?" asked the unfortunate Peret from the sack.

"Throw you into the sea!"

"It's a long walk."

"No matter, even if it takes days!" responded Jeroni. He tied a good tight knot around the opening and hoisted the whole load over his shoulder.

That area is sparsely populated and they came across no one. Walking and walking, Jeroni took the road to Tibi. About half way between that village and Xixona, at a place called the Penya Roja, where the blue line of the sea just comes into view, night was falling and they had to take refuge in a cave. Jeroni put the sack onto the ground beside him.

Peret had spent most the time screaming for someone to come and set him free, but it was useless and at last his voice went hoarse and the only sound was made by Jeroni who, now and again, gave him a blow that would kill a rabbit to make him shut up. And even worse, an hour before they reached the cave, Jeroni opened the sack and tied a gag over Peret's mouth to muffle all the noise he was making.

And so Peret, lying at Jeroni's feet inside the sack, kept silent, half dead from fear, with no hope of salvation and hardly able to breathe. While Jeroni ate his supper in the glow of a small fire he had built, the only protest Peret could make was to wriggle and squirm every now and then inside the sack. Jeroni, the animal, finally got fed up and gave him a swift kick with the tip of his boot that left him motionless for the rest of the night.

* * *

The next day Jeroni set off again for the coast, with Peret slung over his shoulder. But after he had walked for a while he noticed that the sun felt excessively hot on his pate—because he had left his beret in the cave. He set down the sack beside a pear tree and went back to fetch it.

As soon as Jeroni turned the first curve in the road, losing sight of the sack, Peret thought he heard the tinkling of goat bells and the voice of a goatherd. He immediately started to struggle against the gag—it was already nearly worn through from all the biting and chewing he'd done during the night—and to his great joy, he found that his mouth was free.

"Aii, aii, aii," he lamented, "oh how hopeless I am! Aii, aii!"

The goatherd wasn't far away and found the sack in about five minutes' time.

When Peret heard footsteps nearby he moaned again, "Oh Lord, it's hopeless. I was so happy hidden away on my farm and all by myself!"

The goatherd came up close, puzzled, and asked, "Who's there?"

"Aii, it's terrible," Peret went on. "They're taking me to be king, and I don't want to."

"Who's in there," the goatherd repeated, "and what did you say?"

"Aii, my friend. I was happy hidden away and now they've discovered that I'm a member of the royal family and the king has died and they're forcing me to be the new king! Oh, I'll be so unhappy! You see, just because I don't want to go, they've stuck me in here, half suffocated. Aii, aii!"

In a flash the goatherd saw his chance. "That's what you're afraid of?" he asked.

"Yes, it is ... But please stop talking and let me out so I can breathe in some fresh air."

"All right, I'll let you out ... and if you wish, I'll take your place in the sack and become the next king. That would be a whole lot better than living up here in the mountains, always cold or hot or hungry or thirsty."

He opened the sack; Peret got out, looked the goatherd up and down and said, "It's a deal. You could be the next king; you look a bit like me."

"And even if I didn't," said the goatherd enthusiastically, "it wouldn't matter, since they haven't seen you at the court."

So they quickly made the change. Peret helped him into the sack and tied it securely at the top. Then he said, "The only thing is, you must be careful not to talk, because the man who's toting the sack knows my voice. When you get to the court, he'll deliver the sack and go back home, and then the dukes and marquis will let you out."

That said, Peret very hastily took the goats to a ravine covered over with pines which was close to that spot.

* * *

On the afternoon of the following day Jeroni arrived with the sack at the edge of the sea. He went straight to Cape Horta and, from the top of some high cliffs there, threw the unlucky goatherd into the waves. As he did so he let out a great sigh and exclaimed, "Thank the Lord I've finally killed you, Peret! Now you'll never deceive me again!"

He had a fine dinner and slept like a log in the village of Mutxamel, and the next day back to Castalla, on the same road by which he had come.

He was close to the Penya Roja pass when he heard some cheerful songs echoing through the rocky embankments above the path.

His heart skipped a beat.

"That's Peret's voice! It's Peret's voice; but it can't be because I threw him with my own hands into the sea to drown."

Lirorirori
Larà, li la, liiiirarà...

"And he's singing his favorite song, the dance of the Tibi festival!" Jeroni was chilled to the bone. He shouted as loud as he could: "Peret, Peret!"

"Who's calling?" said Peret, as he appeared at the top of the slopes with his herd of goats. "Ah," he said suddenly, as though he were surprised, "it's my old friend Jeroni!" And he slowly and majestically made his way down, followed by the pretty goats.

"Not going to give your old buddy a hug?" he asked with a smile.

Jeroni was stupefied. "You must be the Devil himself!" And he fell like a shot to the ground. "How can you be here after you died?"

"Now, now, Jeroni. I'm a bit upset with you ... It turns out that the sea where you threw me has a magic power. The deeper down you go, the more and finer animals you get out. You were lazy and you threw me in close to the shore ... And you see, I got a herd of 70 white goats; but... if you had thrown me 200 yards farther out my friend, where the sea is really deep, I would've got a herd of cattle—bulls or cows."

Jeroni marveled and began to feel ambitious. "Is it true?"

"Eh! ... Here we go again ... so you don't believe this, either?"

"Yes, Peret, I believe it! ... Do me a favor; find me a sack—the closest place is Tibi. I'll wait here. Don't waste any time; the magic might fade away. Come right back and put me in the sack and throw me into the sea. Maybe at last my luck will change and I can really make a fortune."

Peret didn't dawdle; he carried out Jeroni's request to a T.

He was back in an hour. Jeroni was waiting seated on a rock. Peret put him into the sack and hoisted it onto his shoulder and in a few hours reached the sea, where he cast it in without a moment's hesitation. Then he went back to Castalla as happy as a clam at high tide, saying to himself: "Deep sea waters for the greedy, and life for those who know how to live."

Note

1 This refers to a regional dish, *gaspatxo de Castalla*, which consists of a hash made of various kinds of game, especially rabbit or hare, seasoned with aromatic herbs and served on a large piece of flatbread.

10 Joan-Antoni[1] and the Blockheads
(a story from Castalla)

Once upon a time there was a man who lived in Castalla, and his wife was a blockhead. Ever since they were married, when he realized the full extent of her simple-mindedness, he did all in his power to teach her to do the housework and to till the fields. But it was like beating his head against a brick wall; she just couldn't get any of it through her skull. One day she'd burn the stew; the next day the vegetables were raw. When the clothes needed mending, she sewed on garish, motley patches, and out in the fields it was even worse. She mixed up the seed bags and planted oats instead of wheat; she cut down the carrot stems thinking they were alfalfa.

"Yes, wife of mine, you've turned out to be a real blockhead," he'd say, feeling sorry for himself. And him so clever and sensible!

At last he got so fed up with his wife's dim-wittedness that one fine Sunday morning, cursing and complaining, he set off on the road to the east to see whether he could find anyone else in the rest of the world as dumb as she was. If he couldn't find any, he'd unmarry her on the spot. And if he could, well, he'd take some consolation and would go back home to her.

These thoughts were running through his mind: *I've never known anybody in Castalla as simple-minded, ignorant and backward as my wife. But that doesn't mean there's not the same, or worse, in other towns. So if I don't find any simpletons like her, either men or women, I'll admit it was my mistake—they sold me a rotten apple. But if there are others like her out there in the big, wide world, I'll take comfort and accept my lot, because it must have been the will of God.*

He walked and walked and came upon a nice little village high up in the shady mountains covered with pine trees and lovely terrains with olive trees and newly-planted vineyards. It seemed to be a cheerful place; the chiming bells echoed through the olive groves and people were enjoying the March sun in the streets and squares.

It was almost 12, and Joan-Antoni was feeling peckish. But he struck up a conversation with an old man, inquiring about the townsfolk, their character and their customs, to find out if there were any blockheads in that region. Their conversation turned out to be a long one, and they soon grew

DOI: 10.4324/9781003324232-10

tired of standing in the street, so the old man said, "Let's go into my house, my friend, where we can sit down and chat."

Well, they did. And when they were seated the old man's wife came out of the kitchen and said that dinner was on the table.

"Say," the man proposed to be polite, "since you're here, why not have lunch with us?"

To which his wife interjected in a flash, "Hah! Well I never, Jordi! ... Surely he wouldn't show up here without having eaten!"

"Your wife is right," said Joan-Antoni, rising to leave, "Though I haven't had lunch yet, I had a big breakfast this morning. But to get back to what we were talking about, Uncle Jordi, is everyone in town as clever as your wife?"

"What are you saying?" answered Jordi. "Why, I married the dumbest one!"

Joan-Antoni walked out muttering to himself, "No use asking around anymore. The people in this place are as clever as foxes!"

He left the town and started up the hills to the east, toward the coast.

He had a bite to eat in a sheltered spot and later, as night was falling, he espied a hamlet of 50 or 60 houses at the foot of a broad, high mountain with a snow-covered peak.

"Good. I can spend the night there," he said to himself.

He crossed a stream, walked on through broom and holly, went up a small slope and found himself in the village. He saw a dim light through the half-opened door of the first house he came to.

"Ave Maria!" he said aloud, as he pushed on the door.

A young woman came to see who it was and led him into the kitchen, where quite a few people were sitting around the fire. They all turned to look his way.

"What is it, friend?" asked the patriarch of the family. "But first come in and warm yourself." They made room for him in their circle.

"I was looking for a place to sleep," explained Joan-Antoni, "but ..." And he stared in wonder at the crowd of parents and children and in-laws. All of them, young and old, were red-faced and chubby, as is usual in that healthy mountain clime.

"As you can see," he continued, "the night has caught me before I could get to the coast; and since I don't know whether there's an inn in town, I stopped here. I'd be happy to pay for a night's lodging."

"Of course, of course," said the head of the household, "and no need to pay. Don't even think of it!"

Joan-Antoni said thank-you, and the customary questioning began. They were all astounded to hear the things he told them about his town of Castalla.

The smaller children started to play in the kitchen. The older one listened to the stranger for a while, but soon also tired and joined the other kids. After a while he spoke to one of the little ones, "You know what Mamma said today when she was hoeing in the garden?"

"What did she say?"

"That she'll buy a piggy this summer."

"Oh, that's nice," remarked the little one. "How many legs will it have?"

"The same as you," said the elder, "two in front and two in back."

"That's just when I'm crawling,"

Joan-Antoni didn't miss a word of this nonsense.

"Did you hear that?" said the woman to the visitor. "It's amazing how much kids know these days. Aii, Mother of God! What'll it be next?"

"No," admitted Joan-Antoni, "no doubt about that."

The children went on talking.

"The piglet will grow up to be big and fat," the eldest predicted, "and father will kill it and make gravy and I'll eat it and you won't!"

As soon as he heard this, the younger one, not all that young, as he was around ten, threw himself onto the floor and started kicking and screaming. "Mommy, daddy!" he cried. "Pep will get gravy and I won't!"

Then their father and mother and the patriarch's mother-in law and father-in-law and two spinster sisters-in-law all stood up, alarmed, and chaos broke out.

"Children! Now, now, children!"

"Daddy, he won't give me any gravy! Oh daddy, he'll get gravy and I won't!"

"All right, big guy," said the father, grabbing the oldest son by the nape of his neck, "with God as my witness, I'm telling you to let him have some gravy!"

When the younger one heard that he was going to be allowed to eat gravy that would be made from a hog that hadn't yet been bought as a piglet and that might not ever be bought and, if it were, might not even grow to be a hog, he started to dance and laugh for joy. And the whole family did, too.

"Good! Good!"

"We'll all eat gravy!"

"Hooray!"

Joan-Antoni was astonished by those mountain folks' imbecility. And his heart was lightened to see that there were people in the world not only like his wife, but a hundred times worse. This was another kettle of fish! Because he had begun to worry after the visit he'd made to that Jordi's house in the previous town.

Later that night, after eating supper by the fire from the provisions he had in his rucksack, he went to bed in the hayloft. And the next morning he took his leave, thanking his hosts for their hospitality, and set off toward the coast.

He climbed mountains and crossed ravines, and around mid-morning came to a pleasant village whose houses gathered round a superb church made of hewn stone. As he entered, nodding to everyone he encountered, Joan-Antoni was struck by the idiotic stares on their faces. *It looks to me*, he said to himself, *like this place also has its fair share of blockheads.*

They couldn't even walk in a straight line; every three and a half steps they tripped over their own feet.

Soon he reached the church. "And what an ugly church it is!" he observed, examining it up and down. "There's something off ... but I can't put my finger on it ... Oh, yes, it hasn't got a single window! It must be as dark as the gullet of a wolf inside!"

Then he saw lots of people in the square holding threshing sieves up toward the sun. After a while they looked at the sieves carefully and ran with them into the church.

"What are you folks doing?"

"Oh, stranger, it's such a problem ..."

"What is?"

"When they built the church it turned out dark, and now, on the mayor's orders, we're gathering sunlight in the sieves to carry it inside. But as soon as we step through the door, it disappears."

When he saw how seriously the citizens of that town pronounced such hare-brained rubbish, Joan-Antoni raised his hands in dismay. But he thought it would be better to earn himself a bit of money than to try to give them advice and explanations. (He was carrying some tools.)

"I could fix it so you wouldn't have to work so much. But you'd have to pay me 100 pounds."

They took him to the mayor's house, and the deal was struck.

Joan-Antoni asked for three ladders used for olive picking. He tied them securely together end to end and climbed up to the ceiling with his pick. He quickly removed eight or ten tiles and then opened a hole about 12 by 18 inches in the roof. It was getting on for noon so, through the dust and bits of plaster a bright ray of sunlight immediately came into the dark church.

The onlookers stood there gawking in surprise. "It's Our Lord!"

"Well, whoever it is," ordered the mayor, "give this man his money right away and get him and his tools out of town. If he starts up knocking holes in our houses, in no time flat the whole village will be torn down!"

And so it was. Joan-Antoni chuckled as he walked away, feeling better and better about his wife's stupidity. Going downhill among pines and mastic trees, he whistled the tune of that old song that goes like this:

Mother, I want to get married,
But I can't decide with whom,
It's better not to get married
And never to be a groom.

If I marry a big tall woman
She'll need a gigantic frock;
And there won't be cloth enough to make it
On Alacant's main dock.

*If I marry a younger maiden
She'll still be coy and shy:
The minute I try to touch her
She'll either laugh or cry.*

*If I marry a true believer
That'll be even worse;
She'll go to church in the morning
And at night read Bible verse.*

*If I marry a cook or a servant
I know just what they do;
When the master isn't looking
They eat the master's stew.*

*If that's what she does to the master
Then that's what she'll do to me;
It's better not to get married
And live life single and free.*

With the 100 pounds he'd earned safely stashed away in his rucksack, Joan-Antoni was as happy as happy could be. Downward and downward he walked, as the day got warmer and the wind grew milder. A sure sign that he was headed toward the sea.

"Now this," he said to himself, "is what I call a nice climate. It isn't cold in March. Right now my poor wife is probably fighting the frost in the carrot patch ... This would be a nice place to live ... not that I don't like my town; because ... it's true your fingers go numb when the north wind blows down over the marshes, so fine they say it's woven by the monks in Onil; but I'll wager its healthier. And good health is the finest gift there is ... Anyway, from what I've seen so far, most other places have it beat for blockheads. Seems to me, the harder you look, the more you find."

He passed the whole morning with these and other similar reflections and had a bite of lunch beside a tiny spring. Then he noticed down below, at the foot of a mountain whose frightening peak was crowned with mist, a village as white as a flock of doves.

It was dark when he got there and all of the houses were closed and the streets deserted.

He was just going to knock at a door when he heard strange noises inside, "What in the world is *that*?" he wondered. It sounded like people running to and fro inside and punching each other, mixed in with an occasional scream.

He went to another door, where it was the same.

This looks like the Devil's work! he thought, and decided to go to the inn, which was also closed and locked.

Soon the innkeeper stepped out. His hair was disheveled and he had a large club in his hand.

"Come in, my brother, come in. I apologize ..." he said sadly, "but we have a terrible situation all over town."

Joan-Antoni went in and the innkeeper told him the whole story. They had an invasion of mice. Hundreds and hundreds of mice. In the kitchens, in the stables, in the pantries, in the larders, in the cellars, in the closets, in the attics, on the roofs ...

"But how can that be?" asked Joan-Antoni, slumping into a corner next to the fireplace. (There was no fire burning because, as we know, the weather wasn't cold.)

"Well, you see, my friend ... we club them, but there's just so many. They breed and they breed and they've got us outnumbered."

"But, don't you have any cats?"

"Cats?" Everyone in the inn looked dumbfounded. "What is that? Cats? We've never had anything like that in our town."

"And people from outside haven't ever mentioned them?"

"Nobody from anywhere else has ever come here. You're the very first one."

"Then listen to this," said Joan-Antoni, who was gaining experience while at the same time raking in the dosh. "If you lend me a fast horse I'll go this very night to where they have this thing called a cat. I'll bring a male and a female so you can breed them and they'll take care of all the rats and mice."

The innkeeper told the mayor and he brought Joan-Antoni a horse in person, requesting him to please go as soon as he'd had supper to fetch those animals he was talking about.

And so it was. After his supper Joan-Antoni mounted the horse and galloped out of town as fast as he could. And at last he came to a town where they knew what cats were. He knocked on door after door, raising a ruckus at that time of night, and finally managed to buy a pair of cats that he stuck into a sack and hurried back to where he'd come from.

He got there in the early morning and the mayor, quite excited, received him in a room upstairs in his house. When Joan-Antoni let the cats out of the bag, at the first hisses and meows they made on finding themselves surrounded by so many unfamiliar people, all the folks who had gathered there fled down the stairs and into the street.

The tomcat was big, as big as a badger, with spots and darker stripes. As soon as it caught a whiff of the mice, it shot away and started to hunt them down. Who knows how many it caught? In the blink of an eye the mayor's house was mouse-free.

The female was let loose in the inn and made short work of the mice in that big building as quickly as the tomcat did in the mayor's house.

Joan-Antoni stayed in the village four or five days, taking the cats from house to house. But no one dared to touch them; they thought they must be the Devil's spawn. To be sure, everyone in the whole town, trying with sticks and stones, hadn't been able eliminate the mice. And now, they see with their own eyes how the pests disappear from one day to the next. Because of course, once the cats had eaten a few hundred their smell spread all over and the remaining mice ran for their lives through fields and ditches.

Nevertheless, if the cats didn't stay there, the place could easily be invaded again by the mice, or so thought the mayor, a person known for his prudence. So he sought out Joan-Antoni and addressed him thus:

"My friend, we're very pleased with what you've done."

"Thank you very much, Mr. Mayor."

"But I've been told that you're thinking of going away. So I must ask you if you intend to take the beasts that exterminated the mice with you when you go?"

"Well ... I thought ... You see, Mr. Mayor, they did cost me a pretty penny."

Joan-Antoni's heart began to race; he knew what was coming next.

"Of course, of course. That makes sense, my boy. The village is happy now, so if you leave the cats here we'll give you the horse you rode on and, in addition, 100 pounds. How does that sound?" said the voice of municipal authority.

"That sounds very good, Mr. Mayor. I accept," responded Joan-Antoni.

Soon after that, stuffing the money into his pocket, he took leave of the townsfolk and, following a good lunch, set off again. It was all downhill, going toward the sea, which shouldn't now be far away. But in less than 15 minutes he heard his name being called: "Joan-Antoniii, Joan-Antoniii!"

So he halted his horse. "Wha-a-a-t?"

A crown of people from the village was coming his way.

"Stop, stop!"

"I have sto-o-o-ped!"

They came up closer, but Joan-Antoni had halted at the top of a hill, so they stood below and shouted up to him.

"Liste-e-en, frie-e-end. When the mice are all gone, what should we feed those animals you bro-o-ought?"

Joan-Antoni put his hands to his mouth and shouted, "They'll eat what yo-o-o-u do-o-o!"

But what they heard was, "They'll eat yo-o-ou to-o-o!" And they took off helter-skelter toward town, with the mayor, more frightened than all the others put together, at their head.

Armed with clubs and stones and axletrees, they hunted down the two poor cats, very soon finding them perched on a windowsill and cleaning their whiskers with their paws, as is their wont.

"Look at 'em, just look at 'em," said the mayor. "They're up there thinking, 'You and you and you. It's your turn now'."

And so, in two shakes of a nanny goat's tail, the pair of unlucky cats was done away with.

Joan-Antoni couldn't figure out why these people had turned into a mob like that; but he supposed it was because they were bigger blockheads than his wife would ever be. It made him feel like giving up his travels and going back home right away, satisfied.

But the charming, grandiose panorama of the coastal region, known as the Marina, worked its spell and he continued on his way. After a two hours' ride he was out of the mountains and approaching the coast. Some distance away to his left, the perfect, flame-colored shape of Puig-Campana rose like a magic mountain. To his right there was a line of small hills and vales covered with oleander and aloe that in many places blocked off the sight of the dark blue sea nearby ... It was all too lovely for him to turn back now. Just a little farther! And he had that handsome horse, with its easy, graceful gait. What's even more, now he was making money in these towns filled with knuckleheads.

Suddenly a bolt of lightning ripped through a line of large clouds over the horizon to the east. It was getting dark, and soon a few drops of rain were falling onto the dusty road.

Joan-Antoni spurred the horse to a trot and in little time they came to a roadside inn. That night, over supper, it occurred to him to ask which town in the vicinity had the most blockheads. It turns out the most doltish place was some distance away but, if he started out early next day he could probably get there before nightfall.

He got up at dawn, bought provisions for the day at the inn and set off in the direction they had indicated, along the coast. And after crossing steep mountains and treacherous ravines, deep blue bays and picturesque rock formations rising from the sea, he came to the village they had told him about just as evening was coming on.

He spent the night in a large inn on the High Street. All of its rooms had the pleasing smell of newly-washed clothes. Too tired to look around or ask any questions, he went directly to bed.

The sun was shining brightly the following day, and the mountains and countryside had lovely tones of shadows that contrasted with the clear, crisp morning light. The village, located between two small headlands, stretched from the foot of a line of hills to the nearby sea, which was as quiet and still as a pond. Joan-Antoni strolled about, taking in the scenery and listening to the townsfolk, who all seemed very busy.

A group of men had gathered in the main square in front of the church. He went closer and saw an alderman excitedly giving orders.

"No, no. No need to worry any more. From this day on we'll be free of that pug-ugly dandelion!"

Joan-Antoni pricked up his ears. "What does he mean—a pug-ugly dandelion?"

It didn't take long for the question to find an answer; for a very big dandelion was growing from between two stones just beneath the cornice of the bell tower, high up close to the large bell. And it was a very big dandelion indeed, dark and ugly, with dried-out leaves and at least ten branchlets, because every year it had withered in the winter and grown back out again the following spring.

"Okay," continued the alderman, "we'll put a pulley up there and tie Batistet l'Alficòs's donkey to a rope down here. Then we'll string the rope through the pulley and ... tugging with all our might, we'll lift the donkey up to the dandelion. You know how much donkeys love dandelions. It'll eat it right up!"

"Hurrah! Yes!" cried the people in the crowd. They were full of admiration, as though the alderman, having come up with such a brilliant plan, were the wisest man the world has ever seen.

Joan-Antoni could hardly stifle his laughter.

Next he witnessed how they put the plan into action. Some of them brought Batistet's donkey; while others attached the pulley in the slot at the top of the bell tower. Then they passed a rope through it and dropped it downwards till it reached the ground. They tied a loop with a slip knot and placed it around the donkey's neck. The others immediately set in to haul on the rope to the cries of the alderman, who roared and roared: "Pull men, pull!"

And the poor donkey was hung up like a captured shark.

Joan-Antoni knew they had tied a slip knot and that it was going to be a disaster. In truth, these blockheads were the biggest morons he'd found thus far, because here their stupidity had a victim—the poor donkey. But he kept his mouth shut, for he wanted to see how far this band of imbeciles would go.

The donkey was rising higher and higher along the wall of the tower: ten feet, fifteen feet, almost to the dandelion. But it was choking all the while. The noose was squeezing its neck and its tongue was hanging out something awful. And these blockheads didn't notice a thing!

At last its head was level with the plant. A shout of joy came from the crowd: "It's licking it!"

Licking? It wasn't licking at all. It had been strangled to death! And there it was, with half a foot of tongue sticking out of its mouth until, urged by Joan-Antoni, they brought it back down and saw that it was dead.

And what a commotion ensued! Batistet went straight for the alderman, aiming to give him a beating that would rearrange his ribs.

Joan-Antoni didn't stick around to see any more. That donkey was a fine example of its long-suffering race, and he was saddened by its senseless death. He went back to the inn, intending to pay his bill and leave that town behind forever. But when he reached the High Street, mounted on his dashing, glossy horse, he saw that everyone was running toward the square again. Because the alderman had come up with another brilliant idea.

His curiosity piqued, Joan-Antoni followed them to see what it would be this time.

He found the alderman standing on a soapbox above their heads and haranguing them as follows: "Are we going to let that evil dandelion play us the fool us like that? No! No! Everyone, bring all the barrels in town! We'll make a tower as high as the plant! Two little boys can climb up it and when they get to that dandelion, they'll attack the wall with a hoe and a pick till not a single leaf is left!"

"Hoorahhh!" shouted the crowd.

And everyone rushed through the streets to bring back barrels and casks. They placed them as ordered, one atop the other. The two lightest boys they could find, as skinny as crickets, stepped up onto each new layer. And then balancing precariously with the help of the rope hanging from the pulley, they brought up more barrels from below, risking death at any moment.

After an hour, the tower of barrels was close to the height of the dandelion.

"No more barrels!" someone cried.

And it was true.

"But we're not there yet," said the boys. "We need one more!"

"Wouldn't it have been easier to lower someone down with a rope?" asked a deeply thinking citizen.

"How could they work hanging from a rope?" responded the alderman. "And what's more, they'd be strangled to death like the donkey. Haven't we lost enough already?"

"True."

"But there are no more barrels!"

Then the alderman gave a significant slap to his narrow forehead. "What a bunch of simpletons you are, my friends," he explained, radiating joy. "I know what we have to do! We'll take the one from the bottom and put it on top, and Bob's your uncle!"

And that's what they did.

As soon as Joan-Antoni heard these words, he spurred his horse to the far side of the square. For of course, when they removed the bottom barrel, the whole rickety contraption came tumbling down and all of the barrels went rolling and bouncing through the streets, flattening anyone who happened to be in the way and splattering into splinters when they hit a wall.

And as for the two young boys, they were left holding onto the rope for dear life, like a couple of tethered birds, and everybody was scrambling to and fro like mad to get them safely down.

Joan-Antoni couldn't stomach any more of this spectacle. He galloped out of that town as fast as the horse could carry him.

He had to eat his lunch out in the countryside, in the shade of a tree he'd never seen before, because they don't grow in the cold climate of the Castalla Valley: a carob tree. But now he knew its name, having asked not long after reaching the coast. It was as big as a church, and what deep, cool shade it cast!

He had left the horse near the bank of a stream to get its fill of the abundant sweet-grass growing there. When he finished his meal, he remounted and started on his way, not knowing where he would find another location to collect more news about imbecility.

And as he rode along, absorbed in his thoughts, a distinct sound of voices reached his ears.

Busot, oh yes, I'm from Busot!
Busot, oh yes, I'm from Busot!

they seemed to be saying.

"Oh my goodness me!" he said with a start. "If I'm not mistaken—and I can't be mistaken because I've heard it too often—that *bam, bam* rhythm is the sound of a drum."

He listened hard. The rhythmical "Busot, oh yes, I'm from Busot" went on, and it was getting louder. It must have been coming from a village just behind the hill he was approaching.

The horse soon rounded the hill and a pretty little town came into view. From it he heard a confused hubbub of voices and the music of a flageolet punctuated by a drum. His heart began to beat faster. It was a village dance! Just the same as in Castalla! The words of the song they were playing ran through his brain:

Midgets and giants
Whatever your name,
When we all get older
We'll all be the same.

Then we'll go out
To the village square
And make life hard
For the vicar there.

He spurred the horse on and reached the town in a jiffy.

A man was standing in the doorway of the first house he came to. He looked to be around 30 years of age and was very down in the mouth. The street was deserted.

Joan-Antoni was perplexed because, by the look of things, everyone else must have been in the main square, either taking part in the dances or looking on. So why was this poor fellow here all alone and down in the dumps?

"Is anything wrong, my friend?"

"Oh, don't ask, my good man. I'm so low," he confided, "I don't think things could get any worse."

"Well, don't hold it in. If you tell me all about it, maybe we can come up with a solution."

The man walked out and politely helped Joan-Antoni dismount.

"Come in," he offered, "and we'll have a little drink, even if it's only water. Or if you'd like some wine, I have a muscatel that would knock your socks off."

Joan-Antoni tied the reins to a ring beside the doorpost for that purpose and they went into the sad man's modest house. He brought out the porron[2] and Joan-Antoni took in such a large gulp of muscatel that it brought tears to his eyes.

"That's good wine!"

"Fondillón," he said proudly.

Then they both sat down.

"My problem, friend," explained the melancholy man, "is that my wife wanted to wear a costume to the dance and I couldn't get the notion out of her head. No way!"

"But who's the boss here?" asked Joan-Antoni. He was surprised.

"That's just it ... As I was saying, not only has she gone out to dance; today's the day we bake bread, and she ordered me to prepare the dough. Me? I've never made dough in my life. Mend the clothes, cook a stew, wash the dishes, I've done all that lots of times ... Oh, this is going to get me into a barrel of hot water!"

The poor fellow was seriously fearful.

Joan-Antoni was about to laugh, but he tried to encourage him. "Don't take it so hard."

"How else can I take it? ... And she was so puffed up when she left. Dressed to beat the band. She was wearing a velvet bodice that suits her figure to a T. 'Empire waistline' it's called. And the sleeves—the loveliest thing you've ever seen. Everything fringed with ruffles. You can just imagine how nice she looked ... But I'm getting carried away and off the subject. Like I said, I've taken care of baking the bread for this week. I put the flour in the bowl and mixed in the yeast and it made such a sticky mess I couldn't get it off of my fingers. I kept on mixing it and mixing it, but it just got worse and worse. Come into the kitchen and I'll show you!"

They went in and Joan-Antoni saw a huge, horrible-looking mass of dough. The man must have thrown in everything: bran, flour and yeast, even the chaff of the wheat. It was a terrible mess. Joan-Antoni tried to knead it with one hand, but it got stuck inside like a bird in a trap.

"You'll have to ask your wife about this," he said uneasily. "I don't know how to fix it either."

"But how?" asked the house-husband, looking more frightened than ever. "How can I go and ask her anything at the dance? Don't you see, she'll be right in there with all the others. You'll only hear that racket: clack-clack-clackity-clack, and we won't be able to say a thing. And anyway, I wouldn't want to ask her in front of everyone else ... They'd laugh their hats off at us both, and then I'd really get a tongue-lashing tonight when she gets home ... and too, she doesn't want anyone to know who she is. That's why she's wearing a mask. And if I call out to her ..."

"Okay, okay. I think I know what to do," said Joan-Antoni. He was thinking so hard to find a solution that he hardly heard the poor fellow.

"We'll go to the dance together and when your wife comes our way, snapping her castanets—clackity-clack—you say

Empire waistline,
ruffled dress:
that job you gave me,
the dough's a mess.

And then we'll see what she says.
 The melancholy man's face lit up like the sun.
 "You're my savior!" he said gratefully.
 "Let's go, let's go. No time to lose," urged Joan-Antoni.
 They rushed out and reached the main square in a trice. It was brimming with people. They were crowded onto the balconies, and in the midst of a multitude of onlookers in the square itself the dance was proceeding in all of it splendor and grace; the kings and queens, leaders of the dance, and their followers, all wearing masks and brightly-colored dresses and costumes, glided through the magic ritual of steps, skips and turns.
 Every two minutes, as the circle progressed, a figure in a ruffled dress with an empire waistline passed before them. She was so lithe and attractive, so delicate and graceful in the rhythmical movements of the dance that both Joan-Antoni and her husband stood there staring like slack-jawed fools.
 At last, though, Joan-Antoni reacted. "Now!"
 As she came their way once more, the melancholy man repeated his memorized lines:

Empire waistline,
ruffled dress:
that job you gave me,
the dough's a mess.

His wife, very gracefully, never missing a beat, and to the accompaniment of the castanets, replied:

Clickety-clack, clickety-click,
Add some flour to make it thick

as she passed them by.
 "Well, we're useless idiots, too!" thought Joan-Antoni, reproaching himself for not having thought of such a simple solution.
 So now they knew. They went back to the house and added flour to the dough. And it was just what the doctor ordered.
 The man wanted to give him a reward, but Joan-Antoni thanked him and refused. This was odd, for he had always been eager to profit from his deeds; but this whole affair had affected him.

He left the house, untied his horse and mounted and, with a warm goodbye, headed out of town. When he reached the outskirts he said to himself, "Some are too dumb, and some are too smart. Here the women are the clever ones, and I'm beginning to see with my own eyes that it might be better for them to be the blockheads."

He felt lighter, and maybe the horse noticed the change because it broke into a canter on its own.

Keeping up a good pace for the rest of the day, Joan-Antoni came that night to a large town surrounded by vineyards and some orange trees.

He asked the first person he met for directions to the inn. It didn't take long to find it. He had his supper there, though he wasn't hungry; because he couldn't get the case of the wife with the ruffled dress out of his mind. Afterwards he went straight to his room to go to bed.

He was wakened around eight o'clock by a ray of sunlight and the cheerful ditties of the sparrows perched not far from his window. He quickly got dressed and had breakfast and was soon out and about to see the town.

Besides being big, it was also pretty; but he could see from the state of many of the buildings, as well as other details, that this place had more than its fair share of imbecility.

As he looked here and there, an old woman caught his eye. She was out in the sun on a bit of open ground doing something with one of those wooden trays used to take bread dough to the baker.

His curiosity piqued, Joan-Antoni went closer and saw that she was scrubbing away at one place on the tray with a whitish paste, like glue.

"Might I ask what it is you're up to, my good woman?"

"What else would I be up to?" she answered politely. "My husband and I went to the fair in Cocentaina, a long way away up in the mountains, to trade the she-ass for a donkey, and I saw this pretty wooden tray for taking bread dough to the baker and I bought it on the spot. But when we got back, I noticed that there's a knot in the wood that makes it look ugly, and since I don't know how to remove it I'm rubbing it with this poultice to see if it gets soft and goes away."

"Like when we have a pimple, right?" said Joan-Antoni, amazed by the old woman's blockheadedness.

"Yes, that's right. Last year I had one right in the middle of my forehead that looked like this knot in the tray. You should've seen it ... and with three applications of this poultice it went right away. But now I've been rubbing in this stuff day after day for two months and the knot won't disappear."

"And it never will, like that, my good woman," declared Joan-Antoni. "These knots in wood aren't the same as our pimples. I've got a tool that'll take it off in a jiffy."

Joan-Antoni jumped off his horse and rummaged in his saddlebags for a carpenter's plane. He ran it back and forth over the knot till it was smooth and shiny, just as the woman wanted.

"Oh, you're some kind of angel, you are!" the old woman exclaimed in admiration. "How can I repay you?"

Joan-Antoni pondered. "How can you repay me?"

But that very moment the sound of loud cries and confusion came from around a corner.

"Aii, aii! Mother of God! Oh my Lord, they're going to kill me!" It was a woman's voice.

Alarmed and curious, Joan-Antoni forgot about any payment. He tied his horse to a nearby fence post and ran toward the ruckus.

"What's going on?" he asked the folks in the crowd.

No one seemed concerned. "Oh, it's nothing. It's a wedding," they answered. "They're putting on the bride's stockings."

And what do you think he saw? There was a very pretty bride who had been lifted up to a balcony and some women in the street were holding the stockings up with their tops open. Then the bride was lowered toward them so she could place a foot into each one.

They assured Joan-Antoni that this was how it was done for all the weddings; that most of the brides ended up with bruises and scratches, and that they had to recover in bed for a week or two with the stockings on before they could go to the church for the ceremony. For that reason a lot of the girls never wanted to get married and things in the town were a mess.

"Aiii!"

The bride had fallen to the ground again, without being able to stick her feet into the stockings.

Joan-Antoni was horrified. "Oh my Lord! These people should be put in cages! Hold off, you blockheads. Let me put them on," he offered, "before you beat her to death."

Then the groom emerged from the crowd. "Why you cheeky cad, you! What do you mean, you'll put them on?"

"Rest assured, young man," he said, exuding patience and dignity. "I only wish to rescue your bride. If they keep dropping her like that she'll be a frightful sight at the wedding. But if you don't trust me, give me one of the stockings and I'll put it on myself to show you how it's done without all this hanging and jerking."

They gave him one; he rolled his trouser leg up to his knee and put it on. When they were certain they had learned how to put on a pair of stockings, they gave him a gift, but he wouldn't agree to accept more than ... a 100 pounds. Then he untied his horse, mounted as lightly as always and headed off for another town. For the people there were such animals that he was afraid to stay any longer. There was no telling what they might do to him.

He rode inland and came that afternoon to a very small village located next to a broad ravine stretching uphill toward the west. The area was rich with verdant farmlands, pervaded by a heavenly peace and quiet.

And he happened to pass by a field of alfalfa where six women were cutting the plants and binding them into sheathes. He would have gone on; but he noticed that, behind the women, and although it was already late afternoon, there were only three small sheathes, no bigger than a bunch of parsley.

"Now this is strange! So many harvesters and such a pitiful harvest."

He stopped at the side of the road, dismounted and tied his horse to a nearby quince tree and then walked closer to see what the women were doing. My God! What he saw left him flabbergasted. Each one had a pair of scissors, the kind you use to mend clothes, and they were cutting the stems one by one. That way it would take them a couple of years to harvest a single field!

Who in the world could be so mad!

"Pardon me, gentle ladies, but what manner of harvest is this?"

"Why, we have always reaped our alfalfa like this," they answered.

"But don't you know that you don't reap with scissors?" And, producing a sickle from his bag of tools, he said, "You reap with this!"

"Oh, oh!" they exclaimed, and started as though to flee. "It looks like a snake! Hide, get away from that thing!"

"I'll show you how I hide."

He took two broad strides to the middle of the field. He leaned over above the crop and began to swing the sickle—swish, swish—cutting down great swaths of alfalfa! He made his way through the field like a rocket, leaving piles of the crop in his wake which the women, overcoming their fear, heartily gathered into sheathes. But they murmured among themselves, "This fellow must be the Evil One! This can't be possible! He cuts down more with one swipe than we do in a weeks' hard work."

"It isn't him. It's that animal he's carrying," said one, referring of course to the sickle.

When he finished, they wouldn't let him leave as he intended. By all means, he must go with them to the village, where they introduced him to their husbands and the many folks strolling in the streets in the pleasant late afternoon.

They all rushed to the alfalfa field, which wasn't far away, and they couldn't believe their eyes! At last, the mayor himself took charge of the situation.

As soon as they were introduced he asked Joan-Antoni to give him a demonstration. So the two of them, followed by a gaggle of curious onlookers, went to the mayor's allotment and in no time at all, all of the alfalfa there was lying in piles on the ground.

By now, night had fallen, so they went back to the village and gave Joan-Antoni a good supper at the inn, as well as a gift of 20 pounds. It wasn't much, but he found the people of this village so pitifully stupid and poor that he felt sorry for them.

After giving him the payment, the mayor said, "For you, my friend, we'll gladly grant anything you need; but we'll have to burn that animal you possess."

He ordered that a bonfire be built in the middle of the main square and had Joan-Antoni cast the sickle onto the flames. The handle burnt away immediately; but the blade, of course, only got hotter and hotter, until it was glowing bright red.

As the bonfire burned down, Joan-Antoni left the townsfolk gathered round its dying light and went back to his room at the inn, marveling at the ignorance and savagery of such backward people. When he got into bed, he could still hear the distant shouts and laughter of those benighted fools through his half-opened window.

In the square, the mayor and a large group of citizens kept staring at the glowing iron blade.

"This animal won't die," said the mayor, pointing at the fire. "Look how hot it is." And he poked it with his staff of office. Suddenly the blade bounced up into the air and its tip struck him in the middle of his forehead, causing a considerable burn. An appetizing aroma of roasted lamb chops filled the air.

But everyone started to run when they saw him jump backwards, his eyes round with fear, screaming, "It attacked me, you saw it! It jumped up and bit me!"

Joan-Antoni managed to fall asleep, but he woke around midnight and his brain began to turn things over. He thought and he thought about all that he had seen on his long journey through so many different towns and regions; and he was convinced that in the wide world there were many people as simple-minded and backward as his dear wife, or even more so. So he rose from his bed, packed his rucksack and went to the stable for his horse. He woke the stable boy, paid him the money for his lodging and, in the light of the evening sky, began his journey home, upward along the ravine, toward the distant Castalla Valley.

And when, after several days, he got to his town, he was reconciled with his wife. From that day on he no longer saw her as a blockhead, but merely as a normal, simple, good-hearted woman—which was the most important thing. And they lived for many years in holy peace and quiet.

Notes

1 *Joan*: Masculine name, equivalent of English John. Pronounced joh-ahn.
2 From Spanish, *porrón* (*barral* in Catalan). A small glass pitcher, usually used for wine, with a widened opening at the top and a spout coming from the side. A typical porron contains around 0.75 liters and is passed from one person to another for communal drinking. It is lifted above the head and, when poured correctly, the wine flows from the spout into the drinker's mouth without coming into contact with the lips.

11 The Tale of the Halfling Chicken
(a story from Xixona)

Once upon a time there was an old married couple who lived on a farm in the mountains. They had no children and they made their living breeding fowls. White, black and spotted hens, proud Indian Games, big roosters, Houdans with their long, angled tails, dizzy squawkers and chubby broilers, a motley horde that could often be seen all over the little farm and the nearby fields, sowing havoc wherever they went.

Now the interesting thing is, that old lady knew all of the animals they bred and even gave them names. And she never confused one for another.

One day in May, around ten in the morning, she went out to the threshing floor to give them a few handfuls of corn and a nice serving of cooked bran, as she did at the same time every day.

"Here chickee, chickee," she called.

And the fowls came tumbling in from all directions, some up hills, others from behind the house ... As they were crowding around her, she scattered the corn and set the pail on the ground.

But this is when she got a big surprise. There was a cute, neat-looking half-chicken that held himself back from the feathery mob of the others pushing in around the pail and snatching grains of corn from each others' beaks.

"What's up with you?" the old woman said, shooing it toward the rest. "Don't you want to eat?" But the half-chicken only gave a well-reasoned "cluck, cluck" and moved farther away from its peers.

What kind of chicken is this? the woman wondered. *It's not any animal of mine!*

And it was true. She'd never seen it before.

In the end she had to feed it separately, and then she went round to all the farms in the vicinity to ask if they'd lost a half-grown chicken, neither a chick nor a full-grown rooster, that is, what you'd have to call a Halfling chicken. But no one knew anything about it.

***

The Halfling chicken spent a few weeks like this, foraging on his own when he felt like eating and the lady hadn't come out yet to feed him. Then one day, he started scratching around in a small compost heap in a ditch on the other side of the threshing floor. Scratching and scraping away like a demon, he pulled up a piece of shiny metal in his little claw. He took it in his beak and gave it four quick shakes and, when it was free of dirt, saw it was a coin.

"Cock-a-doodle-doo!" he crowed, raising his crest as much as he could and standing on his toes.

Little half-chicken, bold and brash,
scratching around in a pile of trash
found himself a fortune in cash!

He pops the coin in his craw, turns and says "so long" to the farm and sets right out for the court. He climbs up hills; he goes down dales and through gullies; he walks along streambeds, making his way toward the king's abode. Every now and then he emitted a resounding "Cock-a-doodle-doo" and sang the following ditty:

The daughter of the king will marry me;
I'm richer than he will ever be;
For scratching around in a pile of trash
I found myself a fortune in cash!

Soon he enters some flatlands covered with woods and underbrush and comes to a river that asks him, "Where are you going, Halfling chicken?" To which he replies, "I'm going to the court, because ..." (and here he sings)

The daughter of the king will marry me;
I'm richer than he will ever be;
For scratching around in a pile of trash
I found myself a fortune in cash!

"Only if I let you cross," says the river in its deep voice.

"Then hop into my beak!" orders the Halfling chicken and, *zzzuummm!* He begins to swallow the water, gulp after gulp, until the riverbed is dry and the river is in his belly!

Gaily skipping along, singing his little ditty and crowing his joyous "Cock-a-doodle-doo," he continued on his way.

The trail gradually narrowed till it reached a gorge between a pair of very tall mountains. As he walked through it he came upon a mallet that was pounding big trunks of oak trees to bits.

"Where are you going, Halfling chicken?"

To which he responded, "I'm off to the court, because ...

The daughter of the king will marry me ..."

and we already know the rest.

"Only if I let you get by," the mallet answered, "because I feel like flattening you to the ground with one great blow."

"Then jump into my beak!" shouted the half-chicken. And there goes the mallet—*zzuumm*!—through the air, to disappear into the little fellow's beak.

And so he went on, crowing and singing, toward the court. Soon he came to a thick forest of Holm oaks on a mountainside filled with caves. Out of the biggest one stepped a fox; its eyes flashed like lightning when it saw that delicious canapé hopping toward it.

"Where are you going?" it asked, as it opened its mouth to gobble him up.

"I'm off to the court, because ...

The daughter of the king will marry me;
I'm richer than he will ever be ..."

And the fox cuts him off, "Only if I let you go instead of eating you."

"Then jump into my beak!" the Halfling chicken cries again. And *zzuumm*! the fox hurtles into his beak like a shot from a blunderbuss.

* * *

After several days on the road, and as happy as a lark, the Halfling chicken finally reached the royal court and went straight to the king's abode! As though it were a magic spell, no one noticed all of the cargo he carried inside. He comes to the wall surrounding the palace and hops up onto the main gate with the aid of his wings.

Cock-a-doodle-doo!
The daughter of the king will marry me;
I'm richer than he will ever be;
For scratching around in a pile of trash
I found myself a fortune in cash!

At that time of morning the king was out walking in the gardens nearby. When he heard that barbaric yawp, his face was contorted with indignation, his mustachios curled and he called the guard: "Look at that half-chicken! ... Go catch it and stick it in the corral with the roosters. They're so big and arrogant they'll kill it right away."

Attacked from all sides, the Halfling chicken had no way out. After a brief pursuit, a soldier managed to grab him and he was unceremoniously dragged to the corral.

Neither the king, nor the captain of the guards, nor the soldiers had the slightest idea of what would happen next; they were certain he'd be dispatched in a trice. But when the Halfling chicken found himself all alone before those enormous roosters that were about to attack him with their horrible beaks and spurs at the ready, he said to the fox in his belly, "Come out, fox! It's your turn now!"

Out came the fox; and you can just imagine what it did in a corral full of roosters and hens with thighs and drumsticks ready for a good feast! I'll have that one; no, not that one ... It wolfed them all down in no time flat. And when its hunger was abated, it broke through the fence and scampered away. Out of fear, the fox had not touched the Halfling chicken, and he calmly walked out by the same route.

Strutting proudly through the king's gardens, he went back and perched again on the main gate.

Cock-a-doodle-doo!
The daughter of the king will marry me ...

That is, he once more sang the ditty that had so upset the king. When he hears it this second time the king angrily summons the guard: "Catch it ... this half-chicken from hell! And don't let it get away! Throw it into the vats of olive oil dregs."

So the guards hurry to the gate and manage to catch the Halfling chicken again; and this time, with the captain in the lead, they take him to the palace cellars and cast him into a gigantic vat that was filled with the sediments of the royal harvest.

The Halfling chicken was sure to drown in that stinking, oily substance. But when he hears the soldiers press down the thick wooden lid, he quickly says, "Come out, mallet! It's your turn now!"

Out comes the mallet and, **bam-bam**, with two blows breaks the enormous vat into four pieces. The Halfling chicken rushes out along with the dregs, which spread throughout the king's cellars, making a colossal mess.

The Halfling chicken shakes himself off and, five minutes later, there he is on the main gate, singing his ditty:

Cock-a-doodle-doo!
The daughter of the king ...

Well, you know the rest.

The king is perturbed again: "Where's my guard? Make a bonfire in the square and put that animal on top and burn it alive. Hurry, don't let it get away this time!"

They run off as fast as they can; and again this time, no matter how much he hops and leaps around the garden, the Halfling doesn't escape.

A proclamation is made that all citizens go to the square to see the burning of a half-chicken who presumed no more or less than to wed the daughter of the king. And while soldiers piled up hundreds and hundreds of bushels of thick firewood and large sheathes of broom and pine branches

182 The Tale of the Halfling Chicken

and dozens of bunches of dry twigs for kindling, the people gathered round the growing pyramid.

At the top they place a stake to which the energized and musical little chicken is tied by a leg.

He could hear various comments from the crowd.

"He'll get what he deserves. Trying to offend our king!"

"Someone said it was said that he said he's richer than our monarch!"

"Let him burn! We don't want puffed-up braggarts around here!"

"How could a tiny animal like that marry the king's daughter? You can hardly see its spurs."

"And how. Not even a full-grown rooster!"

"Just a Halfling of a chicken?"

A fat and hungry-looking old man standing right next to the woodpile rubbed his hands in anticipation and said, "Soon we'll have a nice smell of roasted meat!"

And the rabble made many more such clever quips.

The Halfling chicken let them babble on; he didn't even open his beak to crow! The servants finished preparing a dais for the king and his court, who soon arrived with their noses in the air, to witness the execution.

There they sat—the king, the queen and the princess—all prim and pretty as could be at the top of the dais at one side of the square, dressed in their finest attire and surrounded by ceremonious figures of the court. Below them stood the resplendent guard. Then a minor figure came forward with a torch and set the kindling alight. A few clear flames and a column of white smoke rise toward the blue sky and the fire spreads quickly through the whole pyramid, crick-crackle-crack!

"Ooooh!" cried the onlookers, with gaping mouths.

Then the Halfling chicken's little voice could be heard among the whooshing of the bonfire: "River, it's your turn now!"

And the river surges out of the Halfling—it was amazing that such an impetuous flood came from such a tiny body—and puts out the fire, just like that! Then it roars into the king's dais and reaches all of the royal thighs, creating a panic with everyone shouting and running for their lives, devil take the hindmost, and finally rushes out in all directions into fields and groves.

The Halfling chicken, as tranquil as could be, quickly unties his leg with his beak and surveys the now deserted square. Only the king, queen and princess remained at the top of the dais, as though it were Noah's Ark. He begins to sing:

> Cock-a-doodle-doo!
> *The daughter of the king will marry me ...*

But the monarch interrupts him and says, "There's nothing we can do, half-chicken. You win; you have my permission to marry my daughter."

* * *

The wedding took place next day in the city's biggest church. All the church bells pealed and a multitude of adults, youths and children crowded around the doors to get a glimpse of the ceremony and, above all, to see the newly-weds walk out.

Some trumpets suddenly begin to play a glorious march, the doors are flung open, the crowd parts and the couple come out, accompanied by the king, the queen and the royal entourage. Everyone applauds happily. The princess, dressed in a white gown, looked truly charming and the Halfling chicken, standing as tall as he could and giving his wife a wing instead of a hand, struts forward with an easy solemnity, greeting one and all. The townsfolk, for their part, were amazed that such a slender, regal princess could marry a simple half-chicken, no matter how musical and bold he might be. Such an unequal match, between a woman and a chicken, had never before been seen in that water-logged kingdom.

There is a time for everything under the sun, and the thrilling moment for the bride and groom to retire to their nuptial chamber arrived. The princess warmed to the task, for she had always been fond of chickens, so gallant and elegant they were. She begins to pet and caress his little head and suddenly notices a small, hard bump among the feathers behind his comb on the back of his neck. She parts the feathers and is surprised to see something shiny there. The Halfling chicken kept perfectly still and didn't say a thing! The princess carefully grasps it with her fingers and finds that it's the head of pin—a golden pin. She slowly pulls it out of the Halfling's nicely-formed head; and when it is free—**pom!**—there is a peal of thunder and the room is filled with a cool, blue flame and the Halfling chicken turns into a handsome prince, who bows to her with courtly aplomb.

"Thank-you, my princess," he says, voice trembling with emotion, "for breaking the spell. I am the son of the king of the Aitanes and also your husband, if, that is, now that I have regained my man's body, you still wish to be my wife."

Of course, the princess was delighted with his fabulous transformation, and needless to say, she quickly and happily consented. And they lived long and happy lives, as befits all persons of kind hearts and feelings.

Index

Aarne, Antti 14
Aarne-Thompson-Uther system 14
Alacant 2, 5, 7, 8, 23n2, 164
Al-Andalus 24n18, 69
Alcover, Antoni Maria 12, 13, 23n8, 24n15, 25
Alicante *see* Alacant
Amades, Joan 12, 16, 24n14
Andrés Estellés, Vicent 1, 23n1
Asbjørnsen, Peter 10, 15, 16, 18

Balearic Islands 7, 11, 23n8, 24n15
Barcelona 2, 5, 23n5
Basile, Giambattista 12
Biterna 120
Blasco Ibáñez, Vicente 2
Borja Moll, Francesc de 6, 23n8, 24n15
brothers Grimm 10, 12, 15–18, 24n16

Campbell, John Francis 10
Cassana Trilogy 5, 7
Castalla 2, 4, 9, 11, 13, 96, 132, 140, 145, 149, 152, 159–162, 170, 171, 177
Catalonia 11
Càtedra Enric Valor (Enric Valor Chair) 8
Christ 22, 34, 38, 44, 62
Christianity 20, 36, 56, 81, 82
Constantine (Roman emperor) 20, 36, 41
Coromines, Joan 6, 23n7
Creu de Sant Jordi 7

Dumas, Alexandre 5

El misteri del Canadian 5
El Tio Cuc 2
Enllà de l'horitzó 7
Erben, Karel Jaromír 10

Fabra, Pompeu 4, 23n3, 23n5
Flaubert, Gustave 5
folklore 1, 8, 10–15, 18, 19, 21, 24n14
Franco, Francisco 4–6, 9, 23n10
Fuster, Joan 1, 22n1

Generalitat Valenciana 8
Giner Marco, Josep 5, 23n5
Gorg (literary magazine) 6, 23n9

Hernàndez Barrachina, Mercè 2
Hugo, Victor 5

Institut Interuniversitari de Filologia Valenciana 22n1

Jaume I d'Aragó 49, 55n1

La flexió verbal 7
L'ambició d'Aleix 6
Les Misérables 5
"L'experiment d'Strolowickz" 5
Lo Rat Penat (cultural association) 6, 23n4

Madame Bovary 5
Martí Gadea, Joaquim 23n13
Martínez Martínez, Francesc 16, 23n13
Millorem el llenguatge 6, 25
Moe, Jørgen 10, 15, 16, 18
Moors and Christians *see Moros i Cristians*
Moros i Cristians (festival) 124, 137n2
mythomoteur 10

Narracions intranscendents 7
Normes de Castelló 4, 23n4
Nova Planta decrees 9, 25

Obra literària completa 7, 11, 13, 14, 22, 26

Pasqual Tirado, Josep 24n13
Perrault, Charles 12
Philip V 9
phylloxera 2
Pope Sixtus II 82n5
Premi de les Lletres Valencianes 7
Premi d'Honor de les Lletres Catalanes 7

Reconquest *see* Reconquesta
Reconquesta 55n1, 82n4, 137n2
Renaixença 11, 25
rondalla/rondalles 1, 7, 9, 10, 12, 15, 19–22
Rondalles Valencianes 6, 8, 14, 18, 21–22

Saint Hippolyte 124–127
Saint Laurence 81, 82n5
Saint Peter 22, 34, 37, 43–44
Salvador Gimeno, Carles 5, 6, 23n4
Sanchis Guarner, Manuel 1, 5, 6, 11, 22, 22n1, 26
Sant Llorenço *see* Saint Laurence

Satan 42, 123n4
Second Spanish Republic 4
Senent, Joan 6, 23n9
Sense la terra promesa 7, 25
Spanish Civil War 4, 5, 9, 23n7

Temps de batuda 7
Thompson, Stith 14, 26
Three Musketeers, The 5
Tolstoy, Leo 5

Un fonamentalista del Vinalopó i altres contarelles 7
Un habitatge per a l'eternitat 7
Universitat Jaume I 13, 25, 26
University of Alacant 8
University of Barcelona 23n5
Uther, Hans-Jörg 14

Valerian (Roman emperor) 82n5
Valor Ltd. 5

War and Peace 5
World War I 2

Yeats, William Butler 10